LIBRARY OF RELIGIOUS BIOGRAPHY

Edited by Mark A. Noll, Nathan O. Hatch, and Allen C. Guelzo

THE LIBRARY OF RELIGIOUS BIOGRAPHY is a series of original biographies on important religious figures throughout American and British history.

The authors are well-known historians, each a recognized authority in the period of religious history in which his or her subject lived and worked. Grounded in solid research of both published and archival sources, these volumes link the lives of their subjects — not always thought of as "religious" persons — to the broader cultural contexts and religious issues that surrounded them.

Marked by careful scholarship yet free of academic jargon, the books in this series are well-written narratives meant to be *read* and *enjoyed* as well as studied.

D1496267

LIBRARY OF RELIGIOUS BIOGRAPHY

William Ewart Gladstone: Faith and Politics in Victorian Britain
David Bebbington

Aimee Semple McPherson: Everybody's Sister • *Edith L. Blumhofer*

Her Heart Can See: The Life and Hymns of Fanny J. Crosby
Edith L. Blumhofer

Orestes A. Brownson: American Religious Weathervane
Patrick W. Carey

Thomas Merton and the Monastic Vision • *Lawrence S. Cunningham*

Billy Sunday and the Redemption of Urban America • *Lyle W. Dorsett*

The Kingdom Is Always but Coming: A Life of Walter Rauschenbusch
Christopher H. Evans

Liberty of Conscience: Roger Williams in America • *Edwin S. Gaustad*

Sworn on the Altar of God: A Religious Biography of Thomas Jefferson
Edwin S. Gaustad

Abraham Lincoln: Redeemer President • *Allen C. Guelzo*

Charles G. Finney and the Spirit of American Evangelicalism
Charles E. Hambrick-Stowe

Francis Schaeffer and the Shaping of Evangelical America
Barry Hankins

Emily Dickinson and the Art of Belief • *Roger Lundin*

The Puritan as Yankee: A Life of Horace Bushnell • *Robert Bruce Mullin*

Prophetess of Health: A Study of Ellen G. White • *Ronald L. Numbers*

Blaise Pascal: Reasons of the Heart • *Marvin R. O'Connell*

Occupy Until I Come: A. T. Pierson and the Evangelization of the World
Dana L. Robert

God's Strange Work: William Miller and the End of the World
David L. Rowe

The Divine Dramatist: George Whitefield and the
Rise of Modern Evangelicalism • *Harry S. Stout*

Assist Me to Proclaim: The Life and Hymns of Charles Wesley
John R. Tyson

Francis Schaeffer and the Shaping of Evangelical America

Barry Hankins

WILLIAM B. EERDMANS PUBLISHING COMPANY
GRAND RAPIDS, MICHIGAN / CAMBRIDGE, U.K.

Published 2008 by
Wm. B. Eerdmans Publishing Co.
2140 Oak Industrial Drive N.E., Grand Rapids, Michigan 49505 /
P.O. Box 163, Cambridge CB3 9PU U.K.
www.eerdmans.com

Printed in the United States of America

13 12 11 10 09 08   7 6 5 4 3 2 1

Library of Congress Cataloging-in-Publication Data

Hankins, Barry, 1956-
Francis Schaeffer and the shaping of Evangelical America / Barry Hankins.
    p.   cm.   — (Library of religious biography)
Includes bibliographical references.
ISBN 978-0-8028-6389-8 (pbk.: alk. paper)
1. Schaeffer, Francis A. (Francis August)
2. Evangelicalism — United States — History.
3. United States — Church history — 20th century.   I. Title.

BR1643.S33H36   2008
267′.13092 — dc22
[B]
                   2008026250

The author and publisher gratefully acknowledge permission of Good News/
Crossway to quote from *The Complete Works of Francis Schaeffer,* 5 vols.
(Wheaton, Ill.: Crossway Books, 1982).

For Becky

120225

Contents

Acknowledgments

There are several individuals and institutions who helped make this book possible. A Baylor Horizons Grant, part of a Lilly Endowment project, funded the travel necessary to conduct the research, and Baylor provided a summer sabbatical in 2005 during which I was able to write the second half of the book. Doug Henry, Ronny Fritz, and Vickie Dunnam in Baylor's Institute for Faith and Learning were all of great assistance in administering the grant. Wayne Sparkman, director of the PCA Historical Center at Covenant Theological Seminary, was an immense help during the early research stage, not only in procuring documents but also in providing helpful leads about stories and sources concerning Schaeffer's early career. David Malone, David Osielski, and Keith Call at the Wheaton College Archives and Special Collections aided my foray into the Hans Rookmaaker Papers. Editor David Bratt proved to be a good adviser and friend as the book was shepherded into the Eerdmans fold.

I would like to thank all those who were willing to interview with me. They are duly cited in the endnotes. Among interviewees, historian Mark Noll, attorney and religious liberty activist John Whitehead, and author and editor James Sire provided copies of their personal correspondence with Schaeffer. Much of chapter eight is based on this correspondence. (Members of the Schaeffer family were unwilling to be interviewed for this book.) Graduate assistants Randa Barton, Hunter Baker, and Steele Brand (the killer B's) chased down numerous rabbits during the research for the book, always with good cheer. Several individuals read parts of the manuscript, including Da-

Acknowledgments

vid Bebbington, Margaret Bendroth, Mike Hamilton, and Bill Trollinger. Darryl Hart, Sean Lucas, William Edgar, my Baylor colleague Tommy Kidd, and doctoral student Hunter Baker read the entire manuscript. Tommy listened to endless interpretive possibilities at a picnic table next to the Brazos River over barbeque sandwiches from Vitek's Grocery, so thanks to Bill and Sue Vitek as well.

My wife was a constant source of support, serving as sounding board, encourager, and ruthless editor. Her name appears on the dedication page. While all of these individuals offered invaluable criticism and helped me avoid embarrassing factual mistakes and unhelpful interpretations, I take full responsibility for any errors that remain.

Introduction

On Friday, March 11, 2005, several hundred people gathered at the America's Center in downtown St. Louis for the kickoff of L'Abri Jubilee, the fiftieth anniversary celebration of the Christian community in the Swiss Alps founded by Francis and Edith Schaeffer. While one might have expected a lineup of speakers to heap praise on the Schaeffers, this was no time for hero worship. Instead, most of the sessions consisted of serious lectures about the practical work of transforming culture through an authentic exercise of the Christian faith. Dick Keyes, leader of L'Abri near Boston, told of being asked one time at a conference why evangelical Christians seem so ineffective within the larger culture. Keyes told his audience at that meeting to review their conference programs and the kinds of sessions listed. That conference, he said, offered sessions on personal finances, devotional life, the Christian family, and worship, but nothing on the environment, art, architecture, economics, sociology, psychology, or higher education. By contrast, L'Abri Jubilee included sessions dealing with these and other culturally relevant topics. Keyes's own L'Abri Jubilee session was "The Lordship of Christ in All of Life," which could very well have been the subtitle for the entire weekend in St. Louis. In nearly all the sessions, presenters stressed that the Christian faith should not take a believer out of the world, but rather Christians should live deeply in the culture, bringing their faith commitment to bear in all areas of God's creation.

In keynote addresses at the Jubilee's plenary sessions, Harold O. J. Brown stressed apologetics, Charles Colson advocated the political engagement of the Christian Right, while Os Guinness gave a Christian critique of western intellectual history. Ranald Macaulay, a Schaeffer son-in-law and early L'Abri student, argued that while the Schaeffers valued intellectual matters, the central thrust of their ministry was set on April 1, 1955, the first day the family lived at L'Abri. Schaeffer moved unpacked boxes to the side of the living room so he could preach to his family. His text was Joshua 3: "Put your feet in Jordan. . . . God will take care of you."[1]

Those attending L'Abri Jubilee lived out in microcosm this sort of reliance on the providence of God. At the opening session, conference organizer Larry Snyder called the entire assembly to prayer for a L'Abri woman who had just learned she was suffering from multiple sclerosis. Snyder prayed for her by name. When one of the conferees fell ill during lunch on the second day of the conference, leaders halted the luncheon for prayer as paramedics carried the individual to the hospital by ambulance. Jubilee participants honored fifty years of L'Abri by appropriating the varied and complex evangelical influence of Francis and Edith Schaeffer.

It is hard to find an evangelical from the northern or midwestern United States between the ages of fifty and seventy who was not influenced by Francis Schaeffer. Even many people younger than fifty have been influenced by Schaeffer's later works, or by an author such as Nancy Pearcey or Os Guinness, both of whom count Schaeffer as a mentor. In the fall of 1979 I read my first Francis Schaeffer book, probably *The God Who Is There,* although it hardly matters because I immediately read several more. The books had a profound effect on me. Reading Schaeffer was a seminal experience in my decision to become a college professor and pursue Christian scholarship as a calling. If nothing else, Schaeffer inspired within me a desire for more academic study of church history, philosophy, theology, and related subjects, and his books helped me think self-consciously about Christian worldview development.

Schaeffer was among the first well-known evangelicals to emphasize Christian thinking about philosophy and art, and he did this largely in an evangelical subculture that gave short shrift to things of the mind — a subculture still suffering the effects of what Mark Noll would later call *The Scandal of the Evangelical Mind.*[2] I was reared in a denomination that valued religious experience but often denigrated intellectual pursuits. Men and women in my church told of young men in the 1970s during the Jesus Movement who were on fire for God until they went to seminary, cooled off, and became overly intellectual and no longer effective preachers. More than the details or even the essential outlines of Schaeffer's critique, what stood out for me was that he took ideas seriously and conveyed the message that loving God with one's mind meant studying the world God created. This was breathtaking in its implications for many evangelicals in the 1960s and 1970s.

Throughout the 1980s and 1990s, as I completed graduate school and took up residence full-time in the world of Christian scholarship, I met many others whose stories were quite like mine. They too had been inspired by Schaeffer, had come to reject the details of his arguments, but nevertheless viewed his influence as quite positive. In 1997, historian Michael Hamilton wrote the best biographical piece on Schaeffer to date for *Christianity Today.* On the magazine's cover was an artistic rendition of Schaeffer and the caption "Our Saint Francis." In the article, titled "The Dissatisfaction of Francis Schaeffer," Hamilton chronicled Schaeffer's profound impact on an entire generation of evangelicals, his transition from intellectual culture critic to Christian Right activist, and the disappointment many of Schaeffer's followers experienced as a result of that transition. In Hamilton's view, Schaeffer had come full circle from his fundamentalism in the 1930s and 1940s, but in the process had become "evangelicalism's most important public intellectual in the 20 years before his death."[3]

I concur with Hamilton's assessment, at least for the most part. What follows is an attempt to portray Schaeffer in a critical biography. In Schaeffer we encounter one of the most important evangelicals of the twentieth century, and his legacy is varied to say the least. Beginning with deep roots in American fundamentalism, Schaeffer seems to have become in some ways a broad-minded, progressive evangelical without ever forfeiting his past. He and Edith developed at L'Abri a model of Christian community that is still profoundly influential throughout evangelicalism, as the L'Abri Jubilee celebration showed. Moreover, Schaeffer inspired both Christian scholars and Christian Right activists, two groups often at odds with one another. He was a complex and fascinating person, part evangelical and part fundamentalist.

The key to understanding Schaeffer, and the thesis of this book, is his move from the United States to Europe in 1948 and back again in the late 1960s. In Europe, militant fundamentalism's intellectual emphasis on denouncing and refuting liberalism made little sense. While Europe seemed to liberate him from American fundamentalism, in actuality Schaeffer employed the intellectual side of fundamentalism in the service of what can be called apologetic evangelism, and he did this at L'Abri, in the context of Christian community and hospitality. When he returned to America for extended lecture tours and began to participate in American evangelicalism, he once again took up the fundamentalist task of militantly defending the faith against the modern world, and he was willing to divide the evangelical subculture itself along doctrinal lines in the battles over the inerrancy of scripture. This new attempt to defend the faith led quite easily to his political role defending what he believed was the Christian base of American culture. It was not so much that Schaeffer changed fundamentally throughout these three periods, but rather that he adapted the tenets of fundamentalism and evangelicalism to meet the exigencies of the culture where he lived — America in the 1930s and 1940s, Europe from 1948 to 1965, then America again from 1965 to 1984. While militant in battle and fervent in evangelism, he and Edith, and the community of L'Abri, became an exercise in demonstrable Christian compassion of great significance. In an age of communal experimentation in the 1960s, the Schaeffers communicated effectively with young people, adapting and even co-opting the counterculture and putting it to use for the kingdom of God.

While researching and writing this book, I met few who said they had read Schaeffer recently, and some who count him as a major influence in their lives believe the Schaeffer phenomenon, at least in its intellectual permutation, could not have happened in any period other than the sixties and seventies. At least for some, Schaeffer's heavy emphasis on reasoning one's way to the truth does not resonate as well today, in a postmodern era when people are less confident in the efficacy of human reason. Schaeffer's books seem important largely as an example of the way evangelicals and most other Americans thought about ideas at the end of the modern era that began during the Enlightenment of the eighteenth century and lasted until the advent of twentieth-century postmodernism.

The modern era put a heavy emphasis on objective reason as the surest guide to the truth, while postmodernists have argued that all truth is at least perspectival, if not actually relative. Schaeffer was peculiar in that he was in some ways a product of the Enlightenment's emphasis on reason while at the same time critical of where Enlightenment reason had taken the western world. He anticipated the coming of postmodernism by demonstrating that it was impossible to live consistently according to modern Enlightenment presuppositions. Modern thinkers shaped by the Enlightenment divorced religious truth from scientific truth and portrayed religion as little more than an irrational experience. Only through an "escape from reason" and an irrational "leap of faith" could people move from the rational and scientific realm into the arena of religious truth and ultimate meaning. In short, the modern project, Schaeffer argued compellingly, was incoherent because it was built on reason while at the same time requiring an "escape from reason." Ironically, Schaeffer's own method in his intellectual work was akin to the rationalism of the Enlightenment. The primary difference between Schaeffer and the modern thinkers he critiqued was that he believed everything made sense rationally once "the God who is there" became the first premise of the reasoning process.

Of course, it is important to keep in mind when reading Schaeffer that he often overemphasized the particular point he was making in the service of an argument. In this regard, an anecdote is illustrative. Wheaton college philosophy professor Arthur Holmes tells of chasing Schaeffer down after he spoke at Wheaton to ask if he were aware of the positive contributions of existential philosophers such as Martin Buber who defied the negative description of existentialism Schaeffer had just given. Schaeffer answered, "Oh yes, but I'm just making a point."[4] He could sound at times like a Christian rationalist, but he also gave lectures in which he would attempt to balance spirituality and rationality. He sometimes focused so intently on rational arguments that he seemed to suggest one could be argued into the kingdom of God. He did not believe this, of course; he was just making a point.

Many Christian scholars today criticize Schaeffer, not only because of this reliance on modern rationalism, but even more because his interpretation of the course of western intellectual history, what he called "the flow," was problematic in its details. Some Christian scholars who critique Schaeffer's arguments, however, might not be scholars at all if not for his influence. In the 1980s, when a historian who acknowledged being influenced by Schaeffer nevertheless took Schaeffer to task for his interpretative errors and oversimplified view of history, another Christian scholar wrote a letter to the editor of a Christian magazine pointing out that the Schaeffer critic was living proof of Schaeffer's positive influence. The student had learned his lessons so well that he was now teaching the master.

That said, Schaeffer's primary significance is not in a lasting critique of western thought, nor in a reasoned apologetic that would necessarily be persuasive today. His arguments have not stood the test of time in terms of their historical veracity or philosophical soundness. He was not the scholar, philosopher, or great theologian that his publishers liked to claim on his book jackets. Rather, Schaeffer is significant primarily because when he came back to the United States in the mid-1960s, most American evangelicals were still in the throes of fundamentalist separatism, in which Christian public identity manifested itself primarily in an attempt to shun the secular world. Schaeffer was the most popular and influential American evangelical of his time in reshaping evangelical attitudes toward culture, helping to move evangelicals from separatism to engagement. At the same time, as his later years indicate, he was a culturally engaged evangelical whose fundamentalist defense of the faith blurred the bright-line distinction many would like to make between fundamentalism and evangelicalism. What remains of Schaeffer's influence is less the content of what he wrote than his model of Christian worldview development, compassion for the lost, hospitality, cultural engagement, and militant defense of the faith against the onslaught of theological liberalism and secular humanism.

CHAPTER ONE

The Making of an American Fundamentalist

Nothing in Francis Schaeffer's family history or upbringing suggested that he would become an evangelical, let alone a major evangelical figure. He was a second generation German American from a working-class family in Germantown, Pennsylvania. Germantown was first settled by German and Dutch Mennonites from the lower Rhine Valley, who were greeted in 1683 by Pennsylvania founder William Penn. The town incorporated in 1691 and is now a neighborhood in Philadelphia, about six miles northwest of the center of downtown. Germantown was the first significant German community in American history.[1] While it is fitting for Schaeffer's life that the original settlers of Germantown were, like him, religious dissenters, the connection is purely coincidental, because Schaeffer grew up in a home where religion was not taken very seriously. By his own later fundamentalist standards, his family was non-Christian.

Schaeffer's Early Years

In 1869, after a stint in the Franco-Prussian War, Franz August Schaeffer II, Schaeffer's grandfather, emigrated from Germany to Germantown with his wife and child. Ten years later, three years after his son Franz August Schaeffer III was born, grandfather Schaeffer was killed in an industrial accident at the railroad where he worked. Young Frank, as Franz III was called, grew up in the era of child labor, working long hours in a coal-sorting business and completing only the third grade. He ran away from home, joined the Navy, was honorably discharged, then rejoined the Navy to fight in the Spanish-American War of 1898. Honorably discharged a second time, he settled as a workingman back in Germantown and married Bessie Williamson. Bessie's grandfather, William Joyce, had emigrated from England to Germantown in 1846. Bessie's father, Wallace Williamson, died in his mid-thirties, leaving Bessie's mother to care for four children and her own aging father, who lived with the Williamson family. Although a graduate of Germantown Grammar School and thus eligible to become a teacher, Bessie remained with her mother, helping to run a laundry out of their home to make a living for the three other children and the grandfather. It is not clear how Frank and Bessie met, but they were married probably during the first decade of the twentieth century or just after. Bessie was determined not to become a slave to raising children, as she believed her mother had, and for this reason Francis would be her only child.[2]

Francis August Schaeffer IV was born in 1912 in Germantown. According to family lore, the delivering doctor was drunk at the time. He nevertheless handled the birthing duties without any problem, except that the next morning he had no recollection of the event and forgot to register Schaeffer's birth. In 1947, when Schaeffer applied for a passport to travel to Europe, he learned for the first time that he had no official birth certificate.

Schaeffer grew up in a working-class atmosphere and attended Germantown High School, where he was listed in the yearbook as FRAN — Friendly, Restless, Ambitious, Nonchalant. He was involved in school politics as class secretary and was noted as "a straight shoot'n youngster and an enthusiastic member of the Engineering Club."[3] While neither of his parents were intensely religious in a personal way, they attended First Presbyterian Church of Germantown. Schaeffer remembered this church as a mainline liberal congregation, where Sunday after Sunday he listened to the preacher and "realized that he was giving answers to nothing."[4] Eventually Schaeffer became an agnostic.

Shortly thereafter, at the age of seventeen, he began reading Greek philosophy. As Edith tells the story, Francis's Sunday school teacher had invited young Fran to help tutor a Russian immigrant in English. When Schaeffer went to a local bookstore and asked for a beginner's manual of English, the proprietor sent him home with the wrong book, a Greek philosophy text, which Schaeffer decided to read on his own.[5] In the ancient Greeks he encountered intriguing philosophical problems but answers he found unsatisfying, similar to the preaching he was hearing at church. After reading some of the ancient Greeks, he decided to read the Bible. "And I found truth in that Book," he would write later. "In my reading of philosophy I saw that there were innumerable problems that nobody was giving answers for. But in the Bible I began to find answers, not individual answers that shot down problems one at a time, but a series of answers that bound all the problems together. The Bible, it struck me, dealt with man's problems in a sweeping, all-encompassing thrust."[6] As Edith would say later, the reason that Schaeffer would insist throughout his life that the Bible had all of life's answers was that he had found this to be so for himself at a rather young age.[7] It is also worth noting that he would always treat the Bible as something of a philosophical text to be understood rationally, which reflected not only the fundamentalism of Schaeffer's day but also the way he approached ancient Greek philosophy — the difference being that the Bible was the inspired and inerrant word of God.

Even allowing that Schaeffer may have been reading some later understanding back into his first experience with serious Bible study, there is little reason to doubt that this early encounter with scripture was foundational and that it set him firmly on the course of biblical fundamentalism. In 1930, about six months after his initial experience with the Bible, he became a Christian at a tent revival meeting led by evangelist Anthony Zeoli. Like Schaeffer, Zeoli had grown up in Philadelphia, where he got involved in drugs and crime, eventually landing in prison. While he was serving his sentence someone gave him a Bible, which led to his conversion to the Christian faith. He emerged from prison to become known as "the walking Bible," and he engaged in evangelism for sixty years.

Schaeffer graduated from high school the same year he was converted. Although his family put very little stock in the life of the mind and had few books and almost nothing of what might be considered high culture in the home, Schaeffer wanted to go to college. His parents valued physical labor, but the young Francis showed real ability to use his mind. The family emphasis on manual labor together with his own intellectual abilities resulted in his first attending Drexel Institute in Philadelphia to study engineering, but this he found unsatisfying, especially after feeling a call to the ministry. He began talking to his old Sunday school teacher and the headmaster of the Germantown Academy, both of whom were alumni of Hampden-Sydney College in Virginia. They encouraged him to consider their alma mater as an excellent preparation for seminary and the ministry. In January 1931 he switched from Drexel to a night program at Central High School, where he could take Latin and German, then in September he transferred to Hampden-Sydney.

Going off to Hampden-Sydney, a liberal arts college, was an act of rebellion against his father's desire that he become a workingman. His father believed ministers were non-producers; they did not make anything of value and were thus parasites on society. His father tried to talk him out of going, even on the morning Schaeffer was scheduled to leave for Virginia. Schaeffer went to the basement of his home, asked God for guidance in defying his father's wishes, then tossed a coin, praying that it would come up heads if he were to go to Hampden-Sydney. When it did, he tossed the coin again, praying that this time it would come up tails. Then he tossed a third time, praying for heads again. When the tosses came up heads, tails, heads, he went upstairs and told his father he was leaving. His father relented and agreed to pay half of Francis's tuition and expenses the first year.[8]

Hampden-Sydney was, and is, an all-male college named for political activists John Hampden and Algernon Sydney, both defenders of representative government and religious toleration in seventeenth-century England. Hampden died in 1643 fighting on the Puritan-Parliamentarian side of the English Civil War, and Sydney was executed by the Restoration monarch Charles II in 1683 for denouncing the king's arbitrary rule. During the era of the American Revolution, various founding fathers considered Hampden and Sydney heroes for liberty. Princeton president and Scottish Presbyterian minister John Witherspoon suggested the name of the school to the first Hampden-Sydney president, Samuel Stanhope Smith, a Princeton valedictorian, Presbyterian minister, and influential Christian intellectual. Patrick Henry and James Madison both served on the original board of trustees when the college opened in 1775, and the school became the southernmost version of the "Log College" phenomenon, which was started in the early eighteenth century in the colony of Pennsylvania by revivalist William Tennent. Log colleges were Christian schools started in log houses and designed to train revivalist ministers. Like most church-related colleges in mainline denominations, Hampden-Sydney did not maintain its original religious fervor, and by the time Schaeffer arrived, the college, like its sponsoring denomination, had become much more liberal theologically than its staunch Calvinist founders. Still, the president, chaplain, and Bible professor were traditionalist, orthodox Christians who had great influence on Schaeffer. He would say later that his basic approach to the Bible was set by the time he graduated from Hampden-Sydney, even before going to seminary. The college was also a school for southern aristocrats, and many of the three hundred students were the sons of alumni. Into this setting came the northerner Schaeffer from working-class Philadelphia, a ministerial student among classmates who looked askance at the profession. He was dubbed "Philly" by some of the other students, and the nickname stuck for his four years at Hampden-Sydney.[9] Even during his college days he ministered among his classmates, often helping them navigate the dorm halls when they returned to campus drunk on Saturday nights, then taking them to church the next morning.[10] Schaeffer served as president of the Pre-ministerial Student Association during his time at Hampden-Sydney. He graduated in 1935, and that same year he married Edith.

Edith Seville was born in China, the daughter of missionaries with the China Inland Mission. Her father's ancestors hailed from England and Northern Ireland and immigrated to America in the first half of the nineteenth century, settling in Pittsburgh, where her father, George Seville, was born in 1876. He would live to be 101 years old. He attended Westminster College in New Wilmington, Pennsylvania, taught for two years, then attended the Presbyterian Allegheny Theological Seminary to prepare for mission work, having heard of the need for Christian missionaries in China by reading about the famous missionary J. Hudson Taylor. Arriving in China in 1902 at the age of twenty-five, he was soon smitten by a widow named Jessie Maude Merritt Greene, who would become Edith's mother. Jessie Merritt's ancestors on both sides extended well back into the colonial period; the family has ancestral stories from the American Revolution and even the *Mayflower*. In 1894, at the age of twenty-one, Jessie married Walter Greene, with whom she planned to go to China as a missionary. Within a year, as the Greenes worked and saved money to attend Toronto Bible College in preparation for mission work, Jessie gave birth to a baby boy, who died during delivery. Three weeks later, Walter died of a rapid and deadly form of tuberculosis. A widow, Jessie forged ahead with her plans for study and missionary work. After completing three years of study in Toronto, she arrived in China in 1899, three years before George Seville. Jessie had sworn to herself never to marry again, and her initial response to George's advances was a stern "no." Over time, however, George won her heart and hand, and the two were married in 1905. Edith was the couple's fourth child, born in 1914 when her mother was forty and her father thirty-eight. Edith had two older sisters; the Seville's only son died in infancy.

The Seville family returned to the United States in 1919 and lived for a time in Germantown where, unknown to Edith, her future husband resided. They were still planning to return to China, but Jessie could not get the necessary medical approval. Within months of coming to America the family was transferred to California, where they would live for three years. Jessie's family had been Baptist, and the family attended a Baptist church in California, where Edith was baptized by immersion. As an adult, Edith would say that she could not remember a time when she was not a Christian; she never had the crisis conversion experience to which most evangelicals give testimony. Her father attended Gordon College in Wenham, Massachusetts, for a time while Jessie and the children stayed in California, then he became pastor of Westminster Independent Presbyterian Church in Newburgh, New York, where the family would live for seven years, the longest continuous place of residence for Edith until she and Francis moved to Switzerland in 1948. After her first year of high school in Newburgh, the family moved to Toronto, where her father became assistant editor of the China Inland Mission magazine *China's Millions.* After two years, the magazine was moved to Germantown. The Seville family moved to Germantown for the second time just as Edith was set to begin her senior year of high school. The home the Sevilles purchased was within blocks of the lot where Zeoli's tent revival had taken place the year before, the site of Francis's conversion.[11]

Throughout her upbringing, Edith's parents taught her the details and dangers of theological modernism as well as the pitfalls of "worldly" living, which consisted of dancing, smoking, and drinking. With the exception of some forays onto the dance floor in high school, Edith took her parents' words to heart and became a committed and conservative evangelical believer, often arguing against evolution with her school teachers. Edith also enjoyed jazz and classical music, reading, plays, ballet, art, and other culturally sophisticated entertainments. Although her family was not wealthy, she dressed well in clothes her mother sewed from patterns she found in *Vogue*. Her refined and educated Christian parents could not have been more different from the working-class, unbelieving Schaeffers, but she and Francis had in common keen intellects and a commitment to the orthodox, evangelical Christian faith. It is fitting that they met in June 1932 at a Young People's meeting at the Presbyterian Church in Germantown, where the speaker was a former Presbyterian who had become a Unitarian. From an evangelical perspective, the talk was a direct attack on the orthodox Christian faith, and when the speaker finished Edith was about to jump to her feet to defend the faith when Francis beat her to the punch. As Francis rebutted the speaker, Edith asked her friend seated next to her, "Who is he?" When Francis sat down, Edith stood to speak her piece, which consisted mostly of quotes from evangelical stalwart theologians J. Gresham Machen and Robert Dick Wilson. As Edith spoke, Francis asked the friend seated next to him who she was. After the meeting the mutual friends introduced Edith and Francis to each other. Francis asked her if he could escort her home. When Edith replied that she already had a date, Francis replied, "Break it."[12] They began courting almost immediately. One of their dates that summer consisted of reading together Machen's now-classic defense of the evangelical faith *Christianity and Liberalism*. With Schaeffer in college at Hampden-Sydney, a school that expelled married students, the courtship consisted primarily of letter writing; eventually a letter a day went in each direction. Edith enrolled as a commuter student at Beaver College for Women north of Philadelphia, where she would attend for three years before dropping out to marry Francis.

Edith was a hard worker, and as a product of an international upbringing and cultured and educated parents, she became a charming and refined woman who provided a counterbalance to Francis's working-class demeanor. Indeed, while both Schaeffers are remembered for their deep compassion for all kinds of people and their tire-less efforts at L'Abri, Francis had a rough exterior and was prone at times to coarse behavior and a violent temper. Moreover, he seemed to suffer from a kind of speech dyslexia that led to chronic mispro-nunciation of basic words. He frequently mispronounced "galaxy" as "galacacy," and one time at L'Abri gave an entire sermon on the "Jews and the Genitals."

There can be no doubt, however, that Francis Schaeffer was gifted intellectually. When he graduated from Hampden-Sydney in 1935, he was recognized as the outstanding Christian student in his class and was given the Algernon Sydney Sullivan Medallion, which had been established in 1925 by the New York Southern Society. Schaeffer's name was placed on a plaque that is still on display at the school.[13] In 1980 he was inducted into the Hampden-Sydney Phi Beta Kappa chap-ter as an alumnus (there was no chapter when Schaeffer was a stu-dent). In an article covering Schaeffer's induction, *The Hampden-Sydney Record* noted Schaeffer's twenty-one books and two films and reported the college president as saying that Schaeffer's insistence on the logical pursuit of truth was in keeping with the spirit of Hampden-Sydney. With Plato, Schaeffer had argued throughout his career that, in the president's words, "the only viable approach to an honest ex-pression of faith is the well-examined one." The *Record* reporter con-tinued, "Schaeffer has achieved world-wide prominence for his rigor-ous arguments that belief in the infallibility of the Bible as the Word of God is rationally credible and defensible, requiring no existential 'leap of faith.'"[14] Graves H. Thompson, a 1927 alumnus, presided at Schaeffer's induction and was quoted as saying that had there been a Phi Beta Kappa chapter when Schaeffer was a student, he would have been inducted then because of the promise he showed, promise ful-filled later by Schaeffer's intellectual achievements. Graves told Schaeffer that while induction into the Hampden-Sydney Phi Beta Kappa chapter was an honor, "in accepting our invitation to member-ship, you also do us an honor."[15]

While Edith would rarely receive such accolades and never gradu-ated from college, she displayed a rare combination of talents. She ran a household, indeed virtually an entire village, cooking for and hosting dozens of visitors to L'Abri, enjoying with Francis their late-night ritual of cereal and conversation, and then, often after midnight, retiring to her room to work on one of her many books, catching a nap, and then rising at 5:00 a.m. for aerobics in preparation for a new day. She lived a dynamic, full life on three to four hours of sleep a night. As one former associate puts it, "Francis, taken alone, without Edith, would probably never have amounted to a hill of beans. The reason is that Francis alone was a morose and depressed individual — a weeping prophet. He needed to be buoyed up, and that is what Edith did. Edith was energetic and ebullient."[16] While Francis might have accomplished much as a pastor and lecturer without Edith, there would have been no L'Abri without her, and without L'Abri, Schaeffer would never have drawn the audience that made his many books possible and led to the type of recognition that he received at his alma mater in 1980.

Schaeffer's First Foray into American Fundamentalism

Schaeffer came of age spiritually and intellectually in the 1930s, just after the fundamentalist-modernist controversy, and he would be shaped by the fundamentalist defense of the Christian faith against modernism. In short, modernism was the attempt to modernize Protestant theology in light of developments in science and literary criticism. In the decades following the publication of Charles Darwin's *Origin of Species* in 1859, evolution became dominant in the sciences and was then applied to other areas of scholarship as well. Modernist theologians interpreted the history of Christianity using an evolutionary model. This meant that whereas traditional evangelical Protestants insisted that the Bible contained the purest, most authoritative form of the faith, modernists saw the Bible as Christianity's early and rudimentary expression. In the 1900 years since the era of the apostles, the Christian faith had grown and developed in an evolutionary way, much like the natural world, so that the faith of the modern era eclipsed the religion found in scripture. Liberal preacher Henry Ward Beecher was fond of saying, "Why should we study acorns when we have oak trees among us?" He believed that the acorn of scripture had grown into the oak tree that was modern Christianity.

If scripture was no longer authoritative, then what was? The modernist answer was religious experience. Religious modernism was influenced by nineteenth-century romanticism, the idea that one could intuit truth with the senses better than understand it with the mind. Under this romantic influence, the Christian faith itself was no longer viewed as a set of propositions or doctrines to be believed, followed by a supernatural experience of salvation, made possible by Christ's sacrificial death and literal resurrection. Instead, the Christian faith was a natural experience. God was no longer transcendent but instead was immanent — that is, very near to human beings — and humans were no longer radically separated from God by sin, but were instead viewed as basically good with a capacity to experience God quite naturally. Liberal preaching moved away from the emphasis on doctrine and the idea that humans were sinful and in need of Christ's redemptive work and toward an attempt to touch the romantic sensibilities of church members, so they would realize they were already children of God.[17]

This emphasis on the authority and sufficiency of natural religious experience could be quite subtle, and therefore difficult to recognize as a radical departure from traditional, evangelical Protestantism. Much more obvious was the way modernist theologians interpreted scripture. Using the tools of modern textual criticism developed by German scholars, modernists called into question many standard views of the Bible. This approach to scripture became known as "higher criticism," and in many instances it amounted to analyzing the Bible like any other ancient text. Modernist biblical scholars who employed the tools of higher criticism questioned authorship and traditional dates for various books of the Bible, the historical accuracy of many biblical stories, and eventually the concept of supernatural, verbal inspiration. Many critics saw the Bible as an ancient book filled with myths that point humans toward God, not as supernaturally inspired and authoritative revelation. Key doctrines found in scripture that were presented as supernatural were reinterpreted as mythic, owing to the pre-modern worldview of the Bible's authors. Many modernists found the virgin birth, the bodily resurrection of Christ, and miracles too fantastic for modern people to believe. Doctrines such as the incarnation (God becoming flesh in the person of Christ) were reinterpreted to mean that Jesus had merely realized more fully the divine potential that all human beings possessed.

Machen and the other fundamentalists that Schaeffer would follow began in the late nineteenth and early twentieth centuries to make a concerted defense of the faith against the radical changes wrought by modernists. During the first two decades of the twentieth century there developed a coalition of traditionalists that was diverse and not yet called fundamentalist. This eventual name would come from one of the rallying points for the traditionalists, the publication of twelve volumes of pamphlets known collectively as *The Fundamentals.* Financed by two wealthy California businessmen and published between 1910 and 1915, they were mailed to virtually every Protestant pastor, associate pastor, and YMCA director in the country. *The Fundamentals* consisted of articles on various points of doctrine written by a wide array of traditionalist theologians and pastors. The pamphlets were intended as a defense of the faith, and the tone was moderate and reasoned.

By 1920, however, fundamentalists and modernists in the northern Presbyterian Church U.S.A. (PC-USA) and in the Northern Baptist Convention (today's American Baptists) were locked in a fierce battle. World War I had made many rank-and-file Protestants suspicious of German philosophy, which had helped spawn German theology and higher criticism of the Bible. Many traditionalists reasoned that authoritarian government and militarism in Germany, with its "might makes right" ideology, were outgrowths of the same philosophy now infecting American Protestant denominations. What had been a theological debate before the war became a full-blown culture war after, as many traditionalists became militant defenders of the faith. Evolution became the most visible issue by the 1920s, mostly because it combined theological concerns with other cultural hot-button issues, such as education. In 1920, a Baptist editor coined the phrase "fundamentalist" to identify those who were willing to "do battle royal" for the fundamentals of the faith, and for a few decades thereafter virtually everyone on the conservative, traditionalist side of the controversy was called a fundamentalist, whether they liked the term or not.[18]

Machen was the most reasoned and eloquent defender on the conservative side of the controversy. A fine biblical scholar, he did not fit the stereotype of a fundamentalist. His Calvinist faith put a premium on the intellectual and doctrinal while downplaying the revivalistic emotionalism of many other fundamentalists. Moreover, he drank in moderation and did not support Bible reading and prayer in schools. He was, however, the most erudite defender of the faith. For years he was a professor at Princeton Theological Seminary, fighting to keep that school in the orthodox fold, but in 1929 Machen and others left Princeton and started Westminster Seminary in Philadelphia.[19] They envisioned Westminster as a school that would continue Princeton's fine intellectual tradition while adhering scrupulously to the evangelical faith. Edith was familiar with Machen and his Princeton colleague Robert Dick Wilson, and Francis had read Machen with approval, so Westminster seemed like a natural choice for the recent Hampden-Sydney graduate.

Schaeffer spent two years at Westminster. At the end of his second year the school split, with a group of professors and students leaving to form a new seminary. There apparently had been rumblings of trouble at Westminster even before Schaeffer arrived. He had confided in a letter to Edith in 1935, while he was a senior at Hampden-Sydney, that some of the students and young faculty at Westminster were dissatisfied with the lack of fervor and direction of the seminary's old guard. Edith cautioned him not to accept at face value the reports of young enthusiasts concerning their older, seasoned Christian leaders. Edith knew that younger Christians often fault older leaders for a lack of fervor, and she was clearly pro-Westminster.[20] One of the features of fundamentalism that became more and more important during the fundamentalist-modernist controversy was the doctrine of separatism, the insistence on the part of many fundamentalists that it was a scriptural duty to separate from modernist theology. This led to the development of new seminaries, such as Westminster, as fundamentalists withdrew from the mainline modernist controlled schools and denominations or were expelled. Once unleashed, this separatist tendency often went further than mere separation from modernists. Soon, fundamentalists were separating from each other over various matters of doctrine and lifestyle, and this phenomenon spread to Westminster during Schaeffer's second year there. The split at Westminster was facilitated by Machen's death in 1937; his absence as the leading intellectual force of the seminary was destabilizing.[21]

Led by Allan MacRae and the firebrand fundamentalist Carl

McIntire, the group of faculty and students who left Westminster originally intended to form a seminary at Wheaton College in Illinois,
where J. Oliver Buswell was president. When the money for that ven-
ture failed to materialize, the group instead started a new school in
Wilmington, Delaware, known as Faith Seminary. Buswell joined the
others at Faith briefly in 1940. Schaeffer transferred to Faith with the
MacRae-McIntire group and is usually considered the new seminary's
first student. The Faith group formed not only a new seminary but
also a fundamentalist denomination called the Bible Presbyterian
Church, which actually began in the spring of 1937, just months before the first fall semester at Faith Seminary. Shortly after graduating
from Faith, Schaeffer became the first minister ordained by the Bible
Presbyterians.

Schaeffer identified three major issues that led to the split from
Westminster. The first had to do with Calvinism. While both the Westminster and Faith groups were Reformed Calvinists, Schaeffer believed Westminster was too Reformed — what he called at one point
"Hyper-Calvinistic." Later in life he would recall, "The Reformed emphasis was very much beyond what I was sure the Bible taught and in
fact what Calvin taught."[22] He told a prospective student that the
Westminster professors "have so stressed the sovereignty of God that
they have reduced man's free agency to mere responsibility," which
for Schaeffer undercut evangelism.[23]

The second divisive issue was temperance. As mentioned above,
Machen was not a teetotaler, and moderation, not total abstinence,
became the position of Westminster and the Orthodox Presbyterian
Church (OPC) formed by the Westminster group. McIntire, Schaeffer,
and the others who formed Faith Seminary and the Bible Presbyterian
Church adopted the total abstinence position, which had developed
within some branches of Protestantism during the great crusade for
prohibition in the late nineteenth and early twentieth centuries.

Premillennialism was the third issue that divided MacRae,
Buswell, McIntire, Schaeffer, and the Bible Presbyterians of Faith
Seminary from Machen, Westminster, and the OPC. Premillennialism is the belief that Christ's second coming is imminent, and
that the world will progressively worsen until he returns. Typically it is
accompanied by a premium put on evangelism over social reform, as
the goal is to see as many sinners as possible saved before the world

13

comes to a (fast approaching) end. The most highly developed form of premillennialism is dispensationalism, which divides history into seven periods, known as dispensations, and argues that God has related to humankind differently during each period and even establishes a different type of covenant with humankind during the various periods. Dispensationalism became a grid through which many fundamentalists interpreted scripture, in which the meaning of particular passages often depended on which dispensation the verses were intended to address. The most startling example was the view, held by many fundamentalists, that the Sermon on the Mount was not meant as a guide for the behavior of Christians in the present dispensation but was instead a description of life in the kingdom age that is yet to come. Schaeffer and most Bible Presbyterians were not dispensationalists, but they were premillennialists who placed a fair amount of emphasis on end-times prophecy that Machen and the others who stayed at Westminster did not share. This is not to say that Machen and the Westminster group were postmillennialists (those who believed the world would improve and a golden age would be ushered in *before* Christ returned), but rather that they did not attach as much importance to prophetic passages of scripture as did the premillennialists and did not interpret those passages as having direct application to the events of the twentieth century.[24]

In addition to these issues that Schaeffer recalled, there were two other points of contention that divided the Faith Seminary group from Machen and Westminster. The first of these was the use of the Scofield Reference Bible, which tied into the disagreements over dispensationalism and premillennialism. First published in 1909, the Scofield Bible contained reference notes explaining various passages in sometimes dispensationalist terms. Scofield's Bible became the preferred Bible of fundamentalists, especially dispensationalists, but Machen thought it was weak on Calvinist conceptions of sin and grace. McIntire, however, advocated use of the Scofield Bible.

The second was the controversy over the relationship of the Independent Board for Presbyterian Foreign Missions to the larger conservative Presbyterian cause. The Independent Board, founded by Machen in 1933, was not approved by the PC-USA (the mainline, northern Presbyterian church). Because of the Independent Board's association with Machen and Westminster Seminary, some PC-USA agencies refused to license Westminster graduates. In other words, association with the Independent Board was enough to make Westminster grads suspect, especially as Machen became increasingly critical of the PC-USA. Some conservatives actually left Westminster because they believed the association of the seminary and the Independent Board made it impossible to place conservative ministers in the PC-USA. These were conservatives who still hoped to save the PC-USA from liberalism. With the departure of conservatives still hoping to work within the PC-USA, McIntire and his group took control of the Independent Board. They had no desire to place pastors in the PC-USA, so they cared not a whit what the PC-USA thought of the agency. Instead, they wanted only separatist fundamentalists who would pastor churches in their new denomination, the Bible Presbyterian Church. McIntire and his group turned the Independent Board into a separatist fundamentalist mission agency and elected a president who was not even Presbyterian.[25] A decade later, the Independent Board was the agency that sent the Schaeffers to Europe.

These splits were often hotly contested and acrimonious affairs. Identifying himself as a fundamentalist first and a Presbyterian second, Schaeffer charged in 1937 that Westminster men, in their zeal to form a thoroughly Presbyterian church, had "unkindly and foolishly alienated themselves from the entire body of American fundamentalists."[26] The next year he told a friend that Westminster professors were slandering his Faith Seminary teachers in an effort to keep students from leaving Westminster. He believed that the Westminster/Faith schism was a tragedy that resulted from a lack of toleration on the part of those who stayed at Westminster.[27] Ironically, of all the fundamentalists who had been at either Westminster or Faith, McIntire would prove to be the most militant, contentious, and divisive. While Schaeffer would eventually weary of McIntire's militancy, he never lost the separatist tendency that developed within fundamentalism and that was part of the split from Westminster. For the rest of his life, Schaeffer believed it was important to stay clear of theological modernism and to battle it wherever and whenever possible. His separatism would significantly inform the Christian critique of secular culture that he developed later in life.

Fundamentalist Pastor

When Schaeffer graduated from Faith Seminary in 1938, he became pastor of the Covenant Presbyterian Church in Grove City, Pennsylvania, and there began his career in the new Bible Presbyterian Church. Covenant was a fledgling split-off from the mainline Presbyterian church in town and had a mere eighteen members. With no church building, the new congregation met in the American Legion Hall. Schaeffer was undaunted. He was a separatist fundamentalist pastor called to lead just such congregations. In June 1938, he believed the prospects for ministry in Grove City to be good. He asked MacRae to pray specifically for his preaching, as he was running out of sermons he could take "out of the barrel" and would soon have to spend more time preparing new ones from scratch.[28]

Schaeffer's early sermons, not surprisingly, were often aimed at refuting modernism. He began preaching on God, and soon found himself contrasting the God of the Bible with the God of the modernists. "The people not only liked it," he reported, "but the ones who had children in the old [modernist Presbyterian] church went away determined to get them out."[29] When a speaker came to Grove City College and advocated the modernist view of the Bible, Schaeffer responded by rounding up as many as he could from the mainline Presbyterian denomination and preaching a sermon entitled "What Bible?" Impressed with his own sermon, he considered turning his notes into an article to send to McIntire's periodical *The Christian Beacon.*

The speaker at Grove City College, whom Schaeffer identified only by the last name Cotton, was in Schaeffer's view fairly orthodox except that he accepted higher criticism of scripture "without blinking an eye lash." Cotton tried to utilize the approach to the Bible of neo-orthodox theologian Karl Barth while still criticizing the Swiss theologian's anthropology and view of history, but Schaeffer would have none of it. A little bit of modernism was as dangerous as the whole. But what especially caught Schaeffer's ear was the subjectivism he identified in Cotton's message and by extension in the theology of Barth and the modernists. Barth, as we will see later, provided an alternative to modernism by attempting to recapture the transcendence of God and the sinfulness of humankind, but what alarmed

Schaeffer, even as early as 1938, was the apparent severing of the authority of the Bible from the religious experience of the individual. Because Cotton followed Barth in retaining higher criticism, holding out the possibility that parts of the Bible may not be literal and historical, Schaeffer believed he was left with no absolute standard of authority. "Really I do not see very much difference between the Barthian School and the experiential school he tried to combat," Schaeffer told MacRae.[30]

Eventually, these comments on Barth developed into a full-blown critique that Schaeffer pursued in his preaching and early writing. Moreover, this early emphasis on subjectivism became a central part of Schaeffer's larger critique of western intellectual history. In order to better understand western thought, Schaeffer, on MacRae's recommendation, purchased a copy of Gaston Maspero's 1894 text entitled *The Dawn of Civilization.* He reported back to MacRae, "I have literally spent hours with it and your notes. For the first time I have a grasp of the situation."[31] The young preacher would work into the night preparing sermons on the relationship of scripture to secular history, which he would deliver to his fledgling congregation along with a steady diet of fundamentalist biblical sermons in which he agonized over the dating of Old Testament historical events and what they might mean for premillennialist prophecy in the twentieth century. After one period of study, done in light of early events of World War II, Schaeffer speculated that the end was coming soon, only to have his mentor MacRae gently chide him. "Such upheavals as we are now witnessing have occurred at many periods in history," MacRae wrote, "although modern mechanical inventions make them cover a wider territory within a shorter interval. Also, the radio and similar news-spreading devices make us more immediately aware of what is going on."[32]

MacRae's influence on the young Schaeffer was crucial in many ways, and Schaeffer once confided that he wished his elder mentor could be around all the time "to talk over the 100 questions that arise each day."[33] Ten years older than Schaeffer, MacRae had a theological degree from Princeton Theological Seminary and an Ivy League Ph.D. from the University of Pennsylvania. He also studied at the University of Berlin and the American School for Oriental Research in Jerusalem before taking faculty positions at Westminster and then Faith Seminary. In 1971, he, along with several others, left Faith because of disagreements with McIntire and founded Biblical Theological Seminary in Hatfield, Pennsylvania. MacRae became the founding president.

In addition to offering his young student spiritual advice, MacRae told Schaeffer to slow down, take rests after lunch, and get sufficient exercise. Schaeffer needed the advice; he was working at a breakneck pace. In 1939, after barely more than a year in full-time ministry, Schaeffer was already experiencing fatigue, and his doctor ordered him to be in bed by 11:00 p.m. Such advice notwithstanding, Schaeffer was often writing letters and sermons as midnight approached. In 1940, Schaeffer suffered an attack of influenza and then a relapse that MacRae attributed to overwork.[34]

When the Schaeffers moved from Faith Seminary to Grove City, they already had their first child, Janet Priscilla, who had been born in 1937 just before the move. Susan, their second daughter, was born in May 1941, only a month before they moved again, this time to the Bible Presbyterian Church of Chester, Pennsylvania, where Schaeffer had been called as an associate pastor. Like Covenant, Bible Presbyterian in Chester had split off from the local congregation of the mainline Presbyterian church, under the leadership of seventy-six-year-old pastor A. L. Lathem. Unlike Covenant, however, Bible Presbyterian was a large church, with about five hundred members. As associate pastor, Schaeffer preached on Sunday evenings, worked with young people, engaged in many pastoral visits to ill and troubled members, and did evangelism among non-Christians. He was also active in the building program that had been in place before the Schaeffers arrived, putting to use some of the engineering knowledge he had acquired in his first year of college at Drexel Institute. He stayed at the Chester church a little more than two years before moving to St. Louis in the summer of 1943 to become pastor of its Bible Presbyterian Church. There he succeeded John Sanderson, who had been his classmate at Faith Seminary. Sanderson had become the church's first permanent pastor in 1940, about eighteen months after the church was founded in 1939. Along with Sanderson, Carl McIntire also played a role in the church's early years.[35]

In Grove City, the Schaeffers lived in a small town, and Francis often found himself calling on farmers, talking with them as they milked cows. In Chester, the Schaeffers lived in a shipyard city on the Delaware River about halfway between Wilmington and Philadelphia, part of industrial America. There Schaeffer often attempted to share the Christian gospel in the bars and on the docks among the working-men of the eastern seaboard. With roughly 800,000 people, St. Louis was a large city with a diverse culture. In addition to native-born whites of European ancestry, St. Louis had 100,000 African Americans and a large foreign-born population — 14,000 Germans, 6000 Russians, 4000 Poles, 4000 Austrians, and a smattering of Japanese and Chinese immigrants. The St. Louis economy was dominated by heavy manufacturing in textiles, metal works, and chemical industries. The city was also a Midwestern intellectual center. St. Louis University was already a major Catholic university, Washington University was and is a fine selective liberal arts institution, and Lutherans had a major seminary there as well. There were parks, a zoo, working-class neigh-borhoods, and old-style mansions along tree-lined streets. Compared to the areas in Pennsylvania where the Schaeffers had lived, St. Louis presented much greater opportunities for ministry and for settling in and raising a family.[36]

Bible Presbyterian Church in St. Louis had a handsome building, unlike Grove City or Chester. While the Schaeffers were in Grove City's Covenant Presbyterian, the congregation purchased an old white clapboard church building that had been abandoned in a valley that was to be flooded to form a lake. Church members dismantled the ed-ifice board by board and reassembled it on property they had secured. This enabled them to move out of the American Legion hall into their own building. In Chester, while Schaeffer was there, the congregation met in the basement of their new building while the building itself was being constructed above. In St. Louis, by contrast, Bible Presbyte-rian Church suggested stability. It had a red brick classic church building with high arched ceilings, a choir loft, pipe organ, stained glass windows, and dark wood pews. The church building, which is still at the corner of Union and Enright streets, was in a fine residen-tial area with a park nearby.[37] On the same block were two much larger churches, Union Avenue Christian and Pilgrim Congrega-tional, and a few blocks away on Delmar Street was Westminster Pres-byterian.

For Schaeffer all three neighboring churches would have been everyday reminders of the mainline denominations that had gone over to modernism. In the 1940s the fundamentalist-modernist controversy was still the context in which Bible Presbyterian operated, and while Schaeffer made only passing reference to the mainline congregations in the neighborhood, his members simply assumed that people in those churches were liberal unbelievers. Later, some who grew up at Bible Presbyterian would learn there were evangelical believers in those mainline churches who had not adopted the modernism of their denominational leadership, but Bible Presbyterian was a militantly fundamentalist and separatist church that stood against mainline liberal Protestants.[38]

With Francis settling in as the head pastor of an established congregation in a fine area of one of the Midwest's leading cities, the Schaeffers were able to purchase a three-story, thirteen-room home with a study. Having preached only on Sunday evenings in Chester, Schaeffer now had to prepare sermons for both Sunday morning and evening worship services as well as a Bible study for Wednesday night prayer meeting. He also organized a Council of Churches that was the local version of the fundamentalist American Council of Churches headed by McIntire.

The Schaeffers plunged into neighborhood work as well. The children's ministry was called Empire Builders. On a designated day of the week, the children of the congregation and neighborhood would go to the church for various after-school activities. On some occasions Schaeffer would pack as many children as would fit into his 1936 Chevy and drive into Forest Park, to the boulders by the city's zoo. Schaeffer would tell Tolkien-like fantasy stories and take the kids on adventures through the park, sometimes leading them across a narrow walkway over a stream and small lake. It was great fun for the kids, as some remember to this day. Summer vacation Bible school at Bible Presbyterian was four weeks long and attracted hundreds of children from all over St. Louis, including Asian children from a Chinese Gospel Church. The Schaeffers were assisted by Elmer Smick, who later taught at both Covenant and Gordon-Conwell Seminaries. Smick often drove a busload of kids singing "When the Saints Go Marching In" back to their homes in various parts of the city after the day's activities came to an end. The children received report cards for reciting scripture. Will Barker, who went on to become president of

Covenant Seminary from 1977 to 1984, remembers getting a flag sticker on his report card on the Fourth of July during the summers just after World War II. The kids were drilled on the books of the Bible, nearly four hundred of them screaming out "Genesis, Exodus, Leviticus," and so on through the sixty-six books, all cramped into the Bible Presbyterian Church building on a hot and muggy St. Louis summer day. These efforts to evangelize and train children would evolve into the Children for Christ ministry that would be instrumental in the Schaeffers' later move to Europe. Even as both Edith and Francis faced long hours in their ministry, their family continued to grow. The third Schaeffer daughter, Deborah Ann, was born in May 1945.[39]

The Schaeffers' ministry during their first two years in St. Louis took place against the backdrop of World War II. Edith recalled in her 1981 memoir, *The Tapestry,* the air raid drills and city-wide blackouts she and the girls experienced, often while Francis was still out making ministerial calls, attending meetings, or traveling to Philadelphia as a member of the Independent Board of Presbyterian Foreign Missions. Edith found wartime significance in Debbie's birth, five days before Germany's surrender, while Debbie's future husband, Udo Middelmann, was a five-year-old German boy in an anti-Nazi family.[40]

While the mundane details of family and church life took up much of Francis's life, the bigger picture of denominational and doctrinal strife formed the larger stage for his work. During the 1940s, an important group of pastors and theologians was growing weary of the schismatic separatism of fundamentalism. As part of a new vision of what would come to be called neo-evangelicalism, and eventually simply evangelicalism, various leaders of this burgeoning movement founded the National Association of Evangelicals in 1942, Fuller Theological Seminary in Pasadena, California, in 1947, and *Christianity Today* magazine in 1956. The neo-evangelicals wanted to reengage culture in a way that fundamentalists had not, and they also wanted to present a more positive and constructive theological message. Schaeffer would later identify with these goals, and from the 1960s to the end of his life he would have tremendous influence among what could simply be called mainstream evangelicalism. In the 1940s, however, before he went to Europe, he had little use for what he viewed as a softening of the fundamentalist message. He was still very much caught up in separatism and the defense of the faith against modernism. Writing to McIntire in 1944, he said that separation was a daily matter. One could no more separate once and for all any more than one can, as the apostle Paul said, "die daily" once and for all. "[I]t is very easy to insist on separation for the other man, when it involves nothing for ourselves. What counts is when we are willing to be separate on matters that hurt us personally; when avenues of leadership seem to open to us."[41]

That said, however, Schaeffer still believed in a kind of ecumenical fundamentalism — that is, a unity among all who were truly orthodox and who had separated from modernism. In that same letter to McIntire, he charged that Westminster, in its zeal to be purely Reformed, had isolated itself too completely. "One of the things which grieved me about Westminster was the fact that they were cutting themselves off from all possible contact with other Conservatives," he wrote. "It seemed to me then that this was suicide."[42]

Schaeffer worried almost constantly that the separatist principle would wither within the Bible Presbyterian movement. In 1944, he wrote to a fellow Bible Presbyterian pastor back in Pennsylvania, "It does seem to me that the Bible Presbyterian Church stands at the crossroads, and if the separate principle is allowed to degenerate at this time, the whole matter will be 'confusion worse confounded.'"[43] The occasion of his concern was apparently the invitation of an unseparated church to attend an Easter sunrise service with youth in the Bible Presbyterian denomination. So serious was this matter that the pastor wrote back to say that the invitation to the un-separated youth had been an inadvertent mistake.[44]

There was often great fanfare when a pastor from the mainline PC-USA "came out" from among the modernists to join the fundamentalist Presbyterian movement. When missionary Paul Abbott Jr. did just that in the fall of 1945, Schaeffer invited him to preach at the Bible Presbyterian Church and wanted to advertise in the St. Louis newspapers that Abbott's topic would be "Why I Found It Necessary to Leave the Presbyterian Church in the U.S.A." Abbott, however, preferred the softer title, "How God Led Me to Leave the Presbyterian Church in the U.S.A."[45]

As he promoted newly separated pastors and missionaries, Schaeffer helped organize new separatist fundamentalist churches.

In 1946, he traveled to Gainesville, Texas, to help separatists organize a congregation of the Bible Presbyterian Church. This group had left the First Presbyterian Church of Gainesville and called Robert G. Rayburn as its pastor. Rayburn would later become president of Highland College in Pasadena, California, a school under McIntire's control. (Some from Highland would later split with McIntire in 1955 to form Covenant College in St. Louis, which moved to Lookout Mountain, Georgia, in 1964.)[46] Schaeffer lectured on modernism at the founding organizational meeting in Gainesville. Referencing the two great tenets of the Protestant Reformation, "the Bible only as our rule of faith and practice and justification by faith," he claimed that modernism denied both. He then outlined how German higher criticism of scripture had entered America through Union Theological Seminary in New York early in the century and had grown steadily in the mainline denominations ever since. Modernists, he charged, spoke of love and tolerance until they were able to place their men in the most prominent seminaries and other educational institutions, eventually taking control away from the orthodox leaders who had preceded them. In a reference that would become standard for Schaeffer within the next few years, he called the neo-orthodox theology of Karl Barth the "new modernism."[47]

In this lecture Schaeffer emphasized two ideas that would remain central throughout his life. The first was the infallibility of scripture, something he had insisted on since his conversion. He argued that modernists and new modernists such as Barth denied this bedrock tenet of fundamentalism. Second, he claimed that both old and new modernists believed that something could be historically false and religiously true — for example, saying that while Christ did not physically rise from the dead, the resurrection was nevertheless a spiritual truth that led to authentic religious experience. Developing this idea more fully, as we shall see, he would eventually come to believe that the division of subjective experience from objective reality was not just an error of modernism, but was the central error of modern western intellectual history.

Although a staunch defender of separatism, Schaeffer believed ardently in Presbyterian polity, as opposed to looser congregational associations that allowed each congregation to govern itself autonomously. In 1945 and 1946 the Bible Presbyterians had a series of fights with the Independent Fundamental Churches of America (I.F.C.A.). Founded in 1923 as the American Conference of Undenominational Churches, the organization took the name I.F.C.A. in 1930 at the suggestion of J. Oliver Buswell. It was a loosely organized affiliation of independent churches, resembling a Baptist association, where each congregation voluntarily affiliated with the organization without forfeiting autonomy. At one point Schaeffer and the I.F.C.A. were fighting over Harold Rapp, a good pastoral prospect. Schaeffer recruited Rapp for the Bible Presbyterians with the proviso that he would need more education. Schaeffer urged that Bible Presbyterians act quickly, however, before the I.F.C.A. men "begin beating on him as I am sure they will attempt to do if they have a chance to change his mind." In 1946, Schaeffer wrote to Peter Stam Jr., the stated clerk of the Midwest Presbytery, "[B]e praying for us, as the I.F.C.A. men here in this area are becoming increasingly difficult, and [St. Louis fundamentalist] Ira Miller seems to be determined to cast his lot completely with them." Miller was an older pastor whom Schaeffer believed was soft on separatism. Rapp was received into the Bible Presbyterian Church, prompting Schaeffer to write, "Some of the I.F.C.A. men are not too nice about the fact of Harold Rapp coming into the Bible Presbyterian Synod. Ira Miller is the worst of the lot. They have asked him [Miller] to teach Greek at the new I.F.C.A. school here, and I think it has gone to the old fellow's head. . . . Please do not be too soft about it, because those of us of the St. Louis area feel that it is about time that he decided whether his chief loyalty is to the I.F.C.A. or to the Bible Presbyterian group."[48]

Schaeffer recognized that the momentum of separation from modernism could lead to independent congregations, but he insisted that this was an example of letting the pendulum swing too far. It was one thing to move away from the "machine-dominated" organizational structure of the older modernist denominations, but quite another to move all the way to congregational autonomy. Independent congregations lacked the sort of theological checks and balances that Presbyterian denominations provided, Schaeffer believed. Without such a check, he thought, independent churches tended to fight over minor matters and to have very shallow theological foundations, allowing the minor points to be elevated to an unhealthy status. As someone who had split from a denomination that had split from another denomination, he might have missed some irony in his position, but the point he was making was that congregations should not try to go it alone. They needed the support of a Presbyterian organizational structure.

Schaeffer's separatism was never more evident than when he chose to stay aloof from the National Association of Evangelicals when it was formed in St. Louis in 1942. At the St. Louis meeting, McIntire pled with those present to join his American Council of Christian Churches, which had been formed the year before as a fundamentalist alternative to the modernist Federal Council of Churches. (In 1948, Schaeffer would be instrumental in taking the ACCC to Europe and forming the International Council of Christian Churches, the ICCC.) But the vast majority present at the NAE's founding meeting declined McIntire's offer, preferring a more positive and united witness over the militant attacks on the Federal Council of Churches for which McIntire was already building a reputation. Schaeffer had signed on with McIntire's ACCC, and there he would stay for the next decade. The NAE, in contrast to McIntire, wanted to provide association for fundamentalists who wanted to reengage culture constructively. It toned down separatism and sought cooperation from all Bible-believing evangelicals even if they were still in modernist denominations, thereby manifesting a key component of the fledgling neo-evangelical movement. Schaeffer disagreed with the NAE on the wisdom of associating with non-separating evangelicals.[49] At one point in the 1940s, Schaeffer even resigned from the board of the Summer Bible School Association because its parent organization, Child Evangelism Fellowship, participated with evangelicals still in churches aligned with the World Council of Churches. The alternative to Child Evangelism Fellowship was the separatist Children for Christ organization that Schaeffer was active in throughout the 1940s and into the 1950s. In his resignation he made this analogy: "the Child Evangelism Fellowship is to Children for Christ exactly what the NAE is to the American Council."[50]

In many ways, the ACCC and ICCC served not so much as alternatives to the Federal Council of Churches but as more militant, separatist, and purely fundamentalist alternatives to the NAE. Ironically, while Schaeffer chose McIntire and the ACCC but would later be associated with neo-evangelicalism, fundamentalist Bob Jones would move in the opposite direction. After a brief flirtation with the NAE and neo-evangelicalism, Jones and his successor sons led Bob Jones University into separatist fundamentalism to such an extent that in the 1950s they would denounce even Billy Graham for his cooperation with modernist denominations.[51] By that time, McIntire and the Jones boys were firmly in the same militantly separatist camp, and McIntire called Graham a "cover for the apostates" and his crusades a "ministry of disobedience."[52]

Schaeffer's criticism of the NAE for its lack of separatism extended to Fuller Seminary, another important component of the burgeoning neo-evangelical movement. Harold Ockenga, pastor of the Park Street Church in Boston, became the founding president of Fuller in 1947. Schaeffer was troubled when he heard that his friend and mentor MacRae was considering "going to Ockenga's Seminary," as Schaeffer called it. He compared Fuller, Ockenga, and the neo-evangelical movement to the Counterreformation of the sixteenth century. Of this group of counterreformationists, Schaeffer wrote pointedly to MacRae, "I cannot believe that Allan MacRae, whom I have felt that I have known so well, belongs to their number."[53] MacRae wrote back to say he was not leaving Faith, and he excoriated Schaeffer for dictating his letter to two secretaries. "I suppose that by this time every member of the church there has heard that I have apostacized and deserted the faith for which I have stood in the past." MacRae also went after Schaeffer for comparing the Fuller men to the Counterreformation: "To compare men who stand for the full truthfulness of the Bible as a whole and for salvation by faith alone to those wicked Romanists who sent thousands to the stake on the slightest evidence of trusting in Christ alone for salvation, and destroyed every book that contained the slightest suggestion of this blessed doctrine is as untrue as it is harmful."[54] Schaeffer, of course, did not mean that Ockenga and Fuller Seminary were akin to sixteenth-century Roman Catholics. Rather, Schaeffer meant that just as Luther, Calvin, and the other Protestant reformers had had to deal with the challenge from Catholics who attempted to take Protestants back into the Roman Catholic Church, so fundamentalists were now being faced with the neo-evangelical movement that in Schaeffer's view was a step back toward modernism. Such nuances were frequently lost, however, when fundamentalists fought with each other.

Schaeffer, as we have seen, insisted time and time again on separatism. In 1946, when asked whether pastors who left the mainline Presbyterian Church should bring their congregations out with them, he replied, "I agree with Carl McIntire that in every instance where it is at all possible a minister should bring out a group of people with him. Naturally if it is impossible, it is impossible, and that has to be the end of it; but, of course, it means a great deal to our movement when even small churches can be brought along."[55] Those words were written the year before Schaeffer would make his first trip to Europe, where he intended to advance his separatist message. He wanted fundamentalism to transform Europe, but instead, he was the one that would be transformed. He was about to find separatist fundamentalism inadequate for the challenges he would face abroad.

CHAPTER TWO

The Making of a
European Evangelical

After roughly four years in St. Louis, a restless Francis Schaeffer was again on the move, this time to Europe in a transition that would be permanent and would transform Schaeffer's life. Without moving to Europe, Schaeffer would likely never have become well known in any respect. Europe changed his outlook and opened to him possibilities he never would have realized had he remained in the United States as a fundamentalist pastor. In the Bible Presbyterian movement, he was becoming something of a big fish in a very small pond. In Europe he would be a small fish in an ocean of secular culture. But he would grow.

Fundamentalist Reconnaissance in Europe

The Independent Board for Presbyterian Foreign Missions sent Schaeffer to Europe in the summer of 1947. This was a post–World War II effort to survey the prospects on the continent for reviving orthodox, evangelical Protestantism. At a 1947 meeting of the board, Schaeffer said, "It seems to me that we should find out just what the situation is in the churches. So many have been isolated in those countries during the war — isolated from the new sweep of danger, theologically — and are sending their theological students to study in America without any knowledge of what is being taught. We also ought to find out how children can be given Bible teaching, apart from the churches — something like the Children for Christ work."[1]

Just as the United States was gearing up for the Marshall Plan to rebuild the infrastructure and political institutions of western European countries, Schaeffer and others wanted to rebuild orthodox Christianity by alerting Europeans to the dangers of theological modernism and training a generation of children in the fundamentals of the faith. They hoped that while modernism had flourished in the United States, perhaps the devastation of war had interrupted its growth in Europe, opening a window of opportunity for evangelicals and fundamentalists. They wanted to take advantage of this opportunity by sending missionaries to replant the orthodox faith before modernist institutions could get up and running again. After deliberation, the Independent Board decided that Schaeffer was the one who should go to Europe for three months to survey the landscape for this theological Marshall Plan.

Schaeffer's charge for the summer of 1947 was to gauge the prospects for starting Independent Board and Children for Christ work and to persuade European evangelicals to leave the Federal Council of Churches to join the American Council of Christian Churches. Children for Christ Incorporated was an enlargement of Child Evangelism Fellowship in St. Louis; the larger work started at a meeting of the ACCC in St. Louis in 1945. Schaeffer was named director, and Carl McIntire was on the board. The organization was to evangelize and disciple children and direct them into fundamentalist churches — and away from modernist ones. "Control of Children For Christ," read one of the founding documents, "must be in the hands of those who are not represented by the Federal Churches of Christ [*sic*] in America."[2]

As Schaeffer headed off to Europe, Edith and the children traveled to New England, where they would stay for the summer. The Schaeffers were given a leave of absence from their ministry in St. Louis, and another pastor and his wife moved into their parsonage as temporary replacements. Edith found an old schoolhouse in Brewster, Massachusetts, where she, her sister, the Schaeffer children, and their cousins would stay for the summer.[3]

In Europe, Schaeffer visited thirteen countries and had two appointments a day for the ninety days he was there. Schaeffer wrote long and detailed letters to Edith that amounted to a diary of his travels. He saw the sites associated with Calvin in Geneva, including the church where Scottish Calvinist John Knox preached while living in exile from England while the Catholic Queen Mary was in power from 1553 to 1558. Everywhere he went he met evangelical Christians who shared his concern about theological liberalism. Karl Barth's name shows up frequently in these letters. Schaeffer became increasingly convinced that the influential Swiss neo-orthodox theologian was the primary threat to Bible-believing Christianity; he rarely if ever acknowledged the difference between Barth and the theological liberals Barth opposed. Schaeffer was able to hear Reinhold Niebuhr speak in Oslo, Norway. Niebuhr was well on his way to becoming the best-known American theologian of the era. Like Barth, he was a former theological liberal who had taken on what he called a "Christian realist" critique of his former position. Niebuhr was also a former socialist, and Schaeffer described the American theologian this way: "His interpretation of Barth provides the bridge for a socialistic conception of Christianity, but keeping some of the religious context."[4] In a humorous passage, Schaeffer wrote that he attended a meeting of Norwegian Baptists. He reported, "I understood them better in Norwegian than the World Council people at the conference in English."[5] He also attended a Greek Orthodox service with several hundred Protestant young people. "To see those hundreds of Protestant young people from all over the world in the Greek service with its adoration of the Host (communion), Mary worship, prayers for the dead, and all the rest of it, was bad enough," he lamented. "But far worse was the fact that even this was nearer to my heart than what the Protestant men have been giving here! At least the liturgy had Christian elements in it."[6]

The letters to Edith are also laced with fundamentalist separatism, as Schaeffer spoke to numerous Europeans who shared his view that they must separate from the ecumenical Christianity of Barth and the World Council of Churches. Talking to Baptists and Free Church Lutherans in Norway, a Waldensian pastor in Italy, and the British evangelical preacher Martyn Lloyd-Jones, among others, Schaeffer came away encouraged that there were evangelicals in Europe who were natural allies of American fundamentalists in the fight against liberalism and in the efforts to reach non-Christians with the gospel. That his efforts took place against a backdrop of a war-ravaged Europe shows the extent to which Schaeffer's concerns were almost purely theological at this time. He rarely mentioned the physical needs and suffering the war had caused.

While Edith recognized and valued the theological emphasis of her husband's travels, she also viewed his brief sojourn as an invaluable educational experience. Not only was he introduced to Christians with similar theological views but widely diverse life experiences and national backgrounds, something that was itself a broadening experience, he also took every opportunity to visit cultural centers, especially art museums and historic sites — the Louvre in Paris, ancient ruins in Italy, art centers in Venice. From her perspective, this opened up a whole new world of ideas for "that little boy who had been taught to work hard with his hands, and to ignore cultural things." As she recalled years later, "In a way, the seeds of the film 'How Should We Then Live?,' to be made by father and son years later, were being dropped into fertile soil that summer."[7]

The Schaeffers believed the hand of God was in every aspect of Francis's first trip to Europe, and their belief was confirmed by what they saw as a supernatural event on his return trip to the United States. Schaeffer flew out of Paris, across the English Channel, and on to Shannon, Ireland, then Gander, Iceland, on the way to New York. As the plane started across the Atlantic from Shannon, Schaeffer reported in his last written account to Edith, two of the four engines went down, and the plane plunged three thousand feet toward the sea below. The flight crew told passengers to put on their life vests, and Schaeffer fully expected to "spend the night on the wing of the plane" in the cold North Atlantic. Meanwhile, back in St. Louis, Edith received a phone call at the Schaeffer home, where she had returned with the children in anticipation of Francis's homecoming. Family friend Carl Straub told Edith that he had picked up a report on his ham radio of a plane going down over the North Atlantic. They knew this was Schaeffer's plane, and they began to pray for a miracle. Suddenly, as Schaeffer would tell later, the plane's two stalled engines restarted, and all made it safely to Gander. There the pilots confessed they had no idea how or why the engines restarted. But Edith and Francis knew. As she would write later, "We believe that God is able to start motors, as well as to do other things in space and time and history in answer to prayer."[8]

Schaeffer's summer trip was a great success. As he toured Christian communities in France and Switzerland, he encountered Christians who wanted to know what was happening within American fundamentalism. They asked him about American Pentecostalism and the National Association of Evangelicals, and as Schaeffer lectured and answered their questions he initially became more confident than ever that the separatist ACCC was on the right track. His view on this would change over time, but initially he was enthralled by the possibilities of establishing European fundamentalism. He viewed the trip as "the great spiritual experience of my life, second only to my conversion."[9]

He was also exhausted, not just from the travel and the meetings, but also from having to be away from Edith and the care and nurture she brought to their marriage. Edith interpreted such an extended time away from one's spouse as unnatural and unbiblical. "It is ridiculous," she wrote in *Tapestry,* "for Christian boards, committees, [and] directors to commission men and women to do tasks alone, ignoring the fact that the Bible loudly states that sexual relationship, physical oneness in marriage, is meant to be an ongoing daily thing of fulfillment."[10] She firmly believed that this marital, sexual oneness was an important and basic human need, just as vital as food, sleep, and the other necessities of a healthy life. For this and other reasons, the Schaeffers determined that Francis would no longer travel alone. She would be his companion and personal secretary, attending to the mundane details of travel and appointment scheduling, while he focused his energies on spiritual and intellectual endeavors. When asked to give a report of the first European trip at a meeting of the Independent Board in Philadelphia, Schaeffer made it clear that he would not attend without Edith.[11]

The Schaeffers returned to St. Louis in late autumn 1947 fully intending to resume their pastoral work there. But Schaeffer began to receive letters from Europeans, some from people he had met and some from strangers, filled with questions for Schaeffer and with pleas that he return and help them further establish the kind of evangelical work that was going on in America. Letters also began to pour into the Bible Presbyterian Church of St. Louis from Americans eager to hear about Schaeffer's trip and to see his photographs. Both of these sets of letters put greater demands on Schaeffer's time and travel. The Independent Board recognized this phenomenon as an opportunity, and after Schaeffer's autumn presentation in Philadelphia, the mission agency decided to send the Schaeffers to Europe permanently: "We find from what you have given us in your report that we feel strongly that we should send someone to Europe to help strengthen the things that remain, and the consensus is that the only ones we could send would be you and Edith."[12] Following a brief period of prayer and conversation with the St. Louis congregational leaders, the Schaeffers accepted the offer just before Christmas 1947, and Francis sent an official letter of application to the Independent Board. He would also be under the auspices of the ACCC and would be responsible for setting up the inaugural meetings of the International Council of Christian Churches (ICCC), which had already been scheduled for the following summer.

In February, the Schaeffers packed up all their worldly possessions in St. Louis and traveled to Philadelphia, there to live with Schaeffer's mother for six months before leaving for Europe. Edith recalled later that she cried as Francis preached his farewell sermon, because she saw the move as the end of his preaching and pastoral career, to be replaced by administrative work for the Independent Board, ACCC, and ICCC. The six months in Philadelphia were especially difficult for her, as Francis was away speaking and organizing while she attempted to stand as a buffer between her three girls, now ages ten, six, and two, and her mother-in-law, who had a reputation for being cantankerous and even boorish. Edith was convinced that Mrs. Schaeffer was angry that they were going to Europe, and that she was taking out her ill feelings on the girls. More than twenty years later, Mrs. Schaeffer would move to L'Abri, and those who lived there can tell stories of how the entire community had to patronize and humor the Schaeffer matriarch, all of which was then satirized in Francis and Edith's son Franky's thinly disguised autobiographical novel *Saving Grandma*.[13]

A salutary event during their months in Philadelphia was the acquaintance they made with physician C. Everett Koop. This happened in conjunction with Priscilla's mysterious illness, which caused her to vomit violently. At a Philadelphia hospital, where one doctor had despaired of finding a physical cause and suggested psychiatric examination, the young Koop happened to walk into the room where Priscilla lay. After examining her, Koop determined she had mesenteric adenitis, a malady he had been studying and that usually cleared up following removal of the appendix. In the course of conversation, Edith mentioned that the family was set to move to Europe for mission work and that the operation needed to occur soon. Koop picked up on this line — he had just become a Christian a few weeks before. When the traveling Schaeffer sent a telegram to Priscilla just before the surgery, assuring her that she was safe in the hands of her heavenly Father, Koop was impressed that Christians really lived by this sort of faith. This telegram, along with the entire experience of Priscilla's illness, led eventually to Schaeffer's and Koop's meeting. Nearly three decades later they would collaborate on the Schaeffer film *Whatever Happened to the Human Race?* before Koop would go on to even greater recognition as the Surgeon General in President Ronald Reagan's administration in the 1980s.[14]

Moving to Switzerland

When the Independent Board sent the Schaeffers to Europe, it allowed the Schaeffers to choose the setting for their ministry. Francis had been impressed with Switzerland during his initial visit, and that seemed like the best place to settle. While Schaeffer traveled across America speaking and raising money in preparation for European work, Edith effectively became the family administrator, often making major decisions about the direction the family and ministry would take. In this capacity she arranged for the family's visa to Switzerland and decided which city would be best for them. At the Swiss Embassy she learned that the family would need a visa for a particular city, thanks to Switzerland's historically decentralized political system and the autonomy of its cantons. When the embassy worker from Lausanne proved more persuasive than his coworker from Geneva, Edith chose Lausanne, and thus the family's first home would be there. The embassy worker had scheduled a trip back home to Switzerland just before the Schaeffers were to set sail, so he volunteered to help locate temporary quarters at Madame Turrian's apartment on Rue de la Foret in the La Rosiaz sector of Lausanne. The Schaeffers sailed for Europe aboard the *Nieu Amsterdam,* arriving at their apartment in September. Francis initially spent much of his time in Amsterdam, helping a Reformed church that served as one of his early European bases of operation. He commuted to be with his family whenever he could.

Schaeffer's early meetings in Amsterdam were in the *Kloosterkerk,* a church built in the fifteenth century where the Pilgrims who founded Plymouth colony worshipped when they lived in Holland before coming to America on the *Mayflower.* There he met Hans Rookmaaker, an art critic for two Dutch newspapers and a doctoral student in art history. Soon, Edith met Rookmaaker and his fiancée Anky, and thus began a lifelong friendship. Rookmaaker was instrumental in the development of Schaeffer's own critical appraisal of modern art, which became later one of the themes of his lectures and books.[15]

During their early months in Switzerland, the Schaeffer church consisted of the Schaeffer household and a few friends. Francis preached to Edith, the children, an Irish woman they had befriended, and a recently divorced woman from Boston and her two children, whom the Schaeffers had met in the street. The Boston woman soon brought a German boy along, and the Schaeffers began to exercise the type of international Christian hospitality that would later mark L'Abri. When there were no ICCC meetings to attend, Francis dictated letters to his previous European contacts, and Edith typed and mailed them. These letters then led to speaking engagements to which Schaeffer would travel. Whenever possible, Edith and the three girls would travel with him, often to sing children's songs in an effort to start Children for Christ work. In Schaeffer's lectures and sermons, he often told how liberalism in its new Barthian form was taking control of churches in America and Europe, emphasizing the need to train up a generation of children in the orthodox biblical faith. Edith also lectured on these themes. As a result of a series of Schaeffer lectures in Holland, the Rookmaakers started Children for Christ classes in their home and subsequently inspired others to do the same.

As the Schaeffers settled into their work and began to feel somewhat at home, friends urged them to take up skiing, the great winter pastime in Switzerland, and so they traveled to the mountains over Christmas vacation 1948. A friend then persuaded Edith to return to the mountains during the summer. With Francis busy and ill, Edith traveled to Champery in the Swiss Alps alone in February 1949 to find a summer home. After being shown the only available chalet, she calculated that they could afford it, and she signed the papers.

The family spent the summer of 1949 in Champery, and it was such a positive experience that they decided they wanted to live in the mountains permanently. With train access, there was no need to live in the city. The Schaeffers secured the Chalet des Frenes but had to move back to Lausanne to complete their rental obligations with Madame Turrian for September and October. Finally in November they were able to unpack at Chalet des Frenes possessions that had been packed in St. Louis nearly two years before and had been sitting in storage in Switzerland for over a year. Chalet des Frenes was much larger than Madame Turrian's apartment, with a room for each family member, work space, and a large fireplace. The Schaeffers began to feel as if they were no longer merely in transit. As Edith would put it, "We began to feel really at home."[16]

Champery was their base of operations for the next six years. It was a French-speaking, Roman Catholic village in the canton of Valais, a fact that would prove to be a problem for the fundamentalist Protestant Schaeffers. In December, Francis preached a hastily organized Christmas service in a little Protestant chapel that had been built in 1912 by an Englishwoman who had vacationed in Switzerland. Soon, Schaeffer was preaching regularly on Sundays in the chapel. While many of the attendees were vacationing skiers, as was the case at the first Christmas service, there was also a group of English-speaking schoolgirls from a finishing school that rented a nearby hotel. It was a common practice for Swiss schools to move students and teachers to the mountains for the ski season, offering class work in the mornings and skiing in the afternoons. The girls from this school became a nucleus of the Schaeffers' ministry and were soon visiting Chalet des Frenes regularly.[17] The schoolgirls came from many different national and religious backgrounds, and they provided the Schaeffers with an early opportunity to present Christianity to a diverse audience.

Even before moving to Champery, Schaeffer was convinced that the prospects for fundamentalist work in Europe warranted his staying indefinitely. He told MacRae that he intended to live in Switzerland for a number of years to establish the European work of the Independent Board. As the American Secretary of the Foreign Relations

Department of the ACCC, he had already formed the International Council of Christian Churches by persuading a handful of European congregations to join forces with the ACCC.[18] MacRae expressed his disappointment with Schaeffer's going off to Europe; he was "grieved" that Schaeffer had not discussed this career move with him. MacRae believed there was a real need for good local pastors in Presbyterian fundamentalism, and he worried about what would happen to the movement if the best ones, like Schaeffer, went off "to larger work."[19]

It seems that as Schaeffer determined to stay in Europe, he began to put more than geographical distance between himself and his mentors MacRae and McIntire. Now thirty-six years old, he was outgrowing the tutelage of his former seminary professors. He had felt the earlier rift with MacRae concerning the rumor that MacRae was going to Fuller Seminary; now came MacRae's disappointment that Schaeffer had decided to leave St. Louis for Europe without seeking his advice.[20]

In 1950, with the family settled in Champery, Schaeffer expressed his vision for staying long-term in Europe. "I deeply believe in the possibilities here in Europe and I do think the things that have been accomplished in less than 2 1/2 years bear this out," he wrote to the Independent Board. "I must say that my personal inclination would be to hope that we would have many years here. . . . Thus wherever I accepted a call it would have to be understood that I still would be free to continue the work as Director of Children for Christ." He also made a plea for Edith, saying that her writing had become vital for the Children for Christ work, and that wherever they were sent she must not be so weighed down with housework that she would not have time to continue writing.[21] Eleven months later he wrote to MacRae, "I came to Europe because I thought I had the Lord's leading in it, and will leave if I feel I have the same. As for my personal inclinations — in many ways I would remain here. The only personal pull homeward now is that my Mother lives all alone and is at times lonely."[22] Schaeffer feared that a reduction in funding from the Independent Board might result in his having to leave Europe, and by this time he desperately wanted to stay.

Early Development of Schaeffer's Thought

During this period in Champery from 1949 to 1950, as Schaeffer was angling to stay in Europe permanently, he began to put into print some of the ideas that would become staples of his work in the sixties and seventies. Much of this writing would be in response to Barth. In the summer of 1950, Schaeffer gave an address in Geneva at the Second Plenary Congress of the ICCC entitled "The New Modernism," a term he may have borrowed from Cornelius Van Til, one of his Westminster Seminary professors.[23] Barth's new modernism was, in Schaeffer's view, even worse than the old. The old modernists, whom Schaeffer had been fighting since the mid-thirties, were heretics because they denied fundamental truths of scripture, and they were dishonest in their manipulation of theological terms: they continued to use orthodox language, but with significantly altered meaning. The old modernists, however, were at least intellectually honest in that they "stayed within that circle of sanity wherein one man says, 'What I say is true,' and another man if he believes the opposite thing says, 'No your view is false and mine is true.'" The old modernists, Schaeffer argued, retained a willingness to say, "We are right and you are wrong."[24]

The new modernists displayed intellectual dishonesty, Schaeffer believed, because they tried to say that something could be true and not true at the same time. He was here taking aim at Barth's view of theological paradox and irony, although Schaeffer did not use those terms in his address. Schaeffer understood Barth to be saying that the real truth of a theological concept was something different than its historical truth. "The Bible says that man fell in the garden of Eden," Schaeffer reasoned. "Now these New Modernists say that it does not matter if historically there ever was a garden of Eden, so that they try to lay hold of the truth that man is a sinner yet having cast away what the Bible has to say about how man became a sinner. This is what we mean by their hanging a peg in mid-air; they cast aside the historicity of the Scripture and yet try to hang on to the religious truths that the Bible teaches."[25] Such a division of historical fact from theological truth was incoherent and nonsensical to Schaeffer. "To put it simply," he exclaimed, "they achieve this logically impossible feat, of not denying the Higher Critical views and yet producing an authority, by stepping out of the circle of agreement that a thing that is true is true and a thing that is false is false. To them a thing can be historically false and religiously true."[26]

Just before giving this address, Schaeffer and four other ICCC members, including J. Oliver Buswell, visited Barth. Schaeffer reported that while the visit was too short to discuss everything in his address, it became clear very quickly that the basic problem was truth, specifically the new modernists' separation of religious truth from natural truth. For the new modernist it is as if "religious truth and the truth of the natural world pass each other without contact."[27] At their meeting, Schaeffer gave Barth a copy of the paper and asked for his response. Barth responded in early September with a scathing reply to both Schaeffer's address and an article Buswell had written in *The Bible Today* entitled "Karl Barth's Theology."

Barth said Schaeffer's argument was identical to what Van Til had already argued elsewhere. Barth believed that Schaeffer and Buswell had basically accused him of being a heretic, devoid of truth and logic, so what was the point of dialogue? "The heretic has been burnt and buried for good," Barth wrote.

> Rejoice, dear Mr. Schaeffer (and you calling your-selves 'fundamentalists' all over the world)! Rejoice and go on to believe in your 'logics' (as in the fourth article of your creed!) and in your-selves as in the only true 'bible-believing' people! Shout so loudly as you can! But, pray, allow me, to let you alone. 'Conversations' are possible between open-minded people. Your paper and the review of your friend Buswell reveals the fact of your decision to close your window-shutters. I do not know how to deal with a man who comes to see and to speak to me in the quality of an [*sic*] detective-inspector or with the beheaviour [*sic*] of a missionary who goes to convert a heathen. No, thanks! Yours sincerely. Excuse my bad English. I am not accustomed to write in your language.

Barth typed a note at the bottom to Buswell, to whom he sent a copy of the letter, saying that every word of the letter applied to him also, then added, "Sorry, but it can not be helped! Yours Karl Barth."[28]

Schaeffer replied that he was surprised at the tone of Barth's letter and that he had expected that the two would be able to sit down together and discuss their differences amicably and openly, without minimizing the disagreement. Still, Schaeffer was clear: he wanted to talk to Barth again so that he could convert him. "I am sure before God that the position which we maintain is that which is right before the Lord," Schaeffer wrote, "and I would wish nothing better than to see you come to the acceptance of this same position before Him."[29] Buswell responded also, saying that that he, Barth, and Schaeffer were all in agreement in opposing all types of persecution. Buswell acknowledged that while his and Schaeffer's stand for the truth was steadfast, they were capable of error. Buswell, therefore, wanted the dialogue to continue, and he said he would walk halfway around the world to talk to an important scholar with whom he disagreed. "It is not we who have closed our window shutter," he wrote. Buswell added that while he commended Barth's views on religious liberty, "your views on theology are, we are convinced, leading young ministers astray in serious and important doctrines. We are very anxious not to misrepresent you, for the truth is really true, and if we bear false witness against our neighbor, we are false! Therefore, we came to talk with you. We do appreciate your kindness in talking with us."[30]

Ironically, in his demolition of Barth's position laid out in his "New Modernism" address, Schaeffer said, "The end of apologetics is not to slay men with our logic, but to lead them to the true Christ, the Christ of the whole Scriptures." To reach these new modernists, he said, the "logic of heaven" is the answer: "a combination of consistent thinking and consistent living, both conformed to the revelation given by God in the Scriptures." Consistent thinking meant having one's "worldview" shaped completely by the Bible; consistent living entailed not only the things from which Christians abstained, "as important as that is, but also the exhibiting of the fact, that we do not just desire to prove men wrong, but that our lives are unreservedly given to the purpose of leading them to our Saviour."[31] A consistent worldview combined with consistent Christian living: these words foreshadowed his later ministry with Edith at L'Abri.

The address in Geneva also anticipated the direction Schaeffer's thought would take. Published in pamphlet form by the Independent Board in Philadelphia, the lecture was Schaeffer's first significant public attempt to be an intellectual. As with many early forays into the life of the mind, Schaeffer's address lacked the coherence that would mark some of his later work. The lecture was unsystematic and at times rambling, but it contained within it many of the concepts he stressed for the rest of his life. For example, he attributed Barth's way of thinking to the influence of nineteenth-century German idealistic philosopher Georg Hegel. If Barth is difficult to interpret at times, Hegel is even more so. Scholars who specialize in Hegel often disagree on just what the philosopher meant in certain areas, so one could hardly expect Schaeffer to have mastered Hegel. Fundamental to Hegel's thought is the concept of synthesis. Schaeffer read Hegel's understanding of intellectual history as a pattern in which a thesis stood in opposition to its opposite, the antithesis, and the truth would be found somewhere in the middle.[32] Schaeffer's application of Hegel in 1950 went like this: historic Christianity was the thesis, the old modernism was the antithesis, and the new modernism was the synthesis. Whatever Schaeffer's understanding, the concept of antithesis, which he believed Hegel had destroyed in favor of synthesis, would become central to Schaeffer's thought in the 1960s.

While he utilized ideas from philosophy, Schaeffer was not a professional philosopher. Here and elsewhere throughout his career, he would get some of the details wrong when discussing western intellectual history, though his overall analysis would often be helpful for Christians trying to understand the larger picture. In his discussion of Barth and, by extension Hegel, Schaeffer identified relativism as the key problem. Synthesis, for Schaeffer, meant that the difference or antithesis between truth and untruth was lost, and this is where he believed Barth's theological paradox led. Neither Barth nor Hegel were relativists, but Schaeffer intuited that relativism was going to be a key problem in the second half of the twentieth century, and he began to put Christians on notice that something had gone wrong in western intellectual life and that its errors had crept into Protestant theology. Schaeffer was not sure what to make of this, saying, "Thus we live in an era when Pragmatism or Relativism, or whatever you wish to call it, dominates the day," but he was convinced there was a problem and that Christians had better start paying attention.[33]

In addition to pragmatism, relativism, and synthesis, Schaeffer also used the word "subjective" to describe Barth's theology. The new modernists "give scathing denunciations of the Old Modernism as subjective," he argued, "but they themselves are more deeply imbed-

41

ded in the subjective."[34] By the 1960s, he had clarified this connection between the subjective and relative. Subjective truth, advocates claimed, was located within an individual and need not correspond to objective, external reality. One individual, therefore, has personal truth that might differ from another individual's truth, and the result is relativism. Again, he had not put this all together by 1950, but it is clear that the groundwork was being laid.

In the 1950 address Schaeffer continued to connect the fundamentalist war against modernism with wider intellectual currents, just as he had early in his career as a pastor when at MacRae's suggestion he had read *The Dawn of Civilization.* He had begun to see that the problem was more than merely theological, but this time he was finding out not from books, but from daily interactions. He was beginning to spend time with European young people who were not part of fundamentalism or the wider evangelical world. From his enrollment at Westminster in 1935, through his years at Faith Seminary, and then for a decade in the pastorate, Schaeffer had worked and lived mostly among other American Christians. During his first three years in Europe, as he traveled and spoke, and as Edith and the girls brought young people to the Schaeffer home for Children for Christ meetings, Schaeffer began to encounter secularized youths who believed in nothing. "I have been impressed that many of the non-Christian students whom I have met on the continent not only do not believe in anything but do not even feel capable of making the judgment necessary not to believe in anything," he told the ICCC congress. "It is a lack of belief in certainty even beyond that of materialistic atheism. To them the world is a mass of flying unrelated particles and they feel upon them the necessity of running away and standing still at the same time."[35] Tying this back to his theological message, he said that the new modernism was "the same type of insanity" as what he saw in the young people he had met, and it was consistent with the modern thinking of the twentieth century just as the old modernism was consistent with the thinking of the nineteenth century.[36]

Schaeffer's contact with non-Christian young people in Europe, such as the schoolgirls who visited Chalet des Frenes, was significant in another way as well. Not only did they alert him to the connection between the theological battles he had been fighting for fifteen years and the larger world of western intellectual life, but it is quite possible that they taught him most of what he came to know about various thinkers. While there can be no certainty on this point, it is highly unlikely that Schaeffer ever actually read Hegel, Kant, Kierkegaard, and the other modern thinkers he would later critique in his lectures and books. It is doubtful that he even read Barth in depth. Schaeffer's knowledge of these thinkers was superficial, and as mentioned above, he made mistakes with regard to the details. Schaeffer was a voracious reader of magazines and the Bible, but some who lived at L'Abri and knew him well say they never saw him read a book. It appears highly likely, therefore, that Schaeffer learned western intellectual history from students who had dropped out of European universities where secular thinkers from the eighteenth through the early twentieth centuries were believed to have eclipsed traditional Christian ways of thinking about important issues. This trend only increased after the founding of L'Abri and the increased traffic of young people who stayed there.

Of course, some saw this approach as a virtue, not a weakness. "Rather than studying volumes in an ivory tower separated from life, and developing a theory separated from the thinking and struggling of men," Edith would write later, "Fran has been talking for thirteen years now to men and women in the very midst of their struggles."[37] He talked to existentialists, logical positivists, Hindus, Buddhists, liberal Protestants, liberal Roman Catholics, Reformed and secular Jews, Muslims, practitioners of the occult — people of a wide variety of religions and philosophies, as well as atheists. "In it all," Edith said, "God has been giving him an education which it is not possible for many people to have. The answers have been given, not out of academic research (although he does volumes of reading constantly to keep up) but out of this arena of live conversation."[38] Indeed, while this superficial way of learning certainly had its weaknesses, the positive effect was that Schaeffer never divorced the intellectual from the relational. He understood that the lack of intellectual coherence in the minds of his young European friends resulted in meaningless and self-destructive lifestyles. This was why they looked for meaning in aberrant sexual behavior and experimentation with drugs.

While Schaeffer's fully developed approach to these issues was still more than a decade away in 1950, and he was not yet self-consciously constructing a Christian worldview that would encompass the deepest questions of modernity, he was beginning to come to grips with the inadequacies of fundamentalism. Europe placed before him questions that transcended concerns of whether Christians should drink alcohol, dance, or go to movies, and issues such as end-times theology were not central to the problems of twentieth-century Europeans. He was not finished with fundamentalism, though, and in his 1950 address he continued to hammer modernism for its deficiencies. The new modernism was relativistic and subjective in all but one area, the Bible. "We have said that there are no clear doctrinal lines in the New Modernism, but we must make one exception," he insisted to the ICCC members assembled in Geneva. "The New Modernists do raise a definite chorus that the Bible *is not* the Word of God [emphasis in original]. Their well known words are, 'The Bible is not the Word of God, but contains the Word of God.'"[39] This attack on modernism was an aspect of fundamentalism Schaeffer would never relinquish, and it would be more important in his later career than many people realize. On other matters, however, Schaeffer, even while preparing and delivering his 1950 "New Modernism" address, was becoming disillusioned with fundamentalism and was already in the process of breaking with the movement.

The Break with Fundamentalism

The intellectual side of Schaeffer's disillusionment with fundamentalism centered around infighting, especially regarding the issue of separatism. His outspoken support for separatism notwithstanding, Schaeffer had always harbored private fears about how far this doctrine should be taken. Even as early as 1938, he confided to a friend his fear that separatism could lead to an overemphasis on fighting against other Christians, especially over issues of Calvinism, and a lack of attention to fighting the real enemy of theological modernism.[40] Those early doubts grew, especially after he went to Europe. In 1951, even while reiterating that separatism was correct, he began to argue that separatism was not enough. Christians needed a better balance, it now seemed to Schaeffer, between militant separatism and positive spiritual growth. Schaeffer accused McIntire and the small group around him of having missed the forest for the trees: "I do not think we can throw everything that we can lay our hands on at even the World Council, let alone the N.A.E., and curse those who happen to differ from us in our own work and expect the blessing of which should be the desire of our hearts. I think we have to be involved in combat, but when we are fighting for the Lord it has to be according to his rules, does it not?"[41] He did not necessarily believe there should be less warfare, but rather a balance between combat and personal spirituality geared toward following the Holy Spirit's lead. Instead of that balance, Schaeffer believed, "We have tended to act as though ecclesiastical separation towered so over every other issue that everything was sacrificed to the pursuing of this battle into a wider and wider circle."[42]

Clearly, Schaeffer was beginning to envision a larger work that would take him beyond the separatism of American fundamentalism. When the owners of Chalet des Frenes decided to sell the place at a price the Schaeffers could not afford, the Schaeffers moved to the more modestly appointed Chalet Bijou in 1951. Their new home had a hayloft that became Schaeffer's personal place of solace. He retreated there often for prayer and reflection, pacing back and forth across the full length of the loft. Emerging from his reflections there, he began to tell Edith that he was dissatisfied and restless not only about the separatist fundamentalist movement but also with his own spirituality.[43] As he put it years later, there were two things weighing most heavily on his heart: "[F]irst, it seemed to me that among many of those who held the orthodox position, one saw little reality in the things that the Bible so clearly says should be the result of Christianity. Second, it gradually grew on me that my own reality was less than it had been in the early days after I had become a Christian. I realized that in honesty I had to go back and rethink my whole position."[44] The first point referred to the unloving and unproductive spirit he detected within separatist fundamentalism. The second concerned his own doubts. He concluded that he needed somehow to go back to his days as an agnostic and work back through his entire belief system in an effort to find a deeper spiritual reality.

Later that year, after many days in the hayloft, and more than a year after his "New Modernism" address of 1950, he wrote a long letter to MacRae saying that his three-and-a-half years in Europe had given him, for the first time in a long time, a period in which he could rethink some of his positions. He characterized his time in Europe as the most profitable time of his life, rivaled only by his three years in seminary. Schaeffer was a few months shy of forty when he wrote this letter, and he was clearly experiencing a theological midlife crisis, exacerbated by his move to Europe. Reflecting on his age and the passing of time, he wrote, "[I]n a couple of months I'll be 40 now and as I look at [my daughter] Priscilla I realize indeed that time has been passing. If God will spare me I will have more time yet ahead than has yet passed me since I came to mature thinking, but it does not seem to stretch forever as it did even when I first came to Europe four years ago."[45] "Gradually," he wrote, "my thinking has changed — I have realized that in many things previously I have been mistaken."[46]

Whereas seven years before he had argued that separatism had to be practiced daily, invoking Paul's admonition to die in Christ daily, he now criticized an overemphasis on this aspect of fundamentalism: "Once people have 'separated' it seems now to me a mistake to spend too much time on that subject — once that battle is past, then it should not be counted as an end in itself, but only one step in a close and profitable walk with the Lord."[47] He claimed that talking too much about separatism fed spiritual pride, causing people to forget the many other kinds of battles that needed to be fought and won. And for Schaeffer, strikingly, a former ally was now the personal culprit in this unbalanced emphasis on separatism: his former seminary professor Carl McIntire. He criticized McIntire's newspaper, *The Beacon,* saying that any article that criticizes the World Council or National Association of Evangelicals was sure to be published, but that editor McIntire ignored much of what Christian people needed to read for spiritual edification.[48]

As Schaeffer began to make the connection between the fight against modernism and the larger intellectual world, he grew weary of McIntire's insatiable desire to fight against other evangelical Christian individuals and institutions. He called McIntire's brand of fundamentalism "the movement," and characterized it this way: "And then came the struggle against the old church machine, and then against Westminster, and then against the N.A.E., and gradually 'the movement' loomed larger and larger." Schaeffer acknowledged that much of that fight had been correct, but for himself and many others, "the correct perspective got mislaid in the process. . . . I wonder if that is

not what happened to the church of Ephesus in Revelation 2?"[49] In
that biblical passage, the author of Revelation commends the church
at Ephesus for not tolerating evil and for exposing false prophets, but
then the author writes, "But I have this against you, that you have left
your first love."[50] Schaeffer talked about how everything became part
of "the movement" and that anything that got in the way was
"blasted," including the NAE, which, although wrong, was made up
mostly of brothers and sisters in Christ. He even questioned what he
saw as an ethical double standard: "And if someone cuts corners in a
way that even the world would question, but he is strong for the movement — hush, hush — don't speak of it — even if the speaking of it
might overcome his weakness."[51] All had become subservient to the
movement, Schaeffer charged, and the movement had to be preserved
and made to look good on the outside. Schools and mission boards
were used to further the movement rather than to be schools and mission boards.[52]

These strong charges notwithstanding, Schaeffer claimed he had
no intention of leaving the movement. In retrospect, however,
whether intending to or not, he was laying the groundwork for his departure. He told MacRae that when he returned to the U.S. following
his first trip to Europe in 1947, he knew that his dream for the ICCC
was not the same as McIntire's. Schaeffer wanted the ICCC to be a
place of fellowship and learning, but he was convinced that McIntire
wanted the organization to be a vehicle for "pushing American labels
and thinking down European throats."[53] "But not for me," he wrote of
the narrow focus on separatism. "[B]y God's grace — the mountains
are too high, history is too long and eternity is longer, God is too great,
man is too small." Rather than continue down the road of separatist
fundamentalism, his desire was to "win as many as I can, to help
strengthen the hands of those who fight unbelief in the historical setting in which they are placed, to know the reality of 'the Lord is my
song,' and to be committed to the Holy Spirit — that is what I wish I
could know to be the reality of each day as it closes."[54]

In addition to the profound theological differences that began to
divide Schaeffer and McIntire, personal and institutional matters
widened the rift. Schaeffer's lack of trust in McIntire went back at
least to 1938. That year, while still pastoring in Grove City, Schaeffer
sent a news item to McIntire. Part of the item was an announcement

about the upcoming Bible school in Grove City, and the other was about a woman who had been put out of the choir and her Sunday school class at the local mainline Presbyterian church but had decided to stay in that church nevertheless. Schaeffer told McIntire that the bit about the woman was confidential, but McIntire published that item and left out the Bible school announcement. McIntire never told Schaeffer he did this, and Schaeffer heard about it from others and was embarrassed.[55]

Once in Europe, McIntire wanted Schaeffer to spend most of his time and energy organizing and administering "the movement," in the form of the ICCC, but Schaeffer, especially in light of his 1950 "New Modernism" address, saw himself as a thinker, lecturer, and evangelist to modern individuals struggling with the question of whether life had meaning. He told an associate in early 1951 that he did not see administration as his primary gift, and that he would go back to the U.S. and be a pastor before he would be a full-time administrator with the ICCC.[56] In this respect, he preferred his and Edith's activities with Children for Christ, because they worked directly with young people, teaching them the Bible and helping them become grounded in the Christian faith. When Schaeffer and McIntire disagreed over whether the Orthodox Presbyterian Church, the denomination founded by Machen and his associates, should be allowed to stay in the ICCC, Schaeffer wrote, "I don't think Carl likes [my efforts to retain the OPC], but I really don't care."[57]

By 1954, Schaeffer and McIntire were in open warfare, and many others in the Bible Presbyterian Church were losing faith in McIntire as well. The firebrand minister was accused by others in the denomination of inflating the membership statistics of the ACCC, and questions arose about finances as well. That year Schaeffer wrote an open letter blasting McIntire's publication of a letter from FBI director J. Edgar Hoover to evangelical leader Donald Barnhouse, who had stayed within the mainline Presbyterian Church. McIntire had published the letter from Hoover to "expose" Barnhouse for having accepted television airtime from the National Council of Churches. Schaeffer agreed that Barnhouse was wrong for staying in the mainline denomination and doing work in concert with the NCC, but he saw McIntire's publication of the Hoover letter as an attempt to vilify another evangelical Christian personally, and this was especially apparent in that McIntire had previously made a joke of Barnhouse's name containing the word "barn."[58] The gist of Schaeffer's complaint against McIntire was this: "It seems to me that in the attitude shown in these cases there could be no other conclusion on the part of logical men than that we were interested in discrediting men and groups, with whom we differ, even when the material used has no relationship to the differences in principle which separate us."[59]

McIntire replied, claiming that after Barnhouse had written an article in *Eternity* magazine criticizing the FBI and the ACCC, Hoover had sent a response to *The Beacon*. The Hoover letter, McIntire maintained, was merely a defense against Barnhouse's criticisms. McIntire then attempted to turn the tables on Schaeffer, arguing that Schaeffer was the one acting in an unchristian manner by writing an open letter rather than coming personally and discussing this matter with McIntire.[60]

By the summer of 1954, the break between Schaeffer and McIntire was nearly complete. McIntire would lead his strident form of fundamentalism throughout the rest of the century, opposing everything from Communism to the Revised Standard Version of the Bible. In 1973, after running afoul of Federal Communication Commission guidelines in his radio broadcasts, he moved the program onto a ship off the coast of Delaware in international waters to escape federal jurisdiction. In the 1960s he purchased a New Jersey hotel that he turned into a retreat and conference center called the Christian Admiral, and he went on to develop a similar property in Florida. He died in 2002 at the age of ninety-five.[61]

The bitterness of Schaeffer's break with McIntire, the ACCC, and the ICCC lasted for many years. A decade later, in 1965, MacRae chided Schaeffer for not paying a visit when he was in Willow Grove, where MacRae lived. Schaeffer defended himself by saying he thought it might prove embarrassing to MacRae if he came to Faith Seminary where MacRae was still president, given that some from the ICCC who had visited Schaeffer after a meeting in Geneva were criticized for having done so. Apparently, Schaeffer was on the blacklist of those whom ICCC fundamentalists should avoid. Schaeffer put this in the context of loyalty to the movement, writing, "It has been my experience that 'loyalty' has been pretty sharply insisted upon in the past." He also referenced the communication difficulties resulting from "what occurred ten years ago."[62]

By the mid-fifties, Schaeffer was nearly done with McIntire's brand of American fundamentalism. He did not yet know precisely what his new work would be, but he was very close to cutting the cord that had bound him to McIntire, MacRae, and the rest of "the movement." Events in 1954 and 1955 would make clear what the future would hold.

CHAPTER THREE

L'Abri

While the split with McIntire and fundamentalism filled Schaeffer with heartache, the decision liberated him for the work that would become the centerpiece of his ministry: L'Abri. The seeds of L'Abri had already been planted in the Schaeffers' work with the English schoolgirls in Champery from 1948 through 1952. One of those girls, Deirdre Haim, recalls that every Sunday she and four of her classmates attended Schaeffer's little church to worship in English. Haim's father was a non-practicing Jew, and her mother was an agnostic and non-practicing Anglican. Haim attended the Church of England sporadically while growing up, just enough to formulate some deep questions about the Christian faith. When she began attending Schaeffer's services in Champery, she thought to herself, "So, this is what Christianity is really about."[1] In addition to Sunday services, the girls visited the Schaeffers' chalet one evening a week to view photographic slides the Schaeffers had taken during their travels around Europe and to snack on Edith's homemade cakes. Those evenings turned into discussion sessions about Christianity, which established a pattern that would continue at L'Abri. Never pushy with the faith, the Schaeffers gently presented the gospel, and three or four of the English girls were converted, including Haim, who would be close to the Schaeffers well into the 1980s. As Deirdre Ducker after her marriage in 1960, she with her husband Richard would be among the first official "students" at L'Abri. An artist, Deirdre would also do illustrations for two of Edith's books, including *L'Abri*.[2]

Finishing the Break with Fundamentalism

In May 1953, during the period when Schaeffer was at odds with McIntire, the Schaeffers began a furlough in the U.S. that would last until September 1954. They moved into Francis's uncle's home outside of Philadelphia. By this time the Schaeffer family consisted of the three girls and also Francis August Schaeffer V, known as Franky, a son who had been born in Switzerland in August 1952. While on furlough, Schaeffer taught at Faith Seminary and embarked on a strenuous lecture and preaching schedule that would take him across the U.S. to churches and summer camps. His lectures and preaching continued on the theme of what it means to live the reality of the Christian life in the modern world, and this was yet another point that put him at odds with other fundamentalists, who wanted primarily to identify errors in the theology of other Christians. When he gave the 1954 commencement address at Faith Seminary that took aim at fundamentalists themselves and not just their opponents, one professor's wife predicted to Edith that there would be a split in the denomination.[3] A year later that prediction came true, as a schism in the Bible Presbyterian Church produced the Bible Presbyterian Church (Collingswood Synod), led by McIntire, and the Bible Presbyterian Church (Columbus Synod), which would shortly thereafter take the name Evangelical Presbyterian Church. The split also led to the founding of Covenant Seminary and College. Robert Rayburn, the president of Highland College in Pasadena, California, and most of the faculty left Highland and formed Covenant College. The next year they moved the school to St. Louis, where the seminary remains to this day.[4] Even before the split, the Schaeffers were almost certain that the Independent Board would not send them back to Europe, so they began to lay the groundwork for the day when they would have to go it alone, raising their own financial support. The board did send them back in 1954, but the relationship between the Schaeffers and the board was about to run its final course.

The return to Europe was filled with anguish for the Schaeffers. When they sailed to Le Havre, France, in September, Franky became ill the last night on the ship, shrieking in pain from a violent stomachache. The next day he seemed fine as the family disembarked and took a train to Paris for a day of rest. Francis and the girls went sightseeing while Edith stayed with Franky. Usually a rambunctious live wire, Franky climbed out of his crib, fell to the floor and cried out, "I can't walk . . . I can't walk."[5] He had contracted polio and would be partially paralyzed in his left leg. Experimental drug treatment seemed to stem the spread of paralysis to his right side, while rehabilitation and later a muscle transplant on his left leg allowed him eventually to live a normal, active life. At the time, however, the ailment was terrifying. Meanwhile, before the month of September passed, Susan contracted rheumatic fever and was bedridden for two months.[6]

Meanwhile, the relationship between the Schaeffers and the Independent Board continued to deteriorate, as they received word that their monthly stipend would be cut by one hundred dollars. Francis was in one of his many dark periods, so to cheer him, Edith began to work on an idea Francis had broached on the ship returning from the U.S. He had told Edith that their place in Champery should be called L'Abri, the French word for "shelter." Edith started a L'Abri folder and sketched a picture of chalets, trees, a few stick figure people skiing, and the words, "L'Abri . . . come for morning coffee, or afternoon tea, with your questions."[7] Her folder was like a handmade brochure. L'Abri would not be located at Champery, however, and in early 1955 it appeared the dream would not become reality at all.

Losing a Home, Gaining a Shelter

To stay in Switzerland, visitors needed a permit renewal every six months. This had been a routine matter for the Schaeffers in their seven years in the canton of Valais. But in early 1955, their renewal was delayed. The Schaeffers began to hear rumors that there was some sort of problem. The cantonal government at Sion summoned Francis to appear before the *Bureau des Estrangers,* where he was questioned about his religious activities — the church services in the chapel, the weekly meetings for Bible study and discussion with the schoolgirls, the meals, and other activities that had become a regular part of their ministry. He was questioned as to whether they discussed politics at these meetings and why they gave free food and drinks to their visitors. As Schaeffer explained the family's activities, the meet ing seemed to go well, and he was encouraged that the situation could be resolved and the family allowed to stay in Champery.[8] He was wrong, however, and in mid-February the Schaeffers received word from the police that they had until March 31 to leave Champery. They were being expelled from their Roman Catholic canton of Valais for bringing a Protestant religious influence.[9] They could not believe that such a thing would happen in Switzerland, a land that claimed to have religious freedom. Many of their Swiss friends thought it had to be a mistake, but when the Schaeffers investigated further, they found that they were indeed being expelled.

With the help of a friend in Lausanne, the Schaeffers filed appeals to the cantonal government in Sion and the national government in Berne. Then they traveled to Geneva to visit the American Consulate, where they were given little hope of overturning their ouster. The consul in Geneva nevertheless encouraged them to go to Berne to report their situation to the consul of the embassy. After arriving in Berne, they were granted a ten-minute audience with the senior consul. As the senior consul greeted them and began to look over their documents, he noticed that Francis was from Philadelphia. When Francis mentioned that he was from Germantown and had graduated from Germantown High School, he and the senior consul looked closely at each other and suddenly realized they were classmates who had not seen each other since their graduation together in 1930. Now the consul took great interest in the Schaeffers' predicament and helped start their paperwork for an appeal. Still, there was nothing more the American Embassy could do, because the U.S. and Switzerland had no mutual agreement regarding visits by their citizens. In the appeals process, as it turned out, there was only one chance for the Schaeffers: they needed a place of residence in a village in the neighboring canton of Vaud. The name of the chalet had to be on the appeals forms, and they had to have legitimate plans to live there. The village would have to express a desire for the Schaeffers to stay, and it would need to communicate that approval to the canton; then the canton would convey that approval up the line to Berne. In short, the Schaeffers needed to start house-hunting, and they had to do it quickly.

Francis and Edith set out immediately for the canton of Vaud, but as had been the case when the family moved to Champery, the house-hunting became a one-woman mission. In a series of steps, fate, fortune, or providence (the Schaeffers would see it as the latter) intervened. Francis had all but given up when Edith requested that he allow her one more day on her own to find a new home. She ran into a real estate agent whom the Schaeffers had talked to days before. Earlier he had told them he had nothing in their price range, but this time, the agent flagged down Edith, told her to get into his car, and took her to the village of Huemoz, where there was a Chalet les Melezes available. Although only fifteen miles from Champery, Edith had never heard of Huemoz, but the chalet seemed suitable. It was not for rent, however; it was for sale. With no idea how the Schaeffers could possibly buy a house, but with so many things seeming to have led her to this particular village and chalet, Edith decided to go home and convince Francis to go with her to Huemoz the next day.

Edith returned to Champery to find that Berne had given the family an extension allowing them to stay in the country until the matter was resolved, but since the canton of Valais still would not budge, they needed to move by March 31. As Edith tells the story, she persuaded Francis to view Chalet les Melezes in Huemoz the next day without mentioning that it was for sale, not for rent. That next day, before leaving, they received a letter from a couple in the U.S. who had decided to send them a thousand dollars from a bonus the husband had received from his company. The couple explained in a letter that they had deliberated for months about what to do with the money. "Now tonight we have come to a definite decision," the couple wrote, "and both of us feel certain that we are meant to send you this money. . . to buy a house somewhere that will always be open to young people."[10] Having read the letter, Edith then told Francis that the chalet they were going to view was for sale. When the money given by the couple was added to other gifts that had come in from friends with whom Edith had been corresponding, there was enough to put a hold on the chalet and to sign a promissory note that allowed the Schaeffers to move in on March 31. They now had a chalet in a village and canton from which they could complete the appeals process.

Shortly after moving into Chalet les Melezes, Edith met the neighbors, two sisters who wanted to hear the story of why the Schaeffers had moved to Huemoz. The sisters expressed outrage at the Schaeffers' treatment and said they would convey the Schaeffer story to their brother. Edith was unimpressed until she learned that the brother was currently serving as the president of Switzerland! The Schaeffers then learned that one of their neighbors on the other side of Chalet les Melezes was an elderly pastor and the uncle of the chief of the *Bureau des Estrangers* in Berne; the nephew was the government agent who would do the final signoff on the Schaeffers' permit. It was in the nephew's absence that his Roman Catholic assistant had approved the original expulsion. A few days later, the two sisters came to Chalet les Melezes with a letter from their brother telling the Schaeffers that the whole matter would be cleared up and that they could plan on staying in Huemoz indefinitely. The Schaeffers received their permit on June 21, and their passports were returned to them with the word *Annulé* stamped over the page that had signified their expulsion.

The Schaeffers were now legally secure in Huemoz, but they no longer had the contacts with the girls' schools, so they wondered how their vision of L'Abri would move forward in a village where they were unknown. Priscilla started studies at the University of Lausanne in April, just thirty-five miles from Huemoz, and brought the first visitor to L'Abri, a student friend named Grace. Within two weeks, Grace sent John Sandri to L'Abri. Sandri and Priscilla would eventually marry.[11] This began a steady stream of students from the university to L'Abri, and many others would come from other destinations as well. Chalet les Melezes was adjacent to a bus stop for a line that traveled to Aigle, where train service connected to Lausanne, Geneva, Paris, and southward into Italy. Huemoz's location was ideal for travelers, as it turned out, and it was also halfway up the mountain on the way to a ski resort. Young people from all over the world would soon be getting off the bus in front of L'Abri.

In June, while settling in at Chalet les Melezes, the Schaeffers decided to end their relationship with the Independent Board for Foreign Missions. They resigned on June 4, 1955. Their break with fundamentalist associations was now complete.

The Schaeffers envisioned their resignation as the start of a new mission that would incorporate four basic principles. First, they decided they would not advertise, but would merely pray that God would send them the people who needed to come and keep away those who should not. Second, without the support of the Independent Board, they decided they would pray that God would send each month the money they would need to run L'Abri. Years earlier Edith had started sending out "Family Letters" to supporters in the United States and other parts of the world. The people receiving those letters would become the network from which much of the money would come. The Schaeffers needed enough to support not only their own family but also the young people who came to L'Abri, because there would be no fees; they believed that the open atmosphere they hoped to foster would be ruined if they charged people to stay. (Later, the ministry at L'Abri would be funded in part by the speaking honoraria and book royalties that Francis and Edith began to earn.) Third, they decided they would not devise a formal plan for how L'Abri would operate but instead would allow the ministry to evolve as God directed. The fourth principle was much like the first: while the Schaeffers were willing to let L'Abri always remain just a small handful of people gathering informally for discussion, if L'Abri grew, the Schaeffers would pray that the right workers be sent to them without their having to advertise positions.

In July 1955, L'Abri Fellowship became the official name of the Schaeffers' new ministry. Edith's father, who was retiring from a career as a missionary, pastor, and seminary professor, offered to be the home secretary for L'Abri. He would receive gifts and send them on to L'Abri and take care of other administrative duties from his home in the States. Edith's mother took over duplication and mailing of the Family Letters.

During the first few years of L'Abri, a variety of young people showed up unannounced and found welcome. Often, Christians who knew the Schaeffers trekked to L'Abri, inviting others whom they met along the way. Some came planning to stay only for a few weeks or months and ended up staying for a year instead. A fairly steady stream of students visited from the University of Lausanne, where Priscilla, then Debbie, studied. These students returned to the university and told their friends about L'Abri, which resulted in even more student visitors. Word of L'Abri began to spread among American G.I.s stationed in Germany, and soon a steady stream of soldiers came on their three-day passes.

While the Schaeffers never kept statistics as to the number of guests at L'Abri, Edith wrote in a letter that during a six-week period in L'Abri's second summer there were 187 visitors to L'Abri, who stayed for varying lengths of time. Edith later recalled being so busy that she sometimes watered the garden at midnight and transplanted plants by flashlight.[12]

Life at L'Abri

Soon after the founding of L'Abri the Schaeffers were able to buy or gain use of other chalets in the village. By the late sixties, L'Abri had grown from the Chalet les Melezes to a number of chalets and a chapel. While it was able to maintain most of their original vision, L'Abri became more organized as the years passed. Eventually, there were four categories at L'Abri — guests, students, workers, and members. Guests simply dropped in for discussion, stayed for a few days, then moved on. Students would come for a set number of weeks. They would study half the day and work the other half, on a sort of Benedictine model. They studied in a chalet that the Schaeffers called Farel House, named for the sixteenth-century Protestant reformer who was instrumental in getting John Calvin to move to Geneva. Farel had preached in Huemoz during the Reformation and was then chased out of the village by authorities — not unlike the Schaeffers' experience in Champery. Farel House began in 1960 and was equipped with several desks and tape recorders. Students worked out their course of study with Schaeffer individually, then spent time listening to tapes and reading books from the developing L'Abri library. While guests paid nothing to stay at L'Abri, students were charged a very nominal fee of a few dollars a day for food and equipment repair. The ongoing staff consisted of "workers," the third type of L'Abri resident. Workers had their various manual labor assignments and would participate in the discussions and hospitality for the guests and students. When funds allowed, they were given a "gift" of thirty dollars a month. Fourth, there were "members" of L'Abri. These were workers who had stayed for at least three years, moved into the inner circle with the Schaeffer family, and become part of the decision-making team. Decisions were made by consensus — an often difficult and time-consuming process.[13]

The L'Abri tape ministry began in 1958 after a businessman from the United States sent a tape recorder to L'Abri, explaining that he felt

God had led him to do so. When it arrived, Schaeffer wanted nothing to do with the machine, convinced that any attempt to tape the conversations at L'Abri would dampen the spontaneity and ruin the discussion. Richard Ducker, who was staying at L'Abri and would eventually marry Deirdre Haim, felt otherwise. Setting up the recording machine in the dining room above the living room where the discussions took place, he ran the microphone cord through a hole in the floor, dropped the cord from the ceiling of the living room below, and hid the microphone in a plant next to the chair where Schaeffer sat while leading discussions.[14] When others present learned that the discussion and Schaeffer's words had been captured on tape, they wanted copies. For the next two years, lectures and discussions were taped periodically; beginning in 1960, there were regularly scheduled Farel House luncheon talks called "The Twentieth Century Climate" that were routinely taped. Those informal talks grew into thirteen lectures that would become known as "The Farel House Lectures."[15] Ducker was in charge of the taping, and when he and Deirdre planned to move away, he trained Jeremy Jackson to take over.[16] Eventually, all Saturday evening discussions were taped, as were Schaeffer's Sunday sermons and various lectures he gave during the week. Copies were housed in a tape library accessible to the students at L'Abri. A volunteer in the U.S. took over distribution of the tapes from his home in Virginia, and the tapes were shipped all over the world. By 1968, there were Schaeffer listening groups across the U.S. and Canada, as well as in Taiwan, Japan, India, South Africa, France, New Zealand, Australia, and nations in South America.[17] Later, tape recordings of Schaeffer's lectures would be turned into books.

Part of the L'Abri community, although financially separate and independent from the Schaeffers, was Chalet Bellevue, a home for children with cerebral palsy. The home was founded by two women, Anne and Mary, who were among the earliest guests at L'Abri. They had gone to Switzerland shortly before the founding of L'Abri to start an occupational therapy school in a hospital in Basel. They shared with the Schaeffers a desire to engage people in intelligent discussion about the Christian faith and its connection to intellectual matters. In June 1955, little more than a month after the Schaeffers had moved into Chalet les Melezes, Anne and Mary paid a visit. They turned into regular visitors and brought many students who were studying with them. These were mostly young women from several European countries and the U.S. After three years, Anne and Mary turned their school over to Swiss control and moved to L'Abri as workers. During their time at L'Abri, Chalet Bellevue, next door to Chalet les Melezes, came up for sale. The spacious building had originally been a hotel, then a Roman Catholic children's home. The two women developed a vision for a home for children with cerebral palsy, hoping and praying that such a place might be opened close to L'Abri so both the patients and nurses staffing the center could participate in L'Abri discussions and worship. When Chalet Bellevue went on the market, Anne and Mary adopted the Schaeffer method of specifically praying for the money to purchase the chalet. Through various appeals, they received the amount they needed.[18]

In addition to students and children with cerebral palsy, by the sixties there were all kinds of young people visiting L'Abri, especially as the counterculture blossomed and word got around that L'Abri was an inexpensive place to stay while traveling across Europe. There were drug addicts, poor single mothers, and pregnant young women, among many others. All were welcomed, and all found a temporary home at L'Abri.[19] Some of those who dropped in were disciples of Timothy Leary, who advocated LSD and other hallucinogenic drugs, while others were from a radical German group that advocated violence against the establishment, and still others were reading Nietzsche, Siddhartha, or C. S. Lewis. They would arrive at L'Abri, announce themselves as Nietzschean or whatever else they happened to be, ask what Christianity was all about, and the conversation would begin, often lasting for hours into the night and early morning. A variety of social misfits, societal dropouts, and even participants in the occult all came calling. One young man went to L'Abri in the late sixties and announced that he had special power that Jesus did not have. He challenged a L'Abri worker to a stare-down, claiming that his power would cause the worker to look away first. With Edith praying in the kitchen, the man gazed intently into the eyes of the L'Abri worker, looked away, and acknowledged that there was indeed "some kind of power in this place."[20]

The discussions were open to all topics. On one occasion a young woman announced her sexual proclivities and challenged the Christians present as to what they believed about sex. Schaeffer never blinked at this or other topics. He would discuss endlessly, often with tears in his eyes, in an attempt to convince all comers that Christianity was the only coherent worldview, the only answer to the deepest questions of the human race. The conversations were never merely academic; they were about truth and how it affected real lives. As former L'Abri worker Os Guinness remembers, Schaeffer was brilliant at reaching these types of young people: "It was apologetics in the pit, down and dirty."[21]

Saturday nights at L'Abri in the mid-sixties started with tea and Edith's sandwiches as the group gathered around the fireplace. Schaeffer sat on a barrel that had been modified as a chair, which put him higher than the others in the room. At some point he would ask who had a question. Sometimes there would be a period of awkward silence, and Schaeffer would prod the group. Once the questions began, the conversation could go on for hours. His answers were usually wide-ranging, as he attempted to get to the reason the question was asked in the first place. Usually around 11:00 p.m. Schaeffer would announce that he needed to wrap things up so he could finish his sermon for the next morning's worship service, and that he had time for one last question. That answer would sometimes take another hour or more, putting the end time for the discussion past midnight.[22] Schaeffer then retired to his room to complete his sermon. On Sunday mornings Schaeffer traded the lederhosen and knickers he had begun to wear for a traditional dark suit. The services included music, often provided by opera singer Jane Stuart Smith and her musician friends who visited L'Abri. The congregation consisted mostly of L'Abri visitors and workers, but occasionally there would be people from around the area.

As word spread, especially after Schaeffer's books began to appear, busloads of people would drop in at L'Abri. A group of Baptist pastors stopped with their cameras, wanting to take pictures of Schaeffer and to have their own photos taken with the "hippies of L'Abri." For many young people, especially evangelicals, L'Abri became a pilgrimage site — one of the "European stations of the cross," Guinness called it. The community became part of evangelical pop culture and was mentioned in songs by Christian recording artists such as Larry Norman and Mark Heard. One Norman song included the line, "We'll honeymoon in Haifa, have lunch in Galilee, hitchhike up through Switzerland, and drop in at L'Abri."[23]

Not all who dropped in at L'Abri converted to the Christian faith, of course, and some who did fell away from the faith after leaving L'Abri. Many young people were merely experimenting with various experiences, including sex and drugs. Having dabbled in Christianity, they moved on to the next high.

There can be no doubt, however, that the Schaeffers had tremendous influence on many Baby Boomer evangelicals. Guinness, for example, recalls his student days at the University of London in the mid-sixties when he first heard Schaeffer. While evangelicalism had a number of good theologians at the time, there was not much engagement with culture. The youth culture was announcing its presence with the Beatles and Rolling Stones, protest movements, and alternative lifestyles. Into this scene came "a funny little man in Swiss Knickers." "For many of us, it wasn't the content of what he was saying, you could disagree with that," Guinness says; "it was his style, his passion for God."[24] After finishing his undergraduate degree, Guinness went to L'Abri for three weeks in 1967. Although having grown up the son of missionaries to China, Guinness had not been a Christian long and had not thought much about what being a Christian might mean intellectually. Three weeks at L'Abri "turned my thinking around so much that looking back, my conversion was more important, but those three weeks were more revolutionary in everything that I've done in my calling since then."[25] Guinness lived at L'Abri for five years, eventually becoming a member. He later returned to England to do a doctorate at Oxford University before becoming an author and independent evangelical scholar. "Almost all the content of my thinking, I owe to [sociologist Peter] Berger," Guinness has said. "But, the vision of 'why think at all,' how you think, and the passion for truth and God — I owe that to Schaeffer."[26]

Another author and scholar who had a life-changing intellectual and spiritual experience at L'Abri was Nancy Pearcey, whose work today is heavily influenced by Schaeffer. Pearcey had rejected the Christian faith of her upbringing, declared herself an unbeliever, and was studying music in Germany when she discovered L'Abri. Like so many others, she was shocked and impressed to see countercultural hippies fully accepted at an evangelical ministry, most of them not even Christians. Even more remarkable than this, however, was Schaeffer's message. Pearcey writes that Schaeffer may have struck people as somewhat odd, but "when he opened his mouth and began to speak, people were transfixed: Here was a Christian talking about modern philosophy, quoting existentialists, analyzing worldview themes in the lyrics of Led Zeppelin, explaining the music of John Cage and the paintings of Jackson Pollack," all in an era "when Christian college students were not even allowed to go to Disney movies."[27] Pearcey returned to the United States and tried out some of Schaeffer's arguments in her college philosophy classes, eventually concluding that a Christian worldview was indeed coherent intellectually. With her mind at rest in the Schaeffer-inspired conclusion that Christianity made sense, she took on authors C. S. Lewis, G. K. Chesterton, James Sire, and Guinness, and then converted.[28]

The Essentials of L'Abri

The stories of the lasting influence of L'Abri on the lives of people like Guinness, Pearcey, and countless others could never be told in one book. A few, however, can usefully illustrate the central components of L'Abri. True, it was a place where ideas and intellectual exchange were taken seriously, but L'Abri was not a place where people were simply argued into the kingdom of God. Here they were also drawn in by Christian hospitality and love.

Marc Mailloux was a seventeen-year-old agnostic Zen Buddhist who had heard about L'Abri from a friend while on the beach in Greece in 1971. He made his way to Huemoz to "crash for a few days" at the inexpensive retreat. His first night there he slept on the floor in a hallway where Schaeffer had to step over him to get to the bathroom. The next day he listened to an Os Guinness tape entitled "The East No Exit," which presented a serious challenge to the eastern worldview Mailloux had adopted. Attempting to defend himself intellectually at one of the evening discussions, Mailloux extolled the virtues of his Buddhist vegetarian position against the "barbarous nature of animal-eating Christianity." He felt he had done well, but at the end of the discussion Schaeffer told him that while Buddhism was a logically consistent worldview, no one could live with it consistently. As Mailloux was leaving the meeting, he was stung by a wasp in his coat sleeve. Instinctively, he crushed the insect with his hat. As it fell to the floor dead, all in the room looked at him and took in the irony of, as Malloux puts it, "the flagrant inconsistency of my reaction with my animal-patronizing discourse of a few moments before."[29] He eventually converted to Christianity, became a missionary to France, then moved to Florida to work with French-speaking immigrants.

William Edgar's story illustrates the two primary components of L'Abri, the intellectual arguments and the loving hospitality. An American, he grew up in Europe before going to L'Abri in the sixties. Edgar's father was employed for several years in Paris before returning to the U.S. about the time Edgar entered high school. His father was an agnostic, but his mother was a devout Episcopalian, and Edgar was confirmed in the Episcopal Church in Paris before attending St. George's Episcopal boarding school in Newport, Rhode Island, after the family moved back to the States. Beyond confirmation and boarding school, Edgar remembers little tangible Christianity in his home. He entered Harvard in 1962, where his three passions were soccer, French existentialist literature, and music. He was a jazz pianist and would major in musicology. In his sophomore year at Harvard he took a humanities course called "The Epic and the Drama" that was taught by legendary Harvard scholar John H. Finley Jr. Edgar's discussion section leader was Harold O. J. Brown, a graduate student in the Harvard Divinity School who would introduce Edgar to Schaeffer and L'Abri.

Brown's own introduction to L'Abri and Schaeffer is a fascinating and significant part of Edgar's story. Brown's sister Judy had been lost on the shore of Lake Geneva in 1959 when she met Priscilla Schaeffer, who invited her to L'Abri. Schaeffer introduced Judy to the Christian faith. As Brown likes to tell the story, Judy told Schaeffer, "I think my brother believes this; he's in seminary." Schaeffer asked her where, and she replied, "Harvard Divinity School," to which Schaeffer replied, "No, he doesn't believe this."[30] But Brown did believe what Schaeffer was teaching, and on his sister's recommendation he visited L'Abri in 1961. Having grown up Roman Catholic, Brown was like a twentieth-century version of Luther: he tried to do everything right, believing he had to in order to be saved. Studying Luther in Germany helped him come to accept salvation by faith at the age of twenty-one. He became a Protestant and enrolled at Harvard, where he would study with the renowned Reformation scholar George Huntston Wil-

liams.[31] At first he dealt with liberalism at Harvard by merely rejecting what he heard. What Brown learned from Schaeffer at L'Abri, however, was that he needed to engage the culture around him, and that it
was more difficult to defend Christianity in isolated points than to
speak of the faith as a holistic and coherent worldview. When he returned to Harvard he began to take on the secular liberal academic
culture there, making connections between the faith and what he
taught Harvard students in the discussion sections he led as a graduate student. Brown worked the Christian point of view into discussions of the epics and dramas of the ancients, and this is what caught
Edgar's attention, opening him to the plausibility of the Christian
point of view.

The summer after Edgar's sophomore year he returned to France
for a bicycle trip with his brother. Brown told him that while in Europe
he should look up Francis Schaeffer at L'Abri. When the cycling
ended, and Edgar's brother returned home, Edgar decided to give the
Schaeffers a call. He spoke with Edith, who invited Edgar to come to
L'Abri and join the discussion group that evening. Edgar had no idea
what L'Abri was. He thought he was just going to meet a friend of
Brown's. He loaded his backpack and headed for Huemoz.

He arrived on a Saturday just in time for a cookout and the standard evening discussion, which consisted of someone asking
Schaeffer a one-minute question and Schaeffer responding with what
seemed to Edgar like a forty-five-minute answer. The discussion, as
usual, ended past midnight. When it was completed, Schaeffer came
over to meet Edgar and was delighted to discover that Edgar was
friends with Brown. Schaeffer told Edgar that the two would talk the
next day. While not familiar with everything he heard that evening
and in the Sunday service the next morning, Edgar was nevertheless
impressed with this group of people who took ideas and the Bible seriously — and, being a musician, he enjoyed the Sunday singing, which
was a Bach chorale. Following the Sunday service Schaeffer took Edgar aside into an anteroom, and the two had a long conversation, with
Edgar asking many questions. Having had a discussion about the
problem of evil while on the train en route to L'Abri, he asked
Schaeffer to explain how a loving and omnipotent God could allow the
existence of evil. Schaeffer replied with the free-will argument for
theodicy, the roots of which go back to Augustine. The basic thrust

was that for love to be authentic, the lover must freely choose to love. The modern version of this argument is that if God created humans to love him, he had to give them a choice, and from this choice they rebelled against God and fell into sin. As Edgar puts it, "At the end [of the conversation], I was a believer."[32] Edgar spent the rest of the summer at L'Abri as a student and returned to Harvard in the fall as a Christian.

Edgar's future wife would also come under the Schaeffer influence, particularly Edith's, and here we see the L'Abri emphasis on hospitality and Christian love. Barbara and Bill became friends in college. Barbara was a student at a woman's junior college called Pine Manor. She was from an upper-middle-class home with a father who worked in the U.S. State Department. Growing up, Barbara lived in France, Italy, Switzerland, and Washington, D.C., among other places. Barbara and Bill met in 1966, about eighteen months after he had become a Christian under Schaeffer, and she recalls that Bill and his friends talked incessantly about L'Abri, the Schaeffers, the ideas associated with them, and the implications of Christianity in all areas of life. Everything that came up in conversation had eternal significance, and she was asked frequently if she had thought about the logical conclusions to her presuppositions — a typical Schaefferian question. This was all completely new for Barbara. In the turbulence of the sixties, she found it very stabilizing to hear about truth. Barbara called her parents and asked if she could skip her second year of college and go to Switzerland instead. Her father, probably calculating that a year at L'Abri would be cheaper than college, gave her permission, so with a thousand dollars and a round-trip plane ticket, she set off for L'Abri. She would live there for six months, helping to care for Schaeffer's mother; then Barbara became a nanny for the children of Ranald and Susan Macaulay, the Schaeffers' daughter and son-in-law, who were starting the England branch of L'Abri. Barbara would spend eight months with them.

Barbara recalls being taken under Edith's wing. She and many others who were complete strangers to the Schaeffers were brought into L'Abri as children in need of nurture and direction. With scores of young people staying at L'Abri, Edith would go out of her way to accommodate individual needs and preferences — substituting a chicken sandwich because a particular individual could not eat fish, making sure the Dutch boys had extra mashed potatoes, and so forth. Barbara was nearly overwhelmed that although Edith had a village full of people to watch over, she cared about "this little American kid" who just happened to show up while skipping her sophomore year of college.[33] While living with the Macaulays, Barbara saw L'Abri Christianity in a smaller setting. With Ranald in school finishing his theological training, money was tight. Barbara remembers him telling the family that there was not enough money for groceries in a particular month so they would have to pray for God's provision. She had never seen this sort of faith and dependence on God. Susan was interested in child rearing and education for children and would later do some writing of her own on these issues. Because of Susan's influence, Barbara went to Geneva for a few months to study Montessori education with, among others, the renowned child psychologist Jean Piaget. While at the University of Geneva, Barbara went to L'Abri for weekends, often taking her university friends with her.

Bill and Barbara would continue to be regular visitors at L'Abri. Bill's parents moved to Geneva while he was in college, so every vacation he was at L'Abri as much as possible. After Harvard, Bill went to Westminster Theological Seminary on Schaeffer's recommendation — a recommendation indicative of Schaeffer's break with McIntire's brand of fundamentalism. Edgar graduated from Westminster with a Master of Divinity degree in 1969, taught music for ten years at the Brunswick School in Greenwich, Connecticut, then returned to France to teach at the Reformed seminary at Aix-en-Provence. While teaching in France from 1979 to 1989, he did his doctorate at the University of Geneva, defending his dissertation and graduating in 1992. Throughout this time the Edgars continued to visit L'Abri, Bill often giving lectures, and they remained close friends with the Schaeffers.

While the Edgars both came from stable and affluent families and brought primarily spiritual and intellectual needs to L'Abri, the Schaeffers and their community rescued Maria Dellu from a much more difficult family situation, nurturing her in the Christian faith and transforming her life forever. Dellu was born and raised in Milan, where she studied to become a translator. She went to England in 1960 to study English and became a Christian after wandering into a Bible study at Tyndale House in Cambridge, a Christian research institute sponsored by Inter-Varsity Fellowship. She had been raised in a serious Catholic household with a father who had contemplated being a priest. This upbringing, especially her conversations with her father, prepared her for conversion. She arrived at Cambridge with many questions; she was deeply troubled in particular by the idea of Christ's crucifixion. Just before going to England she had tried to put her questions out of mind, deciding that even if God existed, he could not possibly care about human beings. She was becoming somewhat bitter about the anguish that her religious questions caused, but she decided that her one last act of searching would be to read the New Testament she had brought with her from Italy. She read the Gospel of John, and shortly thereafter found the Tyndale House meeting where the group was studying the Gospel of John. Through that meeting, she became a Christian.[34]

As her stay at Cambridge came to a close, Dellu expressed to the Christians she had met her concerns about returning to Milan, where she knew no one who was an evangelical believer. A young man told her about Dorothy and Hurvey Woodson, who headed up the Milan L'Abri study group. Opera singer Jane Stuart Smith was also a part of the Milan group and sometimes hosted Schaeffer for Bible studies among the opera singers in Milan. When Dellu returned home she got in touch with the Woodsons, but her family resisted her turn to Protestantism and made it very difficult for her to attend Milan L'Abri meetings. "[M]y parents forbade me to read the Bible or to talk to anybody about my newfound faith," Dellu would write later. "Sincere Roman Catholics, my parents were raised at a time when people were not allowed to read the Scriptures, since the Church wanted to be the sole source of instruction in order to avoid heresy."[35] On one occasion, Hurvey Woodson called to encourage Dellu to attend a particular meeting, even against her parents' wishes, because Schaeffer was going to be there. Woodson believed it was very important for her to meet Schaeffer.

The Woodsons told Schaeffer that Dellu was having difficulties at home because of her faith. Having himself been subject to Catholic resistance in Champery, Schaeffer was attuned to the difficulties Dellu was facing. After the meeting, he told Dellu that if anything ever happened between her and her parents, she would have a family at L'Abri in Switzerland who would take care of her. Convinced that her family would never turn against her in the way Schaeffer implied,

Dellu was angered by the implications of what Schaeffer said. He was right, however, as Dellu's father told her that if she wanted to continue in evangelical Protestantism, she would have to leave home. With Schaeffer's assistance, Dellu enrolled at the University of Lausanne in 1963, where she continued her studies for the next seven years while going to L'Abri to be with her new family nearly every weekend. Eventually, she took the equivalent of a master's degree in Italian and French literature and art history. Debbie Schaeffer was studying at the University of Lausanne at the same time, and she and Dellu became close friends.

Dellu witnessed the significant growth that took place at L'Abri from 1963 to 1970. When she first arrived, a group of twenty or thirty was considered large. By 1970, it was not unusual to have 130 people staying at L'Abri on any given weekend. Describing what L'Abri and the Schaeffers came to mean to her, Dellu, more than thirty years later, still speaks emotionally, tears welling in her eyes and her voice quivering, as she tells how the Schaeffers came through on Francis's promise, "We will be a family to you."[36] For her, L'Abri was a place full of hospitality, deep interest in the lives of those staying there, and, most importantly, love. Dellu, like so many of the women at L'Abri, became close to Edith. She recalls the perfectionist aesthetic that Edith practiced, making tiny sandwiches that compared favorably to what one would receive at a five-star hotel. Edith would often chide her young helpers to do better, sometimes pointing out that they had missed a spot when spreading butter on a slice of bread. In everything Edith did, Dellu remembers, she always had an eye for beauty, usually putting out flowers and other decorations to enhance the setting.

Dellu was instrumental in L'Abri's growth. She and Debbie regularly took non-Christian friends from the university to L'Abri, just as Priscilla and Susan had when they were students at the University of Lausanne. Dellu says Debbie had the Schaeffer family knack for debate, once talking to their American atheist friend for three days, eventually bringing her to conversion. Dellu was not nearly as forceful or persuasive, but she did what she could to share the gospel with her classmates at the university. Over time, as Schaeffer visited Milan L'Abri, Dellu would travel with him as his translator, giving her a chance to spend more time with her spiritual mentor. Traveling with Schaeffer in Italy, she came to appreciate his effectiveness in evangelizing the cultured and intellectually sophisticated young people of major Italian cities. By contrast, Dellu remembers, many Protestant missionaries were successful only in southern Italy and small villages — largely, she believes, because they had not developed Schaeffer's ability to communicate the gospel within a modern culture and to articulate the biblical message in an intellectually respectable way.

One of the many who, like Dellu, experienced family at L'Abri was an Indonesian young man who arrived not speaking a single word of English. Since he could not communicate, Schaeffer gave the young man a camera so he could occupy himself usefully by taking photographs of L'Abri. The young man eventually learned English, converted, and became a photographer. Dellu heard him years later refer to Edith as his mother, calling her the one who gave him life. This struck Dellu as an appropriate reference to the one who served as her own spiritual mother at L'Abri. When Dellu married, Edith signed a card to her, "Your mother and friend."[37]

Through the Schaeffers, Dellu became friends with Hans and Anky Rookmaaker. Because art history was one of her fields of study at the University of Lausanne, Hans offered her the opportunity to come to the Free University of Amsterdam to study art history with him. She studied with Rookmaaker for several months, and while at the Free University she met John Walford, who had come from England. Walford was studying with Rookmaaker as an undergraduate before going to Cambridge to complete his doctorate. He had been converted in the late sixties and had read Schaeffer without really understanding much of what he read. While studying with Rookmaaker, several people told him he should visit L'Abri, but having already been converted and not wanting to take a space at L'Abri that could be occupied by an unbeliever in need of salvation, Walford always responded that he would go to L'Abri only when he had a good reason to go. He found one: Walford and Dellu fell in love, were engaged, and wanted Schaeffer to perform their wedding. Schaeffer was not about to marry the couple without first meeting John and thoroughly checking him out. They visited L'Abri together in 1972, and Schaeffer took Walford up to his room in Chalet les Melezes.

As Walford recalls, "He really grilled me."[38] Schaeffer wanted to know to what degree Walford had taken on Reformed theology since being converted in a low evangelical branch of the Church of England.

Before meeting Rookmaaker, the evangelicalism that Walford had known in the Church of England was, as Walford puts it, like a sausage machine, good for making other Christians but nothing else. Rookmaaker, Schaeffer, and others were instrumental in bringing Walford to the Reformed perspective that one's faith encompassed and engaged all facets of life and culture. Yet Schaeffer also wanted to be sure that Walford possessed an evangelical living faith as well as a Reformed appreciation of cultural engagement. It was like "being interrogated by a potential father-in-law," Walford remembered more than thirty years later. Schaeffer had a sense of fatherly possession and responsibility for Maria — "possession in the sense of protective care."[39] Schaeffer eventually decided he approved, performed the marriage, and gave John and Maria his blessing. The Walfords went back to England, where John completed his doctorate in art history at Cambridge before taking a faculty position at Wheaton College in 1981. Maria, now Maria Walford-Dellu, completed a doctorate in Italian literature at the University of Chicago. In the late 1980s, Walford-Dellu would sum up her experience at L'Abri: "I saw many people being changed at L'Abri. Many became Christians; some did not. But I think that most went away with the knowledge that they had been loved — with a sense of worth and a clear idea of the existence of God, and with the reality of communication on both the divine and human level."[40]

Like Mailloux, the Edgars, Dellu, and so many others, Jerram Barrs was in college in England when he first heard of Schaeffer. He had been raised in the home of an atheist Marxist father and began listening to a college friend's Schaeffer tapes. He was converted after hearing Schaeffer in person in Manchester. When he graduated, Barrs went to the continent and hitchhiked to L'Abri, where he would become Edith's cook and gardener. Schaeffer then sent him to Covenant Seminary in St. Louis, from which Barrs graduated in 1971. After graduating from Covenant, Barrs returned to England to assist Macaulay at English L'Abri. Informed that his father was terminally ill with a mere six months to live, Barrs left English L'Abri, returned home, and tried to lead his father to conversion as he lay dying. Schaeffer came for a visit and wanted to see Barrs's father. Barrs recalls that on the day of the meeting, he knew his father would become a Christian. As Schaeffer told Barrs later, after hearing Schaeffer's presentation of the gospel, Barrs's father said, "How could a worm accept that?" Schaeffer at first did not know what to say, but then replied, "How could a worm refuse?" The elder Barrs then asked Schaeffer if he could speak to and pray for the other two Barrs children, Jerram's brother and sister, to help undo the atheism Mr. Barrs had taught them all their lives. Barrs says that from that time in 1972, every time he saw Schaeffer, Schaeffer would ask how his brother and sister were doing, and whether they had become Christians.[41]

The Mark of the Christian

These stories illustrate the tremendous appeal and lasting influence that L'Abri had on many young people in the 1960s and 1970s. Before meeting Schaeffer, most of them had never been exposed to an intellectual construction and defense of a Christian worldview, and they found it exciting and liberating. Clearly, however, there was more going on at L'Abri than merely an intellectual defense of the Christian faith. Some of those who came to L'Abri were more taken by the community of love they experienced with the Schaeffers than by the intellectual arguments.

Schaeffer taught that the "final apologetic" for the Christian faith was the fulfillment of Jesus' command that Christians love one another. In his little book *The Mark of the Christian,* Schaeffer argued that Jesus had given the world the right to judge whether Christians really belonged to God. The judgment of the world was based on whether Christians showed love for one another. "In other words," he wrote, "if people come up to us and cast in our teeth the judgment that we are not Christians because we have not shown love toward other Christians, we must understand that they are only exercising a prerogative which Jesus gave them." Christians, Schaeffer wrote, were to "be a loving church in a dying culture."[42] Throughout his sojourn in American fundamentalism, Schaeffer had seen more than his share of loveless Christian communities, and he and Edith were determined that L'Abri would be different. "What then shall we conclude," Schaeffer asked, "but that as the Samaritan loved the wounded man, we as Christians are called upon to love all men as neighbors, loving them as ourselves. Second, that we are to love all true Christian brothers in a way that the world may observe."[43] The ways L'Abri embodied both love for other Christians and love for anyone who came served as a powerful witness to the truth of Schaeffer's message. At L'Abri Francis and Edith mastered the "final apologetic."

This could not go unnoticed. From their remote retreat, the Schaeffers were commanding growing attention. By the mid-1960s, word of what was happening at L'Abri was spreading beyond the young people who crossed paths with Schaeffer in Europe. L'Abri was opening the door for the Schaeffers to gain a wide audience in America, especially on college campuses. As his L'Abri talks turned into campus lectures, and the lectures then turned into books, Schaeffer would become one of the most influential evangelicals of his generation.

CHAPTER FOUR

An American Evangelical Star:
The Trilogy

As word began to spread about Francis Schaeffer's ministry, he grew increasingly influential in Europe and America. His growing popularity was noted in a 1960 issue of *Time* magazine. The brief news item, "Mission to Intellectuals," developed by happenstance after a noted journalist visited L'Abri to thank the Schaeffers for their influence over his daughter. Impressed with what was happening at L'Abri, the journalist tipped off the *Time* reporter in Geneva, who then visited L'Abri and wrote the article.[1] In the piece, Schaeffer was quoted as saying, "Protestantism has become bourgeois. It reaches middle-class people, but not the workers or the intellectuals. What we need is a presentation of the bible's historical truth in such a way that it is acceptable to today's intellectuals."[2] The report was positive; here was an American product of fundamentalism living in the mountains of Switzerland talking about ideas and attracting young people from universities and the arts — not a typical fundamentalist scenario.

The article notwithstanding, before 1965 Schaeffer had not yet become an American evangelical presence. Awareness of Schaeffer among American evangelicals began slowly in conjunction with the formation of L'Abri. As the number of student visitors from the University of Lausanne grew following the initial contacts in 1955, a few of them asked Schaeffer to come to the university once a week for conversation. They secured the back room of a small café near the university and there began weekly discussions as they ate sandwiches and listened to the jukebox.[3] Thus began Schaeffer's activities on university campuses, which grew slowly and would be confined to Europe for many years. From 1955 to 1964, Schaeffer lectured to students at Cambridge, Oxford, London, St. Andrews, Durham, and Manchester, but he had not yet lectured at an American university. For a decade he rarely set foot in America, at one point going five years without even visiting the States. He yearned for a wider audience, but Edith resisted extensive travel.[4]

Late one evening, after a typical L'Abri discussion, Francis retired to the Schaeffers' bedroom, pounded his fist on the wall and exclaimed, "Oh, Edith, I'm sure I have true answers. . . . I know they can help people. . . . But . . . no one is ever going to hear . . . except a handful. . . . What are we doing? What am I doing?"[5] Some of those who stayed at L'Abri in the mid-sixties recall the Schaeffers praying earnestly with the community about every speaking invitation that came in, with Francis saying that the doors might not stay open forever.[6] Eventually, Edith relented, and Schaeffer began to travel more widely. In 1964, he arrived in Boston to speak to students from Harvard, Boston University, and other surrounding schools. It was the beginning of a long and fruitful ministry on American college campuses.

The Evangelical College Lecture Circuit

Schaeffer was brought to Boston by Harold O. J. Brown, who was then the minister to students at Park Street Church, an evangelical haven where Fuller Seminary's founding president, Harold John Ockenga, was pastor. Brown, William Edgar, and a few others from InterVarsity Fellowship groups organized a committee to start the Contemporary Christian Thought Lectures (CCTL), funded by a Dutch donor at Park Street. The series eventually included Dutch theologian Herman Dooyeweerd and Orthodox theologian George Florovsky, but Schaeffer was their first guest. Ronald Wells was a Ph.D. student at Boston University, and he remembers that few had heard of Schaeffer at that time. There were a couple of meetings at Park Street, one at Harvard, and one at Boston University.

Wells remembers vividly the meeting at Harvard. There were about thirty students present. "What an electric moment it was," recalled Wells in 2004. He and the others present were thrilled by Schaeffer's intellectual argument from a Christian perspective.

Schaeffer had the trappings of a European cosmopolitan, and his appearance inspired many in the room to move into their life work as Christian intellectuals. Wells would become a historian at Calvin College. For him and others there that evening, it was as if Schaeffer were a prism: "He took our various lights and concentrated them for a moment, then put us out in other ways. . . . It energized a lot of us to believe you could be an intellectual and be a Christian."[7]

The Boston appearances were the beginning of Schaeffer's identity as a lecturer and evangelical star in America. He would be in constant demand from that time forward, especially on college campuses. The following year, 1965, Schaeffer did a weeklong series of lectures at Wheaton College and then presented the same lectures at Westmont College in Santa Barbara, California. He lectured twice a day, Monday through Friday. The transcription of the lectures runs 130 pages and about 55,000 words. Wheaton was one of the leading centers of evangelical intellectual life, but students and faculty there had never seen anyone quite like Schaeffer. Chuck Weber was a Wheaton student at the time and would later join the faculty. He had grown up in Buffalo, New York, and had visited the art museum that housed works by the abstract impressionist Jackson Pollack, a figure Schaeffer often interpreted. Weber recalls that Schaeffer helped him make sense of the Pollack exhibit. Like all those who saw Schaeffer for the first time, Weber recalls the lederhosen and the "odd" pronunciations, especially of the word "Renaissance," which Schaeffer pronounced Ren-AY-sance, the French pronunciation. After the first lecture, in subsequent talks Schaeffer would dive in right where he left off in the previous lecture, as if no time had elapsed. What impressed Weber most was Schaeffer's intellectual engagement with culture. Neither Weber nor his classmates had ever seen anything quite like this.[8]

Weber also recalls Schaeffer's compassion for his subjects. At one point in his lecture Schaeffer read a poem from a magazine called *Destijl* expressing the meaninglessness of life. Students laughed as he read the poem and its strange lines such as, "like a dish covered with hair, like a four-legged suckingchair, like a deaf echotrunk, half full half empty." Schaeffer brought them upright, chastising them, saying they were laughing at people who were going to hell. "I get so tired of Bible believing Christians who laugh at these people — who laugh at them when they look at their tortured paintings. Do you laugh at a man at the door of hell? When evangelicals learn to stop their laughing and take such men and their struggles seriously, then [evangelicals] can again begin to speak to our generation."[9]

Wheaton would become a regular stop for Schaeffer. When he returned to the campus in 1968, Weber was on the faculty. Schaeffer's visit this time was part of a fourteen-city tour in which Schaeffer spoke in the Arie Crown Theater at McCormick Place in Chicago and also appeared live on a morning television show at the NBC Studios. Roger Lundin was a sophomore at Wheaton during Schaeffer's 1968 visit. As a freshman who had been converted to Christianity a year earlier, Lundin heard about Schaeffer practically the minute he arrived on campus. Schaeffer was by this time a hot topic, Lundin later reflected. He remembers the slight, 5'8" Schaeffer standing behind the lectern on the Wheaton stage, with the huge organ pipes behind him, having been introduced by the towering Wheaton president Hudson Armerding. In an era when no Wheaton administrator, only one or two faculty members, and just a few students wore beards, here was Schaeffer with long hair, a goatee, and knickers. It was all part of the package that made Schaeffer an interesting and powerful figure. But more than the appearance was the power of Schaeffer's oratory. He dazzled and beguiled the students. "This was a man who was engaged with the culture and hitting hard with the Christian faith. I think the combativeness was part of the attraction," Lundin recalled.[10] Lundin, who became a professor of literature at Wheaton in 1978, never found Schaeffer's books as attractive and scintillating as his lectures; Schaeffer's pastoral feel for people, his oratorical style, and his ability to integrate ideas across disciplines captured Lundin most. He attributes his own integration of literary studies and theology partly to Schaeffer's influence.

Schaeffer also lectured at Calvin College as part of the 1968 American tour. His talk was covered for an underground newspaper called *The Spectacle* by a young assistant professor of history named George Marsden, who went on to become a leading scholar in the study of religion and American culture. Marsden had been to L'Abri briefly, so he knew Schaeffer's basic message and style. Of the Calvin lecture, Marsden wrote, "For a Calvin Faculty member the most startling aspect of this achievement is that Mr. Schaeffer, without displaying any particular academic credentials and with an apparent disregard for the usual academic standards and precautions, did exactly what we always have hoped to do — make Christianity appear intellectually relevant to the contemporary era."[11] Marsden contrasted Schaeffer's ability to communicate with secular intellectuals over against the predominant view at Calvin that sixties intellectuals and social radicals were "beyond reach." Marsden said that people at Calvin were lucky if they occasionally reached a suburban materialist, let alone the types of intellectuals Schaeffer was attempting to engage.

Marsden was taken aback by the broad scope and sweeping style of Schaeffer's lectures: "Within a typical hour he may present the thought of Antonioni, Aquinas, two Francis Bacons, the Beatles, Bergman, Bernstein, Camus, Cezanne, Cimabue, Francis Crick, Leonardo da Vinci, Eliot, Fellini, Gauguin, Giotto, Hegel, Heidegger, several Huxleys, Jaspers, Kierkegaard, Leary, Henry Miller, Picasso, Rousseau, Marquis de Sade, Sartre, Terry Southern, Schlesinger, Tillich, and Zen Buddhism. Intellectual modesty is not Schaeffer's long suit. One might sympathize if in the audience another scholar who had spent most of his adult life trying to understand, for instance, Kierkegaard, was appalled."[12]

Still, Marsden appreciated that Schaeffer's sweeping style, even if it ignored details and nuance, was one of the strengths of his presentation. Marsden compared Schaeffer's method to a person sketching a map of the world in five minutes. There would be much to criticize about the details, but it would still be quite helpful in distinguishing oceans from continents and apprehending the broad outlines of the globe. Marsden also noted that Schaeffer avoided the two most notable errors of Christian apologists of the time: talking only to other Christians, and quoting scripture to people who did not believe the Bible. In contrast to Calvin College at the time, which had censured the official school newspaper for suggesting that students go to movies, Schaeffer, in Marsden's words, "has seen the dirty movies, read the dirty books, and even heard the dirty words; yet for all that he is a better Christian. Doubtless such evident empathy for the contemporary culture accounts largely for Schaeffer's remarkable appeal."[13] Marsden summed up the gist of Schaeffer's Calvin College lecture, and indeed the central message of most of Schaeffer's lectures during this period of his life, as an attempt to show that only

Christianity is 1) logically non-contradictory, and 2) a system with which one can live consistently. Schaeffer set out to show that a materialist worldview, with its apparent meaninglessness, can be logically consistent, but that those who hold it cannot live consistently with such a view.[14]

The God Who Is There

By the time Schaeffer delivered this message at Calvin in 1968, his first American lectures from 1964 and 1965 had been published in book form. In early 1965, Schaeffer planned to have the lectures he had delivered at Harvard and MIT and in Philadelphia typed into manuscript form, in the hope that they would become his first book. At the same time, Edith submitted her *L'Abri* manuscript for publication, and Schaeffer believed the simultaneous appearance of their books would show the basics of his teaching and the practical ministry of L'Abri.[15] His fist-pounding desire to reach a wider audience was beginning to find satisfaction. Another book soon took shape as well: *Escape from Reason,* a transcript of lectures he gave at Swanwick, England. Richard Ducker helped Schaeffer edit the transcripts of these lectures into book form. In April 1967, the English publisher Hodder and Stoughton informed Schaeffer that *The God Who Is There* had been accepted for publication; later they would publish *Escape from Reason* as well. That same month Edith received word that her book *L'Abri* would be published by another company.[16] In 1968, *The God Who Is There* and *Escape from Reason* were published in America by InterVarsity Press just months after they appeared in England. InterVarsity would publish fourteen of Schaeffer's twenty-two books; the others were published by Tyndale House, Fleming H. Revell, or Crossway.

Schaeffer did not write manuscripts for his books. Rather it was left to Ducker, for the first two books, then InterVarsity editor James Sire thereafter, to turn Schaeffer's transcribed lectures into readable prose. From the third book onward, Schaeffer lectured from notes, and the lectures were taped and transcribed, sometimes by students, and then sent to Sire. Sire edited the transcripts into manuscript form, then sent the manuscript to Schaeffer to ensure the argument was correct. Schaeffer would make minor changes and send the manuscripts back to Sire for final editing. Sometimes the two would dicker back and forth before Schaeffer was satisfied with the ideas and Sire with the words.[17]

Schaeffer's first two books joined a third, *He Is There and Is Not Silent,* to form his trilogy. Together the three books laid out Schaeffer's basic apologetic, that is, his intellectual defense of the Christian faith and his diagnosis for what had gone wrong with western intellectual life. For Schaeffer, the first message of apologetics, or even of the gospel, was not "accept Christ," but instead "God is there." He effectively inserted a new first step in the evangelism process. Only after showing that God is there, Schaeffer believed, "are we ready to hear God's solution for man's moral dilemma in the substitutionary work of Christ in history."[18]

Apologetics had two purposes for Schaeffer: the first was defense of the faith, and the second was to communicate Christianity in a way that a given generation can understand the message. The purpose was not just to win the argument, but to see people's minds changed in preparation for their acceptance of Christ and eventually their bringing all areas of life under Christ's lordship. To accomplish this, he believed that Christian apologists and evangelists had to answer the most difficult questions posed by their generation.

In his review of Schaeffer's talk at Calvin, Marsden mentioned that Schaeffer did not reject the Augustinian notion that faith precedes understanding. But Schaeffer walked a fine line on this point. He actually said that knowledge precedes faith — an apparent contradiction of Augustine. But it wasn't that simple. To Schaeffer, the truth existed before conversion, and it played a role in conversion. As he put it, "Before a man is ready to become a Christian, he must have a proper understanding of truth, whether he has fully analyzed his concept of truth or not."[19] Indeed, before one could see the truth, one had to first acknowledge the very idea of truth — no small step in a relativistic age. Truth for Schaeffer was that which lay behind orthodoxy, the creeds, and even behind scripture: the truth that lay behind these and gave them their meaning was that "God is there."[20] This is not to say that Schaeffer believed that conversion must necessarily be delayed until a person properly understands all there is to know about God; "If we find a man ready to receive Christ as Savior, then by all means we should not talk about presuppositions but tell him the glorious news," he wrote.[21] In the sixties and seventies, however, Schaeffer believed that most young people were not ready to convert. First, they needed some answers. Many youth were being lost to the faith precisely because their parents, churches, and Christian colleges provided unsatisfactory answers to basic questions. Schaeffer's mission, therefore, was to provide answers to the modern dilemma.

The modern dilemma was relativism. Schaeffer never defined this term at length, but his meaning was clear. Relativism was the belief that nothing was absolutely true, that all beliefs were chosen subjectively and arbitrarily, with no notion that they corresponded to anything that was objective and external to the individual knower. Although Schaeffer did not use the term much, usually opting for the term "humanism" instead, relativism was the basis for what he called a "generation gap" or "epistemology gap." The old, traditional way of knowing was based on the belief that there were absolutes, but the younger generation had a very different approach.

This contrast of approaches led to one of Schaeffer's favorite concepts, antithesis. Throughout his books, antithesis was often vague and imprecise. He criticized liberal Christianity's total antithesis between rationality and religious values, which destroys the unity of individuals so that their personhood is divided and their worldview incoherent. Here he was referring back to his critique of Karl Barth and the view that the Swiss theologian had separated the objective truth of scripture from the subjective truth of experience, with the former not necessary for the latter. Most of the times he mentioned antithesis, however, he spoke of a different kind, in a positive way. He believed that historic Christianity was based on the right sort of antithesis. "The basic antithesis," he wrote, "is that God objectively exists in contrast (in antithesis) to his not existing."[22] In *Escape from Reason* Schaeffer argued that antithesis was so much a part of the created order that one could hardly begin to try to refute antithesis without using it. We cannot get away from it, Schaeffer said, because that is the way God made us.[23] Antithesis, therefore, was little more than the recognition that some things were objectively true, while others were false. In short, antithesis stood over against relativism.

Schaeffer's concern for the loss of this right sort of antithesis led to his critique of modern western intellectual life that he first posed in *The God Who Is There* and then outlined in more detail in *Escape from Reason.* The centerpiece of this argument was his famous "line of despair," which almost everyone who heard him lecture in the 1960s remembers well. Often, the first thing people will recall about hearing Schaeffer during that era, aside from his knickers and lederhosen, is the line of despair. Typically, he would begin lectures by drawing the famous line on a chalkboard. The line of despair designated when people stopped believing in absolutes — in other words, when antithesis gave way to synthesis. Synthesis was the belief that all ideas could be harmonized, that all were equally subjective and relative. Below the line was this new way of thinking, the lack of absolutes.

The move below the line of despair began in Germany then spread throughout Europe, so that by 1890 Europe was pretty much below the line. In the United States the move below the line of despair did not come until 1935. It is unclear why Schaeffer chose these rough dates, but it is worth noting that 1935 was when he graduated from college. The move below the line of despair spread not only geographically over time but also from one area of culture to another, from philosophy to art to music to general culture, and then finally to theology. The move below the line in theology he attributed largely to Barth, just as he had when he wrote his pamphlet critiquing the Swiss reformer in 1950. "Barth was the doorway in theology into the line of despair," he wrote in *The God Who Is There.*[24] Schaeffer diagramed this movement with stair steps that led downward below the line from philosophy through the other areas to theology, each area with its own stair step.

Escape from Reason

After Schaeffer introduced the line of despair and traced its development in *The God Who Is There,* he discussed it in more detail in *Escape from Reason,* the second book of the trilogy. Moreover, in the second book he outlined the origin and historical development of the modern western mind. In this history, he began with the thirteenth-century theologian Thomas Aquinas (1227-1274), calling him "a man who changed the world in a very real way."[25] Before Aquinas, Schaeffer believed, the western mind had been Byzantine. This was an unusual use of that word, and Schaeffer spent little time defining the idea. He wrote simply that for the Byzantine mind, heavenly things were considered so all-important that they were not pictured realistically. "[P]rior to Thomas Aquinas there was an overwhelming emphasis on heavenly things, very far off and very holy, pictured only in symbols, with little interest in nature itself."[26] There was, in other words, an antithesis between the things of a holy and sinless God and the things of fallen and sinful humankind, but there was no disjunction between nature and grace. When Schaeffer spoke of there being no disjunction between nature and grace, he meant that the things of humankind, nature, and the things of God, grace, could both be understood with the same rational thought processes. They were not two different spheres of understanding. While not fully intending to, Schaeffer argued, Aquinas began an intellectual process that separated nature from grace. Aquinas did this by arguing that some things could be understood through the natural process of human reason, while others had to be accepted by faith. For Schaeffer, this meant that there were some truths that could not be understood with the mind but only by an irrational application of faith.

Aquinas unwittingly achieved this, according to Schaeffer, because he believed that while the human will was fallen, the intellect was not. This, Schaeffer said, was an incomplete view of the biblical fall into sin, and it led to the belief that human reason was autonomous. This, in turn, led to the separation of philosophy from revelation, with philosophy becoming increasingly free and autonomous. "From this basis of the autonomous principle," Schaeffer wrote, "philosophy also became increasingly free, and was separated from revelation."[27] Schaeffer's treatment of Aquinas consisted of roughly two pages and was superficial, to say the least, as even some who were influenced by him in a positive way would point out later.[28] Ironically, the received view of Aquinas that reigned in Catholic intellectual life into the 1960s was the opposite of Schaeffer's: Catholic theologians and philosophers, and most Protestant scholars as well, viewed Aquinas as having integrated faith and reason remarkably well.

While establishing no connection between Aquinas and the artist Cimabue (1240-1302), Schaeffer claimed that the latter accepted the separation of nature and grace and then passed it to his student Giotto (1267-1337). Schaeffer then moved quickly and seamlessly to the medieval literary figure Dante (1265-1321). "Then Dante began to write in the way that these men painted. Suddenly everything started to shift on the basis that nature was important. The same development can be seen in the writers Petrarch (1304-1373) and Boccaccio (1313-1375)."[29] Schaeffer acknowledged that the interest in nature of Renaissance authors such as Petrarch and Boccaccio and artists such as Cimabue and Giotto was good and proper, but Aquinas had nevertheless "opened the way to an autonomous humanism, and autonomous philosophy; and once the movement gained momentum, there was soon a flood."[30]

The flood was the Renaissance, during which the separation of nature from grace led to nature eating up grace. This essentially meant that all important things would be known by natural reason alone, and there would then be no need for grace. For Schaeffer, intellectual life got off track as a result of the Renaissance. Most scholars of the Renaissance highlight the difference between the Italian Renaissance, with its more secular form of humanism, and the northern Renaissance, where intellectual figures such as Thomas More and Erasmus, while humanist in their desire to go back to ancient texts, remained nevertheless thoroughly Christian. Schaeffer seemed only slightly aware of the difference. For him, the only real difference between the Renaissance in the south and in the north was that secularization, nature eating up grace, came later to the north. He never mentions More or Erasmus. It appears that Schaeffer confused Renaissance humanism with Enlightenment humanism, the latter containing the idea of the autonomous individual.

When Schaeffer moved his argument to the high Renaissance of the sixteenth century, he began to use his upper-story/lower-story dichotomy. Grace was in the upper story, and nature in the lower. The point was, again, that the two had been separated. He traced the nature/grace dichotomy in his brief treatment of the great Renaissance artist Leonardo da Vinci (1452-1519), who appropriated Neo-Platonism, "which became a dominant force for the simple reason that they needed to find some way to put something in the 'upper story.'"[31] If nature had eaten up grace, what would replace grace? Neo-Platonism replaced grace in the upper story with ideals or universals, while the lower story remained the domain of nature and particulars. The problem was how to hold the particulars in the lower story together once they had been set free from grace — that is, made autonomous from God. Da Vinci, Schaeffer argued, tried mathematics because it deals only with particulars, not universals, and he also tried to paint the soul. This can all be confusing, especially since Schaeffer has by this time covered the history of western intellectual life and the development of autonomous, secular thinking from Aquinas through da Vinci in a mere four pages. The upper story/lower story split that began with Aquinas would not be complete until much later in history, when thinkers concluded that there could be no relationship between knowledge in the lower story and experience and meaning in the upper.

If by the high Renaissance of the sixteenth century western intellectual life was already autonomous and secular, why did full-blown relativism and the move below the line of despair not occur until the nineteenth century? Simply put, the Protestant Reformation saved the day, or at least staved off the tide of relativism for three hundred years. Here Schaeffer's antithesis kicked in again, as he placed the Renaissance and Reformation in stark opposition to each other. By reasoning this way, Schaeffer saw the Reformation as recapturing the (good) antithesis that Aquinas had forfeited. The Reformation taught that final and sufficient knowledge was found in the Bible, *sola scriptura.* "What the Reformation tells us, therefore, is that God has spoken in the Scriptures concerning both the 'upstairs' and 'downstairs.' He has spoken in a true revelation concerning nature — the cosmos and man. Therefore, the reformers had a real unity of knowledge. They simply did not have the Renaissance problem of nature and grace."[32] Schaeffer called this "the Reformation base," and he offered it as the answer to the intellectual problems of the twentieth century.

Having established the basic problem, the separation of nature and grace and the opposition of the Renaissance and Reformation, Schaeffer moved to early modern science. Here he featured seventeenth-century philosopher Francis Bacon (d. 1626) as the leading voice among a host of early modern figures who did not see science as autonomous but rather placed it "within the revelation of the Scriptures at the point of the Fall."[33] In this camp he placed Bacon, Copernicus (d. 1543), Galileo (d. 1642), Kepler (d. 1630), Faraday (d. 1867), and Maxwell (d. 1879). As one can see from these death dates,

85

the list ranged over more than three hundred years, but Schaeffer grouped them together because they all retained God at the center of scientific inquiry. Copernicus is usually considered a Renaissance scientist, and Schaeffer acknowledged this when he wrote, "Nature had to be freed from the Byzantine mentality and returned to a proper biblical emphasis, and the Renaissance played a part in this; but it was the biblical mentality which gave birth to modern science."[34] Schaeffer was here acknowledging the role of the Renaissance in restoring science to its proper biblical emphasis while still insisting that the Renaissance was completely separate from the Reformation, which held up scripture as the base. This was difficult to maintain historically or logically.

While Schaeffer did not ignore the Enlightenment of the eighteenth century, neither did he give it the emphasis one might expect to find in a story about the rise of secularism and relativism. He wrote, "After the Renaissance-Reformation period the next crucial stage was reached at the time of Rousseau (1712-78) and Kant (1724-1804), although there were of course many others in the intervening period who could well be studied."[35] Kant and Rousseau were the turning point. "By the time we come to Kant and Rousseau, the sense of the autonomous is fully developed. . . . Whereas previously men had spoken of nature and grace, by the eighteenth century there was no idea of grace — the word did not fit any longer. Rationalism was now well-developed and entrenched, and there was no concept of revelation in any area. Consequently the problem was defined, not in terms of 'nature and grace,' but of 'nature and freedom.'"[36] In short, the problem of nature eating up grace that had started in the Renaissance was completed during the Enlightenment.

The next step in Schaeffer's analysis was his move from Kant to Hegel, then from Hegel to Kierkegaard. This would bring the analysis into the nineteenth century and to the line of despair. "Kant and Hegel," he wrote, "are the doorway to modern man."[37] Kant brought about autonomy, but Hegel went even further, Schaeffer argued, because Hegel "changed the rules of the game in two areas: epistemology . . . and methodology. . . . All things are relativized."[38] Schaeffer was here referring to Hegel's synthesis. Hegel believed history was a reflection of Spirit, and that history unfolded in a series of clashes between thesis, that which is, and the antithesis, that which is the opposite of the thesis. Perhaps the best way to illustrate Hegel's view of history would be in the area of ideas. A particular idea in history is a reflection of Spirit and represents the thesis. The thesis clashes with an opposing idea known as the antithesis, which is also a reflection of Spirit. The clash of the thesis and the antithesis produces a synthesis, which is a wholly new thing and is, like the thesis and antithesis, a reflection of Spirit. The synthesis becomes the new thesis, and the process begins anew as history moves forward.

Schaeffer took this to mean that everything was "both/and" instead of "either/or." He was convinced, therefore, that Hegel was not only a relativist, but quite possibly the first significant relativist in western thought. Schaeffer believed he saw relativism because the antithesis that kept ideas and their opposites apart gave way to a synthesis that seemed to harmonize an idea with its opposite. For Schaeffer, Hegel's clash of opposites was healthy, but Hegel's synthesis of opposites was disastrous. Schaeffer believed that because some ideas were true while their opposites were false, the clash between them should be a war, with the true ideas winning and the false ideas routed from the field of battle. There could be no synthesis between truth and error, for in such a synthesis, "all things are relativized."[39] In this way, Hegel opened the door to the line of despair by junking antithesis in favor of synthesis. Schaeffer acknowledged, "Hegel did not put it this simply. His thinking and writing are complicated, but the conclusion is that all possible positions are relativized, and leads [*sic*] to the concept that truth is to be sought in synthesis rather than antithesis."[40] In short, for Schaeffer, if we are confronted by a thesis and its antithesis, we should have to pick one and reject the other, because one is true and the other false.

If Hegel opened the door to the line of despair, Kierkegaard was the first man through it, the first person to move below the line. Where Hegel emphasized synthesis, Kierkegaard believed that one arrived at synthesis not by reason, but by a leap of faith. "Kierkegaard said this was an act of faith," Schaeffer wrote, "with nothing rational to base it upon or to which to relate it. Out of this came the modern concept of a 'leap of faith' and the total separation of the rational and faith."[41] At this point, Schaeffer used a diagram showing "Earlier Philosophy" at the top with an arrow downward to Kant, then an arrow down to Hegel, the line of despair at Hegel, then an arrow down to

Kierkegaard, who was below the line of despair. Then there was a forty-five-degree diagonal arrow downward and to the left toward secular existentialism and another diagonal arrow downward to the right toward religious existentialism.[42] "What we are left with now runs something like this," Schaeffer went on. "Below the line there is rationality and logic. The upper story becomes the nonlogical and the nonrational. There is no relationship between them."[43] In the lower story, below the line of despair, we have reason, logic, mathematics, and pessimism concerning the human predicament. In the upper story we have faith, which is non-rational and gives humanity hope and optimism. After Kierkegaard, the only way to get into the upper story is through the non-rational leap of faith. Now no amount of human reason can move one toward hope, optimism, and ultimate meaning.

In *The God Who Is There* and *Escape from Reason,* Schaeffer drew a direct line, even if diagonal, from Kierkegaard to twentieth-century secular existentialists such as Sartre and Camus, who were atheists. The other diagonal line from Kierkegaard went to religious existentialism, and this brought Schaeffer back to his long-running critique of Karl Barth that first appeared in the 1950 pamphlet *The New Modernism.* Barth's neo-orthodox theology held out the possibility that the truth of scripture could be separated from its historicity. For Schaeffer this was very much like Kierkegaard's alleged separation of religious experience from what we could know rationally.[44] Schaeffer also believed that Barth and neo-orthodoxy had an insufficient view of the fall of humankind into sin. "Man, in neo-orthodox theology, is less than biblical fallen man," Schaeffer wrote in *Escape from Reason.*[45] By contrast, in the Reformation and the scriptures, while one cannot do anything to save oneself, "he can, with his reason, search the Scriptures which touch not only 'religious truth,' but also history and the cosmos. He not only is able to search the Scriptures as the whole man, including his reason, but he has the responsibility to do so."[46]

Schaeffer understood and made sense of the attempts of secular existentialists to find upper-story meaning, even through drug use in the counterculture of the 1960s. As was apparent when he chided Wheaton students for laughing at modern artists and poets, Schaeffer respected people who attempted to live consistently with their presuppositions, even if those presuppositions were un-Christian. The early twentieth-century intellectual Aldous Huxley was an example. Huxley's use of drugs was a search for an upper-story experience necessitated by his belief that nothing from the lower story of reason could provide upper-story meaning. "The basic reason that drugs were seriously taken," Schaeffer argued, "was not for escape or kicks, but because man is desperate. On the basis of rationality and logic man has no meaning, and culture is becoming meaningless. Man is therefore trying to find an answer in 'first order experiences.' This is what may lay behind the serious drug mania of the 1960s."[47] Along with drugs, "optimistic evolutionary humanism" was another way to find something of value for the upper story. Schaeffer argued that "Optimistic evolutionary humanism has no rational foundation. Its hope is always rooted in the leap of man. In looking for proof one is always diverted to tomorrow."[48] In other words, the evolutionists cannot say why there is meaning, but only that things are evolving. Like drug use and evolutionary humanism, art and poetry served similar purposes as attempts to express non-meaning and to create an experience where there was no rational possibility of finding ultimate reality. Schaeffer even made reference to Michel Foucault's *Madness and Civilization*. He interpreted Foucault's work rightly as the recognition that the Enlightenment failed to make good on its promise of providing a unified answer based on reason.[49] Oddly, Schaeffer never made much of late nineteenth-century nihilist philosopher Friedrich Nietzsche, who began the critique of the Enlightenment and Romanticism and laid bare the inadequacy of reason for finding a unified answer.

Schaeffer's analysis is not without its difficulties, to be sure, but on topics ranging from drug use to art and poetry Schaeffer was getting evangelical young people to think in a new way about their world. Many in his audience had grown up in an evangelical subculture that taught them to separate from worldliness and sin while making little attempt to understand culture. Schaeffer helped them begin to make sense of the culture around them.

He also warned that cultural norms were creeping into evangelical life in ways more profound than most evangelicals had yet considered. The temptation was not so much that evangelical kids would take drugs — although that was always a concern — but that evangelical people would use religion in the same way that Huxley and the counterculture figures used drugs. They would forego propositional theology in favor of a pure experience with Jesus cut off from reason, evidence, and logic. Jesus would become their drug. "When a Christian has made such a statement [about an experience with Jesus cut off from reason]," Schaeffer wrote, "he has, in an analyzed or unanalyzed form, moved upstairs."[50] Schaeffer went so far as to say that when he heard the word "Jesus," he feared that people really meant an experience that replaced the need for propositional truth. "If evangelical Christians begin to slip into a dichotomy, to separate an encounter with Jesus from the content of the Scriptures (including the discussable and the verifiable portions of Scripture), we shall, without intending to, be throwing ourselves and the next generation into the millstream of the modern system. This system surrounds us as an almost monolithic consensus."[51] Schaeffer returned to this theme in later writings, and in an appendix to the complete works edition of *The God Who Is There* he warned again that evangelicals were "jettisoning any serious attempt to exhibit truth and antithesis" and were going over to the new theology's view that scripture could be true even if the Bible's history and science contained errors. In an echo of his separatist, fundamentalist past, he said that to show how serious this issue was, it might be necessary "not to accept an official part [in organizations] if men whose doctrine is known to be an enemy are going to be invited to participate officially."[52]

While Schaeffer respected atheists like the Huxleys and their attempts to live consistently with their presuppositions, in the end he believed it was impossible for any but Christians to actually achieve such consistency. In *The God Who Is There* Schaeffer gave the example of John Cage, a postmodern musician. Cage was famous for deconstructing music, making a point of not conforming to the strictures of melody, time, and key signature, even going so far as to record the sounds in his throat as he swallowed a piece of toast and orange juice, calling this music. Schaeffer told the story of an orchestra playing a Cage composition, with Cage himself serving as conductor. At the end of the piece, when Cage turned to the audience to receive the applause, the musicians hissed at him. Schaeffer said that when audiences or musicians booed Cage, "they are, if they are modern men, in reality booing the logical conclusion of their own position as it strikes their ears in music."[53] Schaeffer then told of Cage's obsession with the regularity and beauty of mushrooms, a hobby that defied Cage's belief that all was chaos. Generalizing from this point, he wrote, "It is impossible for any non-Christian individual or group to be consistent to their system in logic or in practice."[54]

He Is There and Is Not Silent

Throughout *The God Who Is There* and *Escape from Reason,* Schaeffer addressed the impossibility of living consistently with modern presuppositions. He pressed the argument in the final book of the trilogy, *He Is There and Is Not Silent.* There he argued that only Christians could live consistently with their presuppositions, and that orthodox Trinitarian Christianity was logically necessary. This is where the trilogy made its greatest contribution to evangelical intellectual life, but it also brought Schaeffer to dangerous ground philosophically. The contribution was in getting evangelicals to think in terms of worldview. The philosophical problem was that Schaeffer claimed a conclusion that outstripped his argument.

Schaeffer's working definition of "presupposition" was different than the classic Reformed definition of someone like Cornelius Van Til, apologetics professor at Westminster Seminary and one of Schaeffer's teachers. Van Til started with the notion that only God can be the basis for meaning and for predication. God is self-contained and self-testing — that is, there is nothing outside of God by which or through which we can come to know and evaluate God. For Van Til a presupposition was revelation, and the question was how one reacted to that revelation. Believers know God only through the revelation of scripture, not rational argument, and therefore have virtually nothing intellectually in common with unbelievers, who begin their thinking with something other than God. Even to start the reasoning process with something like the law of non-contradiction was problematic for Van Til because it seemed to apply a rational standard to God.

Schaeffer, by contrast, believed there was common ground between Christians and unbelievers, namely human rationality. He believed that all humans were subject to the law of non-contradiction, the coherency theory of truth, and the other basic features of rational discourse. Because of this common ground, a Christian could start a conversation with an unbeliever, because all people reasoned in the same way. Human rationality was part of what it meant to be human; it was part of the created order that we could take for granted. Presuppositions for Schaeffer were like hypotheses that one tested to see if they were correct. In their practical method, Schaeffer and Van Til had a good deal in common. Van Til spoke of getting over to the non-Christian's ground for the sake of argument, which Schaeffer did with great skill largely because he believed there really was common ground between Christians and non-Christians, something Van Til rejected vehemently.[55] One interpreter argues that the key to understanding Schaeffer's view of the common ground between believers and unbelievers is Schaeffer's statement from *The God Who Is There:* "[T]here always is a common ground, not because there should be a common ground, but because, on the basis of the lack of logic of [the unbeliever's] presuppositions, there will be common ground."[56] In other words, the common ground exists only because the non-Christian cannot live consistently with his or her own presuppositions.

Because Schaeffer believed that Christians and non-Christians alike had a common rationality, he argued in *He Is There and Is Not Silent* that everyone had a basic philosophy of life, or worldview. All people are philosophers, Schaeffer believed, and he wanted to help people confront what he believed were the basic truths about humanity in order to get them to reconsider their worldview. He wanted to show that there was a metaphysical, moral, and epistemological necessity for God. In other words, he wanted to prove that God was logically necessary.

Metaphysics is essentially the question: What is the nature of reality? Schaeffer began his metaphysical argument with the two dilemmas that humans face. First, humans are finite yet personal; second, there is a contrast between the nobility and the cruelty of human beings. There are three ways of explaining how human beings became personal yet finite and noble yet cruel. These are: 1) everything that exists has come out of nothing; 2) everything that exists had an impersonal beginning; and 3) everything that exists had a personal beginning. The first is unsustainable, Schaeffer said, and so could be dismissed. The second is pantheism, or what Schaeffer liked to call "pan-everythingism." He couldn't resist a shot at theological liberalism here, asserting that liberal theology is pantheistic, though providing no evidence to prove it. The third answer, of course, is the only one Schaeffer believed could possibly make sense. It alone answers humankind's dilemma by explaining why and how human beings exist.[57]

Why does the third answer alone make sense of humankind's dilemma? First, only the personal, infinite God is big enough. As with Plato, Schaeffer argued, one must have absolutes in order to have meaning, but the Greek gods were not big enough. (Big enough for what, Schaeffer did not say.) Second, the personal God must have unity in diversity. "Without this," he wrote, "we have no answer."[58] He did not say exactly why we would have no answer without unity in diversity, though it seemed that the two-part dilemma of humankind was the reason. Because a human being is personal yet finite and noble yet cruel, an individual has within him or her a diversity of features and yet is still a unity of one person. This being the case, Schaeffer believed, God also has to have unity in diversity, and the unity in diversity of God was none other than the Trinity. "I would still be an agnostic if there was no Trinity," he wrote, "because there would be no answers. Without the high order of personal unity and diversity as given in the Trinity, *there are no answers*. . . . So we have the answer to man's being finite yet personal. It is not that this is the best answer to existence; it is the *only* answer" (emphasis in the original).[59]

Having discussed the metaphysical necessity for the existence of the triune God, Schaeffer next tackled the moral necessity. This argument specifically addressed the problem of human beings being both noble and cruel. Put simply, Schaeffer tried to show that if one begins with an impersonal universe, then there is in the end no final meaning for morality. If one starts with a God of moral absolutes, however, then posits that human beings were created moral but chose to act immorally, four things emerge: First, God is let off the hook for human cruelty, because God did not create humans as cruel creatures, but as moral creatures who chose to act sinfully. Having chosen to rebel against God and against the image of God within, Schaeffer said, human beings actually live in an abnormal state. Second, there is hope for a solution because the abnormality of man is not intrinsic to man's "mannishness." What is intrinsic to the "mannishness of man" is to be in the image of God. Third, there is adequate ground for fighting against evil without fighting against God. This was an answer to existentialist author Albert Camus's famous charge that if there were a God, God was the author of evil, and, therefore, to fight against evil was to fight against God. For the Christian, Schaeffer answered Camus, to fight against evil is to fight against humankind's abnormal state and, therefore, to be part of the process of restoration of humans to what they were intended to be in creation. Fourth, we have real moral absolutes because God is good. As with the metaphysical argument for God, Schaeffer then moved easily from having demonstrated that Christianity answers the moral dilemma of humankind to the claim that Christianity is the only answer. "Again, as in the area of metaphysics," he wrote, "we must understand that this is not simply the best answer — it is the only answer in morals."[60]

Schaeffer believed that this moral argument necessitated not only *The God Who Is There,* the first book of the trilogy, but also *He Is There and Is Not Silent,* the third book of the trilogy. It was not enough that God had revealed himself in the person of Christ, although this was certainly true. Throughout scripture, particularly in Genesis, God had also revealed himself in propositional truth. "He must indeed not only be there," Schaeffer wrote, "but He must have spoken. And He must have spoken in a way which is more than simply a quarry for emotional, upper-story experiences. We need propositional facts."[61] For Schaeffer this meant that the story of Genesis must be taken as factual history, something he addressed more fully in his book *Genesis in Space and Time.* The story of Adam and Eve in the Garden of Eden consisted of real, space-time events, he insisted. Interpreting Genesis as allegory, myth, or parable was to undercut the whole moral argument for the existence of the triune God.

Finally, after having covered the metaphysical and moral necessity for God, Schaeffer moved to his epistemological argument. Epistemology has to do with how human beings can know things and, for Schaeffer, what the nature of truth is. Schaeffer said the epistemological problem was the central problem of his generation and the basis for the generation gap between the youth of the sixties and their parents. He sometimes claimed that there was a generation gap of four hundred years, by which he meant that the parents of the sixties generation were still reasoning on the basis of a Reformation antithesis, while the youth were living in a world of relativistic synthesis. He reviewed the upper-story/lower-story division, once again attributing

94

this divide to Kant, Rousseau, Hegel, and Kierkegaard. The epistemological problem was that individuals are either left in the lower story as a machine with words but no meaning, or in the upper story with values but no rationality. In other words, in the lower story human beings know in one way, through reason and logic, while in the upper story they know in another way, through faith and experience. This results in a divided self.

As was so often the case, Schaeffer again got to the heart of the problem of twentieth-century Americans and western Europeans. How does one find meaning in life that is grounded in something other than subjective experience? And, if one finds meaning in subjective experience cut off from rational knowledge, how can one know that the subjective meaning is real? His answer to the epistemological problem was, as he had argued in *Escape from Reason,* the Reformation. In *He Is There and Is Not Silent* he wrote, "No, there simply was no problem of nature and grace to the Reformation, because the Reformation had verbal, propositional revelation, and there was no dichotomy between nature and grace."[62] A few pages later he shifted from the Reformation to Christianity as a whole: "Christianity has no problem of nature and grace. . . . Christianity has no problem of epistemology."[63] This was a subtle shift that seemed to broaden his outlook but actually reflected Schaeffer's belief that only Reformation Christianity counted as true Christianity. On the next page, the epistemological dilemma disappeared completely: "It is not that we happen to have an answer, but rather that there is no problem in the Christian structure. . . . The Christian does not have a problem with epistemology."[64]

In some of his lectures and books, Schaeffer said clearly that spiritual problems were at root epistemological in nature. Young people went to L'Abri because they were trying to find out who they were and if their lives had meaning. "I have come to try to find out who I am," they would say to him, a rather common quest among young people in the 1960s. For Schaeffer this was not just a psychological disorientation but an intellectual problem that could be solved initially through helping them understand and correct the upper-story/lower-story division that plagued modern thought. The belief in autonomy cut individuals off from meaning that transcended the self and left them adrift. "This is the heart of the problem of knowing," he wrote, "and it is not solved until our knowledge fits under the apex of the infinite-

95

personal, Triune God who is there and who is not silent."[65] Yet in other books Schaeffer argued that the central problem of humankind was moral, not epistemological. "The biblical answer is that the dilemma of the human race, this dilemma that twentieth-century man is wrestling with so much, is moral. The basic problem of the human race is sin and guilt," he wrote in *True Spirituality*.[66] That Schaeffer could hold these two opposing points of view as to the fundamental problem facing human beings is difficult to understand. Of course, here as elsewhere, Schaeffer displayed his habit of overstating his argument when he was making a particular point. On balance, it would be fair to say that Schaeffer believed humankind had a moral, epistemological, metaphysical, and spiritual problem, and that the moral and spiritual elements were more basic and fundamental than the other two.

Assessing the Trilogy

So often, Schaeffer's analysis of western history was compelling in its broad outlines, but problematic in its details. Like so many who were inspired to further study in part by Schaeffer, Chuck Weber, who heard Schaeffer lecture at Wheaton in 1965, went on to graduate school, where he become more critical of Schaeffer's approach to western thought. One of his first classes in graduate school at the University of Chicago was an intellectual history course that dealt with Kant, Hegel, and other modern western philosophers. Weber came to believe there was more to these thinkers than Schaeffer understood, and that Schaeffer had analyzed them superficially.[67] He appreciated Schaeffer's zeal to introduce evangelical college students to the world of ideas and their importance for Christians, but along with many others, he would quarrel with the particulars of Schaeffer's narrative. Those details troubled many scholars.

To start, Schaeffer insisted on a chronological oddity at the beginning of his analysis. For Schaeffer the problems begin with Aquinas, who died in 1274, but they accelerate to the point that nature begins "eating up grace" already in Petrarch (d. 1374), a person born a mere thirty years after Aquinas's death. Petrarch was the earliest exemplar of the Renaissance, the one often referred to as the father of Renaissance humanism. If we were to take Schaeffer's argument at face value, therefore, nature would have eaten up grace and full-blown secular humanism would have existed during the first generation of the Renaissance, long before the Reformation and even longer before the Enlightenment. In light of historical scholarship already available in the 1960s, Schaeffer's analysis would be much more palatable in its details if he had downplayed the secularizing role of the Renaissance, acknowledged the degree to which much Renaissance thinking remained Christian, paid more attention to the relationship between the Renaissance and Reformation and how the former paved the way for the latter, and focused more intently on John Locke (d. 1704), as opposed to Aquinas, as the beginning of a real move toward modern autonomy.[68] Starting the story of secularization with Aquinas's distinction between faith and reason is a move with which few scholars agree. Most see Aquinas as having achieved a "fine blending of faith and reason," which was just about the opposite of what Schaeffer saw.[69]

Had Schaeffer emphasized Locke in the seventeenth century as the beginning of modern individual autonomy, rather than Aquinas in the thirteenth, and acknowledged that even Locke remained Christian in much of his thinking, he could have more properly ascertained the important role of Kant as building on Locke and moving the idea of autonomy toward its logical conclusion. Having proceeded in this way, Schaeffer's statement regarding Rousseau and Kant would have been somewhat more accurate: "By the time we come to Kant and Rousseau, the sense of the autonomous is fully developed. . . . Rationalism was now well-developed and entrenched, and there was no concept of revelation in any area. Consequently the problem was defined, not in terms of 'nature and grace,' but of 'nature and freedom.'"[70] Schaeffer overstated the case with regard to Kant and Rousseau, and he failed to deal with the complicated roles of Descartes and Newton, who preceded Locke. Still, the broad outlines of his summary statement about Kant, Rousseau, and, more generally, the Enlightenment could be accepted by many scholars even today. Once again, while erring in many of the details of his analysis, the broad outlines of Schaeffer's argument were tenable, and he identified an essential problem of modern intellectual history: the move toward individual autonomy.

Another area where Schaeffer's analysis was idiosyncratic was his pitting the Renaissance and Reformation in stark opposition to each other. Most scholars see the Reformation as growing out of the Christian themes of the northern Renaissance. Christian humanists of the northern Renaissance were defined in large part not by their rejection of authority per se, as was more the case in Padua, but by their rejection of *wrong* authority. In rejecting what they believed was wrong authority, they used the humanist methodology of looking to ancient texts in hopes of finding better, truer authority.[71] Christian humanists looked to the ancient texts of scripture in their original languages along with the ancient church fathers of the second through fifth centuries, among them Augustine. When Christian humanists found the Roman Catholic Church of their day not living up to the teachings of these ancient texts, they called for reform. The Protestant Reformation, as its name implies, grew out of this reform emphasis.[72]

With a Ph.D. in Renaissance literature, Sire, Schaeffer's editor, had misgivings about *Escape from Reason* precisely because of the way Schaeffer interpreted the Renaissance. Having accepted the editor's position with InterVarsity Press in 1968, Sire took a train to Chicago to look for a house near InterVarsity headquarters. He read half of *Escape from Reason* on the way there and the other half on the way back, and what he read discouraged him. Sire felt he was coming to a press that was about to publish the American edition of a book he believed was wrong. The problem, Sire believed, was that Schaeffer focused on the Italian Renaissance; Sire was more familiar with and interested in the northern Renaissance, which remained quite Christian. Authors such as Spenser and even Shakespeare were not utterly humanistic, "at least the way I read Shakespeare," Sire said. Sire then read *The God Who Is There* and had the same feeling. He mentioned this to some of the InterVarsity staff, but they were more troubled that he disagreed with Schaeffer than about the way Schaeffer handled the Renaissance. Sire changed his mind about Schaeffer somewhat when he heard him lecture in person.[73] Like so many others, Sire found Schaeffer much more persuasive and effective as a lecturer than a writer.

The most likely reason that Schaeffer missed this connection between the Renaissance and Reformation is that through the time he was in college the interpretation of the Renaissance was dominated by the work of nineteenth-century Swiss historian Jacob Burckhardt. Burckhardt was the first modern scholar to treat the Renaissance as its own historical entity separate from the Middle Ages, and in doing so he was primarily interested in the ways in which the Renaissance presented a full break with the medieval Christian past. For Burckhardt, and then for Schaeffer, the Renaissance humanists were more modern than medieval. Scholars since Burckhardt have found much more continuity between the medieval Christian era and the Renaissance, but because he didn't keep up with the literature, Schaeffer missed this. The result was that Schaeffer, like Burckhardt, saw the Renaissance as completely different from the medieval Christian worldview and from the Christian revival that was the Reformation. As he put it, "To this problem of unity [between nature and grace] of which we have been speaking, the Reformation gave an entirely opposite answer from that of the Renaissance."[74]

Schaeffer's treatment of Hegel and Kierkegaard, like his use of Aquinas, the Renaissance, and the Reformation, was also deeply flawed. However Hegel's system worked, he was not a relativist in the sense that Schaeffer used the term, though it makes some sense that Schaeffer believed he was. For Hegel, Spirit was not a fixed and transcendent reality, but rather something that moved in history. All that takes place in history is a reflection of Spirit. Schaeffer was onto something, because Hegel did posit that all reflections of Spirit contained within themselves their potential opposite. Still, this is hardly the same as modern relativism, which posits that truth corresponds to nothing objective. When he addressed Kierkegaard, Schaeffer acknowledged in the 1982 complete works edition of the *The God Who Is There* that the Danish philosopher/theologian would not have appreciated what people have made of his thought: "I do not think that Kierkegaard would be happy, or would agree, with that which has developed from his thinking in either secular or religious existentialism. But what he wrote gradually led to the absolute separation of the rational and logical from faith."[75] This was a revision of what Schaeffer originally wrote in the 1968 edition and what he had said at the Wheaton lectures of 1965. There, Schaeffer said that it was debatable whether Kierkegaard was a Christian, and "whether, if he came back today, he would be pleased with what had been made of his teaching."[76] It appears that Schaeffer was backing away from the stronger implication that Kierkegaard himself had presented a non-Christian worldview. This was very likely the result of criticism Schaeffer received from Christian philosophers over his understanding of Kierkegaard. Arthur Holmes at Wheaton and his student Stephen Evans, the latter an authority on Kierkegaard, believed that Schaeffer's most egregious error of detail was in his understanding of Kierkegaard.[77]

Christian philosopher Ronald Nash acknowledged that Schaeffer's view of Kierkegaard was an interpretation that was passing in scholarly circles, but one that did have a scholarly history to it. "The point here," Nash wrote in the mid-1980s, "is that although Schaeffer's view of Kierkegaard is in decline, it is not without scholarly support and that he was more balanced than he is often given credit."[78] Almost all Christian scholars today see Kierkegaard as Christian. Father Richard John Neuhaus of the Christian journal *First Things* summed it up concisely in 2005: "As for Francis Schaeffer, his contributions to evangelical Protestant thought are significant, but he painted with a very broad and eccentric philosophical brush. I suppose some might be inclined to, but nobody should, debate whether or not Kierkegaard was a Christian. He was."[79]

Schaeffer faced a range of critics. While Van Til was the most important Schaeffer critic in the Reformed camp, there were others. William White, who taught for a time in the 1960s at Temple University, wrote letters to Schaeffer's good friend Hans Rookmaaker and sometimes to Van Til criticizing both Schaeffer's methodology and theology. In one such letter he wrote, "Yet Schaeffer stated as recently as December 1966 in print . . . , 'Historic Christianity rests upon the truth of what today is called the "brute facts."'" White commented, "At this point the issue is clear and plain either men's minds are amenable to the Gospel of salvation by appeal to commonly accepted 'brute facts' and thus converted by the overwhelming mass of evidence or their hearts are too wicked to acknowledge such evidence and they must be brought to belief by the preaching of the Gospel and the conviction of God's spirit."[80] Clearly, White believed the latter. White had a friend named Harry Schat of Wyckoff, New Jersey, who worked for Fallek Chemical Corporation in New York. Schat also wrote frequently to Rookmaaker and occasionally to Schaeffer. He believed Schaeffer, the neo-evangelicals, *Christianity Today,* Wheaton College, and virtually all things evangelical were not Reformed enough. They were too fundamentalistic and Arminian, he said, and he thought fundamentalists and evangelicals equated Christianity with the American way of life. In 1967, Schat told Schaeffer that he was not going to get anywhere with his "line of despair" because no one in America was in despair. "Believe me," Schat wrote, "nobody in this country knows what you are talking about — things are fine and dandy in this country; how could it be different with pragmatism and religion having taken over?"[81]

To no avail Schat tried to convince Schaeffer that the prevailing philosophy in America was John Dewey's pragmatism, and that Schaeffer's critique of all things European was not hitting its mark. Schat was onto something in stressing the importance of pragmatism in America, but he was clearly wrong to the extent he implied that Schaeffer's message would go nowhere in America, as the explosion of Schaeffer's popularity would attest. Still, the fact that Schaeffer in America became popular almost exclusively with evangelicals, as opposed to in Europe where unbelievers with various philosophical commitments found him persuasive, gives some credence to Schat's critique. White's and Schat's attacks worried Schaeffer, and he did a bit of letter-writing of his own in an attempt to get them to stop their campaign against him, as did Rookmaaker.[82] Seven years later, in his 1974 book *No Little People,* Schaeffer spoke of those who make certain doctrines central, instead of letting Christ be central. He mentioned specifically predestination and the sovereignty of God, writing, "[S]ome of my friends have stressed [the sovereignty of God] so much that the doctrine, not God, has become the center of their ministry."[83] One wonders if he was thinking of Van Til, White, and Schat when he wrote these words.

Schaeffer's idiosyncratic interpretations were the result of his isolation from Christian scholars, his tendency to place history on the procrustean bed of American fundamentalism, and his propensity to view history in terms of decline and fall.[84] The strength of fundamentalism during the early twentieth century was its pitting God's absolute truth against the errors of humankind. As a fundamentalist, Schaeffer knew that the modern view of individual autonomy stood in antithesis to the Christian notion that human beings exist in absolute dependence on a holy God. Lost in this sort of analysis was the sense that history is neither a story of pure antithesis nor a story of steady decline. Parts of the Renaissance, for example, helped Reformation figures such as Luther and Calvin break with tradition and return to the authority of the ancient text of scripture, while there were other parts of the Renaissance and Reformation that opened the way for individual autonomy. Schaeffer, schooled as he was in fundamentalist habits of the mind, needed to pit the entire Renaissance over against the whole Reformation and yield not an inch to the former.[85] Oddly, though not surprisingly, within his general theory of decline and fall, he exempted the Reformation as the "base" that stood apart from the general move from Aquinas to modern relativism.

Schaeffer was on much surer footing when he discussed the shift from nature and grace to the modern notion that nature and freedom eclipsed all supernatural ideas — leaving grace largely forgotten. In one of his clearest definitions, Schaeffer wrote, "What is autonomous freedom? It means a freedom in which the individual is the center of the universe."[86] When young evangelicals in the sixties heard this, it made sense in a way nothing else had in their evangelical upbringing. Many of them had come from churches and homes where they had been taught that the primary problem with modern culture was wild music and long hair. Many non-evangelical youth had come from nominally Christian or secular homes where there was no sense at all that modern people had a spiritual problem. Young evangelicals did not quite know what to make of the counterculture of the sixties, while those from secular backgrounds were participating in the counterculture as an alternative to and protest against their parents' materialism. Schaeffer helped both groups understand that driving the counterculture of rock music, drugs, free love, and all the rest was the modern belief that individuals were autonomous, completely free, and therefore left alone in the universe to create their own meaning. This was a dilemma for modern humanity, and Schaeffer understood it and was able to communicate it better than any other evangelical of his time.

However persuasive Schaeffer's argument, some Christian thinkers were convinced that it was still flawed — and not just in its details. He argued throughout the trilogy that the Christian faith could be demonstrated rationally, and that the triune God was a logical necessity. He did this because he realized, as Marsden noted in his 1968 article in *The Spectacle,* the futility of quoting scripture to people who do not believe the Bible. In his effort to reason his way to the truth, however, Schaeffer's conclusion outstripped his argument. In the mid-seventies, Yale philosophy graduate student Thomas Morris wrote a book critiquing Schaeffer's rational argument for the existence of a personal, triune God. The book was updated and republished in 1987, by which time Morris was teaching philosophy at Notre Dame and Schaeffer was gone, having died in 1984. Morris acknowledged the cogency of much of Schaeffer's reasoning and the very positive influence he had on Christian thinking at the popular level, but Morris also argued that Schaeffer's conclusion went too far. While Schaeffer demonstrated deductively the necessity for something personal behind the universe, he never showed deductively that the personality there need be God, let alone the Trinity of the orthodox Christian faith. For example, three personal gods would have answered the dilemma just as well. Morris believed that Schaeffer should have just acknowledged that these conceptions of God come from Christian revelation, and that on that basis they answer the dilemma of humankind. This, in Morris's view, would not have weakened Schaeffer's argument — unlike claiming a conclusion that goes beyond the deduction.[87]

Schaeffer was greatly troubled by Morris's critique. He was convinced that Morris had based his analysis on an erroneous quote summing up Schaeffer's definition of "presupposition" from an article entitled "How I Write My Books" that appeared in *Eternity* magazine. Schaeffer wrote to *Eternity* saying that the definition Morris had attributed to him was "quite contrary to my own use of the word in all my writings."[88] Schaeffer believed that perhaps the editors at *Eternity* had made a mistake resulting in the erroneous quote. When Steve Board at *Eternity* looked into the matter, as Schaeffer had requested, he found that Morris had not taken his definition of "presupposition" from Schaeffer's *Eternity* article "How I Write My Books" but from *The God Who Is There,* and that Morris had quoted Schaeffer perfectly.[89]

Schaeffer was convinced that Morris's view that the triune God was something to be accepted on the basis of revelation alone and not something that could be logically deduced was "pure poison in the midst of today's concept of the loss of truth. I'm afraid that many evangelicals will simply swallow it without realizing what they are reading and therefore that it will be one more note in the confusion at this point that . . . exists in the evangelical world anyway."[90] Schaeffer was deeply troubled over Morris's argument that all worldviews and even knowledge, including Christianity, depend on non-logical, non-rational moves at some point in the reasoning process; Schaeffer, Morris wrote, "does not fully acknowledge the nonlogical contributions of every human knower to his own knowledge, in whatever area."[91] Moreover, Morris believed that while Christianity offered a plausible answer to humankind's dilemma, it was not the only system capable of logically answering that dilemma. This would never do for Schaeffer. He insisted not only that the triune Christian God answered the metaphysical dilemma of humankind in a plausible way, as Morris believed, but that *only* the triune Christian God who is there logically answered the dilemma. No other system, real or conceived, could do so: "The only answer to the metaphysical problem of existence is that the infinite-personal God is there; and the only answer to the metaphysical problem of existence is that the Trinity is there."[92]

Schaeffer informed his editor, Sire, that he had written a twenty-two-page response to Morris and intended to photocopy several hundred copies to have on hand.[93] Sire responded that the primary problem with Morris's book was that the philosopher had not gone to L'Abri, spent time with Schaeffer, and then placed Schaeffer's writings within the context of Schaeffer's total work. Sire also believed that Schaeffer and Morris had a different view of presuppositions and were therefore talking past each other. Sire discouraged publication of Schaeffer's response to Morris; he believed it would give Morris's book more attention than it deserved. Sire believed that beyond the guild of professional philosophers there would be little interest in Morris's critique, and he was probably correct.[94]

Schaeffer's concern about Morris's book was part of his deep sensitivity to criticism from Christian scholars, which we will see more of in chapter eight. But it also touched a key element of Schaeffer's thought. He insisted that human beings were capable of arriving intellectually at the truth of Christianity by reason alone, even if once convinced in this way they could be saved only by faith in Christ's atoning work on the cross. Schaeffer, like almost all thinkers who came of age during the first half of the twentieth century, was himself a product of the Enlightenment to the extent that he placed such a high value on rational thought. His fundamentalist heritage was in many ways also a product of this Enlightenment emphasis on reasoned demonstration of objective truths and a corresponding wariness of subjective experience. In his unpublished response to Morris, Schaeffer quoted approvingly from Reformed theologian Gordon Lewis: "Only faith which believes God on the basis of knowledge is true faith."[95]

Of course, this high value on reason must be held in balance with what Schaeffer wrote in books such as *True Spirituality* and *The Mark of the Christian*. These and other works show that for all of his confidence in the ability of human reason to discern propositional truth, Schaeffer believed at bottom that the Christian life consisted of God's justification and sanctification, accomplished through supernatural acts.[96] While Schaeffer clearly appreciated the extra-intellectual aspects of the Christian faith, he could not bring himself to consider that even propositional knowledge includes non-rational features.

He was trying to hold back a tide that was washing in around him. By the end of the century, the modern world that had been produced by the Enlightenment was giving way to postmodernism, with its recognition that all worldviews and all rational systems rely to some extent on non-logical moves. Schaeffer, however, had already identified Kierkegaard as the father of all existential philosophy and theology, because he posited the "leap of faith" that is necessary in the area of human meaning above the line of despair. This move into the non-logical or non-rational resulted, Schaeffer believed, in a loss of distinction between reality and fantasy. Schaeffer always maintained that the goal of his work was to evangelize successfully — in other words, to bring people to the place where they made a faith commitment to Christ. The first step in this process, what he sometimes called "pre-evangelism," was to cut the legs out from under modern, non-Christian, and therefore incoherent, worldviews so the people holding those worldviews would be forced to come to grips with their inconsistencies. Such pre-evangelism was threatened by the notion that there might be coherent worldviews other than Christianity.

Love and Logic

Sprinkled throughout the trilogy are anecdotes of encounters in which Schaeffer succeeded in undercutting the worldviews of others. In one case he told of a brilliant man who had moved from South America to Paris to be at the center of humanist thinking. On the verge of committing suicide because he had found the humanist way so ugly, he made his way to L'Abri. There he asked Schaeffer, "How do you love me; how do you start?" Schaeffer answered, "I know who you are because you are made in the image of God."[97] It is interesting that Schaeffer remembered the man at his wits' end because humanism was "so ugly" — an aesthetic problem, not an epistemological one. The most likely approach to such a person would seem to be a demonstration of the beauty, rather than the logical consistency, of Christianity. Schaeffer's point, however, was that for whatever reason, the man simply found his worldview unlivable. This was exactly the sort of recognition Schaeffer wanted.

In the existential drama that sometimes characterized L'Abri, suicide was a valid concern. When he began his method of exposing people to the fact that they could not live consistently with a modern worldview, Edith asked Francis if he were not afraid he might drive one of these desperate young people to suicide. Indeed, at least one young woman at L'Abri tried to kill herself. Schaeffer answered that even if the woman had succeeded, "after walking in the mountains and crying before God, I would have begun the same way with the next person who came."[98] This should in no way be taken to mean that he was callous to the life of the young people he sought to evangelize. Rather, he believed the stakes were so high, the need so great, and the lives of sixties youths so desperate, that the only way he could reach them with the gospel was to show the gravity of the modern dilemma.

Most of Schaeffer's reported encounters with modern students at L'Abri ended rather easily, with his refuting their inconsistent worldviews and showing them the truth. He told of a secular Oxford student who was trying to lead a seminar. Each time the student used the word "data," Schaeffer interrupted and asked, "How do you know, on the basis of logical positivism, that it is data?"[99] Logical positivism was one of the leading scientific and social scientific approaches to knowledge that emerged from Enlightenment thinking. Positivists believed that only that which can be measured, quantified scientifically, or deduced logically really counts as knowledge. Consequently, there is no need for faith, because science can prove positively all that is important. Schaeffer was trying to show this positivist student that something had to be taken for granted, presupposed, or believed before one could even decide what counted as measurable data. Schaeffer said he felt like he was slapping the hand of a child, but he had to expose the student's illogical position. Schaeffer sometimes called this "removing the umbrella from above the heads of modern people" or "taking the roof off."

On another occasion, on a boat traveling from Lisbon to Genoa, he encountered an atheist who was trying to live consistently with his atheistic, materialistic worldview. Seeing that the man was deeply in love with his wife, Schaeffer asked him how, when he took his wife into his arms at night, he could be sure she was real. Schaeffer was quite sure he had spoiled the man's evening and possibly the couple's romantic cruise.[100]

These sometimes amusing, sometimes startling stories reveal the compassion Schaeffer had for people struggling to find meaning in their lives and the deep seriousness with which he approached the world of ideas and worldviews. He spoke of weeping for modern people as well as refuting their worldviews, and this is consistent with the reports of many who stayed at L'Abri. He often wept as he preached and spoke, and he took no delight in showing people they could not find true meaning or happiness if they lived consistently with modern presuppositions. But even with so much obvious emotion and deep love, Schaeffer sometimes failed to take into consideration the importance of the non-logical aspects of knowledge — that is, the extent to which what we know is more than what we can logically prove — as Thomas Morris argued. Some of Schaeffer's supporters recognized this also, even some who were converted through his ministry. William Edgar cited Schaeffer's tendency to see presuppositions as purely a matter of ideas. Edgar wrote, "In fact, it is the heart that is basic to all else that is human. And the heart cannot be reduced to an idea. There is a tendency in Schaeffer of reducing the modes of human existence to ideas."[101]

Schaeffer's emphasis on logic and reason seemed to mask any appreciation for the non-rational aspects of his own apologetic. So many, especially those who came to L'Abri, were convinced of the truth of Christianity not merely because it was logically consistent, but also because he, Edith, and the other L'Abri workers demonstrated the love of God by accepting people where they were and loving them regardless of whether they were Christians. Edgar, for example, had heard all the arguments from Harold O. J. Brown before going to L'Abri, and he was certainly prepared intellectually for his conversion by Brown's witness. It was only within the love of L'Abri, however, that Edgar converted. Borrowing a term from sociologist Peter Berger, Edgar says that L'Abri provided a "structure of plausibility" for the Christian intellectual message.[102]

Sometimes Schaeffer acknowledged that this incarnational aspect of L'Abri transcended all the arguments he could muster. After all, as we saw in the previous chapter, love was "the final apologetic," and the Schaeffers loved their L'Abri children. The students walked the roads of Huemoz every night with Schaeffer like disciples with their teacher. Other L'Abri members likewise gave their time to the visitors and students. The deep sense of love and care became part of the trilogy's apologetic for Christianity. Jerram Barrs said Schaeffer had a gift for answering questions and displaying great love; "his compassion for people" was one of his great gifts. Even if the questioner were hostile and aggressive, Schaeffer could look past the aggression and see the need.[103] Sometimes young people left L'Abri naively believing they had the arguments that would win friends and family to the faith, only to find that the arguments did not work for them the way they worked for Schaeffer at L'Abri.[104] The context of love demonstrated at L'Abri was a powerful apologetic indeed. It was the perfect complement to his reasoned arguments for the Christian faith.

The trilogy and the lectures from which it sprang were Schaeffer's first efforts to reach a broader American audience. He found a receptive audience on evangelical college campuses, where he inspired young people who were already Christians to use their minds to bring a Christian critique to bear on the culture around them. And he continued to show the Christian love and compassion for those caught in the modern predicament that had made his message so successful at L'Abri. Now he would delve more deeply into the culture around him, and what he had to say would resonate with young, restless evangelicals like nothing he had said before.

CHAPTER FIVE

Progressive Prophet of Culture

The first book to appear after the trilogy was *Death in the City,* which grew out of Schaeffer's 1968 Wheaton College lectures. Jim Sire and Jim Nyquist of InterVarsity Press traveled to the Wheaton campus to hear the lectures. By the second day Sire had already told Nyquist he did not think the lectures could be turned into a book. At the end of the Tuesday evening lecture Schaeffer concluded by saying, dramatically, "There's death in the city; there's death in the city; there's death in the city." Then he turned, walked away from the podium and sat down. Sire turned to Nyquist and said, "Well, if we do these lectures, we have the title for our book."[1] When Sire, Nyquist, and Schaeffer met, Nyquist told Schaeffer that if his upcoming lectures at Stanford were something the publisher might be interested in, Schaeffer should let them know — implying that the Wheaton lectures were not. A few weeks after the Stanford lectures, however, Sire got a call from a student group at Wheaton that had taped and transcribed the Schaeffer lectures. After consulting with Nyquist, Sire changed his mind and told the Wheaton students that InterVarsity would do the book. *Death in the City* was the first time Sire took Schaeffer's spoken words and turned them into written prose.[2]

There is a marked difference in the written quality of the books edited by Sire and the trilogy that came before. *Death in the City,* and the books that followed, have sharper, clearer prose than the trilogy, even if there are still many vague generalizations in content. While *Death in the City* was not nearly as popular as the trilogy, literary scholar Roger Lundin believes it was Schaeffer's best book. He read all Schaeffer's books through 1971, and only *Death in the City* (and to a lesser degree *Pollution and the Death of Man*) had much impact on him. *Escape from Reason* and *The God Who Is There* "simply left me cold," Lundin recalled in 2004. "I didn't find the arguments convincing and the presentation beguiling. I was really taken with the pastoral insights, but I did not find the intellectual arguments attractive."[3] Lundin acknowledged that the reason he was unimpressed with Schaeffer's writing was probably because before he read Schaeffer he was already being influenced by philosophy students at Wheaton, and they had a lot to say in critique of Schaeffer. "If you had dinner with them, they would give you an earful about Schaeffer," Lundin remembers.[4] Lundin was also reading Shakespeare's *King Lear,* Bonhoeffer's *Letters and Papers from Prison,* Helmut Thielicke's sermons on the Apostles' Creed, and Dostoevsky's *Brothers Karamazov,* and he was taking philosophy with Arthur Holmes and others in Wheaton's philosophy department, reading Descartes, Berkeley, Kant, Hume, Hegel, and Nietzsche. "By any standard, Schaeffer did not stack up as a writer against those kinds of people," Lundin recalls.[5] "When you're an undergraduate and you're reading the history of modern philosophy . . . , then you go to Schaeffer, you can see that he has a procrustean bed that he's putting things in. . . . It doesn't seem to fit with the nuance and flow of intellectual history. That's what I thought about his books. They were intriguing, but they weren't convincing in their attempts to make large judgments about intellectual movements."[6]

Lundin may have found *Death in the City* to be more compelling because he had heard the book as a lecture first when he was a sophomore and a new convert to Christianity. "When I heard Schaeffer," Lundin remembers, "that would have been one of the early experiences for me of seeing someone attempt to apply biblical understanding and Christian truth to pressing cultural and political issues. That would have been a nascent and early image of [Christian] scholarship for me, of what it might be."[7]

Indeed, much more than in the trilogy, in *Death in the City* Schaeffer brought biblical themes to bear on modern culture. The opening lines of the book read, "We live in a post-Christian world. What should be our perspective as individuals, as institutions, as orthodox Christians, as those who claim to be Bible-believing? How should we look at this post-Christian world and function as Christians in it?"[8] This was an early use of the term "post-Christian," and it is not hard to imagine the effect it would have had in lecture form at Wheaton. As with the 1965 lectures that became part of the trilogy, *Death in the City* was first delivered in spoken form to students from an evangelical subculture that was not yet grappling with the serious issues the sixties had laid before the world. As was often the case, Schaeffer was out front, leading a developing trend. As such, the lectures, then book, would help Schaeffer carve out a niche as a progressive prophet of culture.

Death in the City

In *Death in the City* Schaeffer called for reformation and revival. Reformation meant the reclaiming of pure Christian doctrine in the face of the challenges of liberalism, an old theme for Schaeffer that became more pronounced in his work throughout the seventies. "Revival" referred to reclaiming the Christian lifestyle.

The two were interconnected. Revival of the Christian way of life could not happen without reclamation of doctrine. Like the good preacher that he was, Schaeffer adhered to his texts throughout the book. His New Testament text was Romans 1:21-22: "Because, when they knew God, they glorified him not as God, neither were they thankful, but became vain in their reasoning."[9] This was a reference to the cognitive side of humans, their thinking. For Schaeffer it meant that the Christians in Rome, to whom the apostle Paul was writing, had accepted false doctrine. In modern America, the culture had turned away from its Christian base: "[I]f we are looking across the history of the world to see those times when men knew the truth and turned away, let us say emphatically that there is no exhibition of this anywhere in history so clearly — in such a short time — as in our own generation."[10] In roughly one generation, Schaeffer said, from the 1920s to the 1960s, America had moved away from its Reformation base. "Men of our time knew the truth and yet turned away — turned away not only from the biblical truth, the religious truth of the Reformation, but turned away from the total culture built upon that truth."[11]

Schaeffer was not arguing that the majority of people in America or Great Britain had necessarily been Bible-believing, practicing Christians in the 1920s, but he did believe that had one walked around Columbus Circle in New York or Trafalgar Square in London and done a survey, it would have shown that most people understood the basic concepts of Christianity and accepted them as the foundation of western culture. By contrast, English-speaking culture by the end of the 1960s "had trampled on the truth of the Reformation. . . . It is a horrible thing," Schaeffer said, "for a man like myself to look back and see my country go down the drain in my own lifetime."[12]

For a biblical period that paralleled modern America, Schaeffer turned to the book of Jeremiah, his Old Testament text in *Death in the City*. Schaeffer used the term "Christian" culture, with Christian in quotation marks, to describe Jeremiah's society. As in our own time, the "Christian" culture of Jeremiah's day was giving way to a "post-Christian" culture. The people were turning away from God, and as a result their city was under siege. So it was in the late twentieth century. The problem of modern men and women was that they no longer believed anyone was watching over them in the universe. This left them with no sense of being loved, with no sense that their lives had meaning. In Jeremiah's day, in a city under siege, the people would give anything for bread. Likewise, in modern culture, although no one was starving physically, people were starving spiritually; they were losing their sense of what it means to be human, what it means to be created in the image of God, and what it means to know "the mannishness of man." There was "death in the city, death in the city, death in the city."[13]

In turning to a materialistic view of life, modern men and women had lost their belief that, as the Westminster Shorter Catechism says, "Man's chief end is to glorify God, *and enjoy Him forever*."[14] Even Christians were forgetting how to love and enjoy God. The Christian life was meant to fulfill the whole human being, and should, therefore, never appear to the onlooker as the negation of life. Modern culture, by contrast, was based on a materialistic philosophy that said this life was all there is. Such a worldview led to meaninglessness and despair, which was reflected in the art and literature of the late twentieth century. Schaeffer cited specifically the surrealistic art of De Chirico as well as the novel *On the Beach* by Nevil Shute, which contemplated life on Earth after nuclear war has destroyed civilization.[15]

As in Jeremiah's day, the specter of judgment loomed over twentieth-century western culture. For having turned away, God had allowed the Hebrews to be carried off into captivity in Babylon. The Hebrews believed that because the temple of God was with them, all would be well, but God was not pleased with their empty religion. Likewise in the twentieth century, Schaeffer argued, there is much religion, but it is the new theology that is full of compromises. In a note Schaeffer sounded repeatedly in the 1970s (as we will see more fully in the next chapter), he said in *Death in the City* that even some within evangelicalism were compromising with liberal theology. He lamented that increasingly from the 1930s to the 1960s the evangelical church had stopped using the word "apostasy."[16] In a reference back to the trilogy, Schaeffer said that instead of "calling apostasy, apostasy, we are all too easily infiltrated with relativism and synthesis in our own day."[17]

In the late sixties and early seventies, Schaeffer was still an independent and prophetic voice within evangelicalism. This was before evangelicals had taken sides in what would become known as America's culture war, and a figure like Schaeffer could speak independently with little concern for staying on the right side of political battles. Thus Schaeffer criticized evangelicals on issues often considered the province of left-wing evangelicalism — affluence, for example. Turning to Jeremiah 5, Schaeffer described what happens to an affluent society. "They are like fed horses in the morning," he quoted the prophet. "If a horse is well fed, says Jeremiah," Schaeffer amplified, "it turns to sexual things." What would Jeremiah say to the sexually liberated culture of the sixties? Schaeffer paraphrased, "O affluent United States and northern European Reformation countries, turning from the Reformation faith. They are as fed horses in the morning; every one neighed after his neighbor's wife."[18] In addition to sex, Schaeffer believed that members of the sixties generation were finding their escape in drugs much as their parents had in alcohol and adultery. The problem was partly relativism, which Schaeffer defined simply as individuals no longer believing in absolutes. The only thing keeping society intact morally at all was that people were living on the memory of the absolutes of the Christian faith in which they no longer believed. Americans were affluent in material wealth but had lost the absolute standard of morality taught by Reformation Christianity.

While Schaeffer acknowledged that evangelicals were not as deeply into a materialistic philosophy of life and the sins of amoral affluence as the wider culture was, he argued that much of the religion of the late twentieth century was but an echo of the world.[19] This was a reference to liberal theology. Liberal theology was little more than modern psychology and sociology put in theological terms.[20] Jeremiah's word to liberal preachers, according to Schaeffer, was "Woe be unto the pastors who destroy and scatter the sheep of my pasture."[21] Here Schaeffer referenced Malcolm Muggeridge's article "The Death Wish of the Liberal," in which the English author and recent Christian convert attempted to show that having eliminated moral absolutes, liberals had lost the distinction between love and non-love. Without such distinctions, Schaeffer added, we get Michelangelo Antonioni's film *Blowup,* advertised as "Murder without guilt, love without meaning." "The sheep are scattered," Schaeffer declared.[22]

Schaeffer believed that the first step in speaking to such a culture was to say honestly that something is deeply wrong. Too often, he chided, evangelicals are overly quick to tell people the answers without first convincing them that there is something deeply wrong with the culture. Evangelicals also needed to convey a sense that everyone is in this mess together. They must really live among the hurting and show solidarity with those caught in the maelstrom of meaninglessness. "We cannot shout at people or scream down upon them. They must feel that we are with them, that we are saying that both of us are sinners, and they must know these are not just words, but that we mean what we say."[23] Schaeffer believed that modern men and women sensed something was wrong, but that they often had no one to tell them what was amiss and why. He was convinced that such truth-telling was the first and necessary step for evangelism.

A dead orthodoxy would not do. Evangelicals needed correct theology accompanied by true Christian love. Schaeffer cited China in the ninth century and Arabia in the sixth as having a substantial Christian presence, only to see the church routed by competing worldviews — by Islam in the case of Arabia. In these cultures, as in parts of Africa and Armenia, a dead church had lost out to other faiths or ideologies.

A central part of the Christian message to modernity, Schaeffer said, was that human beings were made in the image of God and were therefore not bound by the determinisms of twentieth-century intellectual life. Schaeffer cited the chemical or biological determinism of the Marquis de Sade in the eighteenth century and Francis Crick in the twentieth, the psychological determinism of Sigmund Freud, and the environmental determinism of B. F. Skinner. Then he moved from Jeremiah to Romans 1:21-22: "When they knew God, they glorified him not as God, neither were thankful, but became vain in their reasoning, and their foolish heart was darkened. Professing themselves to be wise, they became fools."[24]

Schaeffer warned evangelicals to avoid giving the appearance that if humans were sinful, they were nothing. Psychological and environmental determinism posited human beings without will or meaning, reduced to their psychological urges or responses to environmental stimuli. If Christians piled on with nothing more than the message that humans were also depraved sinners, they could drive modern people even deeper into despair. The biblical message is that human beings are sinful, but they are still created in the image of God. "Man is lost, but great," Schaeffer said.[25]

Salvation was the answer, but salvation was not just for individuals; it was also for the culture. Salvation established an individual's vertical relationship with God, but it also reestablished proper horizontal relationships among humans. In a statement that must have surprised, perhaps even confused, those who had read the trilogy, Schaeffer said that in this sense Christianity was a most existential religion. He explained that there are two ways to use the term "existential." The first, as he had used it throughout the trilogy, was to describe a philosophy that held that human beings must create their own meaning in the present, because there is no transcendent meaning for them to find. The second, however, was to use the term to mean something like "moment by moment reality." Christianity was existential in this second sense. Christians were to find meaning in this present existence, not merely in the life to come.[26]

Schaeffer used Acts 14:15-17, Acts 17:16-32, and Romans 1:18–2:16 to show how the apostle Paul talked to "men without the Bible" — that is, to Greeks who were not schooled in the Old Testament scriptures. Schaeffer believed Paul should serve as a model for how to evangelize in a modern secular culture among people who no longer knew the Bible very well. In each of these biblical examples, most completely in Romans, Paul argued from human nature and human history to show that the deep needs within human beings are evidence of a creator, and that humans themselves are created in that Creator's image. "Primitive man, cultured man, ancient man, modern man, Eastern man, Western man," Schaeffer exclaimed, "all have a testimony that says man is more than their [*sic*] own theories."[27] Even in an age built on evolutionary science there are glimpses of this, Schaeffer continued. Einstein, for example, at the end of his life turned to mysticism because he came to believe there was something beyond what science could explain. Sartre pondered the question, Why is there something there instead of nothing? Scientist Murray Eden at the prestigious Massachusetts Institute of Technology used a computer to calculate the probability that the complexity of the universe could have arisen from chance alone and concluded it was virtually impossible. Charles Darwin himself, according to Schaeffer, near the end of his life said, "I cannot believe with my mind that all this was produced by chance."[28] Schaeffer used these stories to illustrate his belief that deep in every human being was a sense that there was something beyond us. He believed, therefore, that if Christians pressed the issue correctly, they could help modern people with little knowledge of the Bible see their need for God.

Even in matters of God's judgment for immorality, Schaeffer believed Christians could reach men and women who were indifferent or hostile to the Bible. This could be done by showing that no individual consistently extends to others the kind of moral consideration one demands for himself or herself. In other words, every person who has ever claimed to have been wronged morally, everyone who has uttered the words "That's not fair," has to acknowledge that by the standard he or she uses to judge fairness and equity, each has failed to apply such fairness in all relationships with others. All stand guilty by measure of their own moral standards. The only way to get around moral judgment is to give up the holiness of God, who has created morality and expects human beings to live by it, or to give up the significance of human beings, so that they are not responsible for what they do. To those with the Bible, Schaeffer said, drawing on Romans 2:17, God said he will judge by an even higher standard. The upshot is that both the Jews and the Greeks, both those with and those without the Bible, stand condemned. Regardless of which standard is being used, the moral standards humans apply to each other or the biblical standard, all are guilty. How, then, can humans be saved without compromising the holiness of God or ignoring the significance, and therefore the responsibility, of humankind? Only by Christ's having taken our place on the cross. "Thus three great things fall into place," Schaeffer exclaimed: "God's holiness, man's significance, and the possibility of man's redemption. I don't know about you, but I believe it is time to stand up and sing the doxology. Here is an intellectual answer that nothing else has ever presented."[29]

Along with this intellectual answer, Christians needed to show compassion for those still lost in sin. "What do you think when you see the newspaper pictures of those starving and displaced people? Do you have any compassion? What I find in much evangelicalism," he lamented like the weeping prophet Jeremiah, "is not only weakness in sensing the lostness of the lost, but a tremendous weakness of compassion for the needs of my kind in the present life."[30]

Schaeffer claimed he had never met a person who thought the message of sin and the need for redemption was ugly if presented as he outlined them in *Death in the City.* Perhaps thinking about his own early career in McIntire's wing of American fundamentalism, he said, "What men find ugly is what they see in Christians who hold to the orthodox doctrine that men are lost, but show no signs of compassion. This is what is ugly. This is what causes men in our generation to be turned off by evangelicalism."[31]

Schaeffer concluded *Death in the City* with his story "The Universe and the Two Chairs," which would later be published separately as an article in *Christianity Today.*[32] In this little analogy, the universe consists of one room, with windows closed and doors locked. In the room are two men, one a materialist, the other a Christian, the only two men in the universe. They sit in two chairs facing each other. The materialist describes the universe to the Christian scientifically and presents the Christian with a stack of books that explain things further. The Christian spends months, even years, studying the books, until he has become an expert in all the materialist believes about the structure of the universe. Both now know how the universe works biologically, chemically, astronomically, psychologically, and so forth. The Christian then tells the materialist that his explanation is incomplete. The Christian adds another book to the stack, the Bible, and explains to the materialist, "I have a book here, the Bible, and it tells me things that you do not know. It tells me the origin of the universe. Your scientific investigation by its very nature cannot do that."[33] The materialist, the Christian argues, has discussed only half the universe, the natural half. "To really understand reality in our universe, you have to consider both halves — both the seen and the unseen."[34] Schaeffer went further, however, and argued that the two stories are incompatible and cannot be synthesized. Christians could certainly glean a good bit of detail from the materialist's observations, but in his comprehensive worldview the materialist is arguing that the material is all there is. The Christian knows otherwise. There are only two chairs, and the Christian must acknowledge that he or she is in one or the other. "If courses in a Christian college are being taught as though the professors are sitting in the materialist's chair, is it any wonder that there is an unreality?"[35] This, in the guise of a story, was Schaeffer's call for worldview thinking. There would be many more such calls to come.

The Call to Christian Environmentalism

Schaeffer next turned his attention, and his call for worldview thinking, to the environment. In 1970, a year after *Death in the City,* Schaeffer published *Pollution and the Death of Man,* a fifty-five-page booklet outlining a Christian approach to ecology. Starting with the example of the effect of DDT on aquatic plant and animal life, he said that if humankind cannot solve the ecological crisis, then the resources necessary to sustain life are going to die.

"The distressing thing about this is that orthodox Christians often really have had no better sense about these things than unbelievers," Schaeffer wrote. "The death of 'joy' in nature is leading to the death of nature itself."[36] He used an article by historian Lynn White Jr. as his starting point. White argued in "The Historical Roots of Our Ecologic Crisis," an article that appeared in *Science* magazine, that the Christian view of dominion over nature was to blame for the ecological problem. He believed that dominion had led to destructive tendencies. White advocated a return to Saint Francis of Assisi's view of the kinship of all the natural world to replace the view that humans were superior and given dominion over the rest of nature. This approach, Schaeffer worried, could be extended into a full-blown pantheism. Pantheism is the view that all of life is part of the divine, and that all living things are sacred. The appeal of pantheism for environmentalists, Schaeffer said, citing sociologist Richard L. Means, is that human beings will be less likely to degrade nature if they see it as sacred and see themselves as equal to the rest of nature.[37]

Schaeffer critiqued this pantheistic solution by demonstrating that pantheism turns human beings into something less than they actually are — making them less responsible in the process. In the Christian worldview, humans are created in the image of God, superior to the rest of the created order. As such, human beings alone are endowed with a moral responsibility. If everything is equally divine, then humankind's moral responsibility is destroyed, and the moral problem of ecology becomes merely pragmatic. Critiquing Means, Schaeffer wrote, "He started off with a moral crisis, but suddenly all one is left with is a pragmatic problem."[38] Why should human beings treat the environment well? The pragmatic approach suggests that if we do not, we will suffer. Schaeffer then pointed out that there is no reason for humankind to avoid suffering if there is nothing special about human beings. The problem with pantheism is that while unity has meaning, particulars do not. The whole has meaning because it is divine, but human beings, as particulars within the whole, do not have individual meaning, and if "particulars have no meaning, then nature has no meaning, including the particular of man. . . . Pantheism gives you an answer for unity, but it gives no meaning to the diversity. Pantheism is not the answer."[39] Schaeffer argued that those, like Means, who proposed pantheism as the answer to the ecological crisis were actually devaluing humankind, because "without categories, there is eventually no reason to distinguish bad nature from good nature. Pantheism leaves us with the Marquis de Sade's dictum, 'What is, is right' in morals, and man becomes no more than the grass."[40]

Along with pantheism, another inadequate answer to the ecological crisis was "Byzantine Christianity," Schaeffer's collective label for Roman Catholic and Orthodox Christianity before the Renaissance. Byzantine Christianity valued only the things of heaven, he said, while devaluing the things of this world. As in every other area of life, the only adequate answer to the question of how human beings should relate to nature was what Schaeffer once again called "Reformation Christianity." Reformation Christianity's doctrine of the creation taught first that created things have an objective existence — that is, they are really there. Moreover, creation is not an extension of God, nor is nature a dream in the mind of God. Rather, God created nature as other than himself.

Within the created order, human beings are part of nature and share some things in common with all other created things. At the same time, however, human beings are different from all the rest of God's creation, because they alone were created in the image of God. Only human beings are personal. Human beings, therefore, are both like and unlike God, as well as like and unlike the rest of nature. There is a chasm between God and everything in the created order, including human beings. Yet human beings are made in God's image, meaning there is also a chasm between God and man on one side and the rest of nature on the other. "[M]an is made in the image of God, who is personal; thus he has two relationships — upward and downward."[41] This meant that human beings were separated from nature, which is lower than human beings, but at the same time related to nature, because humans, like everything else, are part of God's creation. We have a common lung system with dogs and cats, but this relationship we have with other animals is not our basic relationship. Rather, Schaeffer argued, our basic relationship is to God, in whose image we are created. This eliminated the possibility for the autonomy of human beings, and Schaeffer attacked and rejected the autonomy of human beings as well as the autonomy of the rest of nature: "The value of the things is not in themselves autonomously, but that God made them — and thus they deserve to be treated with high respect."[42]

Schaeffer very briefly brought the incarnation and resurrection of Jesus Christ into his discussion of nature to show that God valued the human body and not just the human soul. There should be no platonic division between body and soul for the Christian. God became real flesh in the incarnation and was resurrected as real flesh before ascending into heaven. The scriptures, moreover, promise that believers will be resurrected in real flesh and blood human bodies. The spiritual and material, he insisted, are not opposed to one another.[43]

For Schaeffer, therefore, all of creation deserved to be treated with respect because it was all created by God, but human beings deserved to be treated with more respect because they were made in the image of God. Schaeffer related his view of creation to Dutch theologian Abraham Kuyper's concept of sphere sovereignty. Kuyper taught that there were different spheres of creation and that human beings were to be Christians in each of the spheres — the church, the state, the family, and so on. God was sovereign over all, and humans were called to live for God in all, yet at the same time their roles were different in each sphere. Extending this concept, Schaeffer believed that Christians should acknowledge the various spheres of nature and treat each aspect of nature properly and with integrity, "each thing in its proper sphere by creation."[44] The problem with pantheism was that it flattened out creation, devaluing humankind to the level of all other created things.

When it came to nature and the ecological crisis, Schaeffer proposed what he called "substantial healing," a concept he developed further in his little book *True Spirituality*. Substantial healing is that which can take place in the here and now — recognizing that full redemption will not come until the future kingdom. Human beings are divided from God spiritually, from themselves psychologically, from each other sociologically, and from nature ecologically. The Christian faith does not teach that these can only be overcome in the hereafter; rather, it proclaims that there can be substantial healing in this life as well. In the area of ecology this would mean that when Christians have returned to a proper fellowship with God, all proper relationships should be restored, including in their use of nature. "We are to have dominion over it," Schaeffer wrote, "but we are not going to use it as fallen man uses it. We are not going to act as though it were nothing in itself, or as though we will do to nature everything we can do."[45]

Christians should not be destroyers, he insisted. They may cut down the tree to build shelter or to heat themselves, but they should not cut down the tree just to cut down a tree, and they should not cut down all the trees. They may have to kill ants to protect their homes, but they should step over an ant when walking down the sidewalk. The same principle applied to hunting and fishing. Taking game for food was one thing, but these creatures do not exist to be slaughtered. Having argued that it was heresy to push to the point of pantheism Saint Francis's view of the relatedness of all created things, here he cited Saint Francis as theologically correct for recognizing that there is a relationship among all of God's creation. The ant is not created in the image of God, but "The ant and the man are both creatures."[46] Schaeffer cited the rock group The Doors, who expressed this when they sang of nature as "our fair sister"; he even used "Our Fair Sister" as the title to chapter one of *Pollution and the Death of Man.* Problems arose only when the order of nature was confused and the spheres denied. A fish, Schaeffer argued, should not be treated like a human baby, but neither should it be treated in the same way as a block of wood.[47]

In matters of ecology, Schaeffer concluded, the church should become the "pilot plant." Just as companies often build a smaller pilot plant that models what the larger plant will be, so the church should model how human beings can find substantial healing for the alienation of humans from themselves, from each other, and from nature. Christians can do this by saying no to such nature-destroying activities as strip mining, even if this means lower profits. If it takes more time and money to mine in a more ecologically sensitive way, that is the price to be paid for treating nature as part of God's creation. The same is true in business relationships, Schaeffer argued. Christians must model a creation ethic that refuses to view workers as dehumanized modes of production or as means to an end. If Christians treat other human beings as machines, soon they will view themselves as machines, the wonder of nature will be lost, and the environment will be destroyed. "When we learn this — the Christian view of nature," Schaeffer summarized, "then there can be a real ecology; beauty will flow, psychological freedom will come, and the world will cease to be turned into a desert."[48]

Christian Aesthetics

The sense of wonder for nature that was part of Schaeffer's Christian environmentalism was related to his aesthetic sense, which also included his appreciation for art. Schaeffer was the first prominent evangelical to bring a Christian worldview to bear on the visual arts. Before Schaeffer, evangelicals had had little positive to say about any of the arts. In 1947, when he traveled to Europe for the first time to survey the possibility for fundamentalist work, he visited museums.

After moving to Europe permanently, he came under the influence of Christian art critic Hans Rookmaaker.

Rookmaaker was a fascinating figure. The son of a colonial administrator, he grew up in the Dutch East Indies (present-day Indonesia). He started collecting jazz and blues records at the age of twelve and would eventually have one of the most extensive collections in the world. Rookmaaker attended the Dutch equivalent of the U.S. Naval Academy and was a midshipman when the Germans invaded Holland during World War II. In 1942, after the Germans had defeated the Netherlands, Rookmaaker was taken to a prisoner-of-war camp. His Jewish fiancée and her family were taken to a concentration camp and eventually killed at Auschwitz.

Rookmaaker began to read the Bible as a prisoner. When he was transferred to a camp in Stanislau in the western Ukraine, he met an older serviceman, Johan Mekkes, who had done doctoral work at the Free University of Amsterdam under Reformed thinker Hermann Dooyeweerd. Mekkes influenced not only Rookmaaker's conversion to Christianity, but also his eventual career path in the world of scholarly study.

Rookmaaker was baptized after being released following the war, and he would go on to graduate school, but not before meeting some more key figures in his life. Rookmaaker set out to find his fiancée with the help of her friend Anky Huitker. They found out that the object of their search had been killed in the Holocaust, but their efforts bore some unexpected fruit: Anky and Hans became friends, fell in love, and were engaged in 1948. During their engagement, Anky worked as an administrative assistant for the founding conference of the International Council of Christian Churches (ICCC) in Amsterdam, a meeting organized by Francis Schaeffer. Rookmaaker was looking for Americans he could talk to for leads about acquiring jazz and blues recordings to expand his record collection. Anky thought Schaeffer might be able to help, so she introduced the two. While Schaeffer was not much help with the music, he and Rookmaaker found they had a mutual interest in art and ended up talking long into the night. Hans and Anky were married the next year, and the Schaeffers became their model and mentors for Christian marriage and family, while Rookmaaker mentored Schaeffer in art criticism.[49]

Rookmaaker completed his doctorate in 1959 at the University of

Amsterdam, writing his doctoral thesis at the same time he worked on a book on jazz, blues, and spirituals. He completed his thesis on Gauguin in English, but there was some question among the faculty as to whether it was passable English. Rookmaaker turned to Schaeffer for help in proofing the work for language errors. Schaeffer found Rookmaaker's use of English to be adequate, so he wrote a letter to the faculty attesting to the English proficiency of the thesis. With Schaeffer's endorsement, Rookmaaker was awarded the doctorate. Rookmaaker's biographer Laurel Gasque says that he "just squeaked through." Nevertheless, in 1964 Rookmaaker was invited to become the founding professor of the art history program at the Free University of Amsterdam.[50]

Rookmaaker enjoyed helping non-experts develop an appreciation for art, taking numerous Christian groups on tours of museums, sometimes after art discussions at L'Abri. Like Schaeffer, he was deeply interested in the intersection of Christian faith and western culture. He also shared Schaeffer's love for scripture and a deep sense of calling to use his training to spread the gospel by critiquing culture. In another sense, however, he was Schaeffer's inverse. As Gasque puts it, "Schaeffer was an evangelist who could be intellectual; Rookmaaker was an intellectual who could be evangelistic."[51]

There can be no doubt that Rookmaaker was the major influence on Schaeffer's thinking about art. As we have seen, Edith and Francis were cultural separatists when they first went to Europe, and some who knew the Schaeffers in the pre-L'Abri years remember them as opposed to the arts. Deirdre Haim recalls that in the early 1950s the Schaeffers attended neither films nor live theatre and generally discouraged converts from going into the arts. Haim studied at the Chelsea School of Art anyway, the Schaeffers' discouragement notwithstanding, and there seemed to prove the Schaeffers correct by drifting away from the faith. "At art school I, admittedly, backslid as a Christian on occasions as I continued to feel a little guilty at not studying something more 'Christian,'" Haim wrote in 2005. When she returned to visit Schaeffer at L'Abri some years later, however, Schaeffer told her about his wonderful friend Hans Rookmaaker. "From this time Fran's attitude to art, and especially the theatre & film totally changed," Haim (then known by her married name, Ducker) recalls. "Because of Rookmaaker and Schaeffer's joint exploration of the arts from the Christian point of view the whole Evangelical world changed its attitude to the arts."[52]

Schaeffer's earliest mention of art in print came in the "New Modernism" address of 1950. There he argued that art was the most honest expression of modernity, more honest than the new modernist theology. While the new modernism of Barth was relativistic but wanted to retain some things as absolutely true, modern art expressed the full incoherence, flux, and meaninglessness of the modern condition. "By this standard perhaps," he told the International Council of Christian Churches gathering in Geneva, "the modern artist is the most honest of non-Christian men." By contrast the "transcendental theologian" (a none-too-veiled reference to Barth) was "the greatest cheat" because he had "divided truth and yet builds such a heinously clever counterfeit of revealed Christianity."[53]

Schaeffer's new embrace of the arts was evident in his little booklet *Art and the Bible,* originally published by InterVarsity Press in 1973.[54] There he admonished evangelicals for their tendency to "relegate art to the fringe of life."[55] He said that evangelicals understood poetry better than visual art because the Psalms show explicitly that the Bible affirms poetry. But scripture affirms the visual arts as well, he argued. Since all of life falls under the lordship of Christ, and since in Christianity there is no Platonic division of mind, body, and soul, Christians needed to understand that the artistic, aesthetic side of humankind was part of God's economy. Christianity was not just true in its doctrine, he insisted, but was "true to what is there, true in the whole area of the whole man in all of life." Modern Christianity had not been attentive to the visual arts, however, producing little more than Sunday school sketches.[56]

When Schaeffer began to speak of Christianity and culture this way, there were some who believed that because he was speaking intellectually, he must not be drawing his insights from the Bible. He did not back down, however. After all, God had commanded cherubim representations of gold as well as candlesticks in the Tabernacle. The temple was then covered with precious stones to make it beautiful. Good art was more than just religious representation, however; he cited King David from the Old Testament as someone who offered beautiful music as praise to God. An artist who sought to praise God could do so even if the subject were not necessarily religious and even if no other person saw it as praise. King Solomon's poems about love between a man and a woman have intrinsic as well as allegorical value in that they affirm and represent that which God has made beautiful, the love that is exhibited between male and female.[57]

Schaeffer considered art a legitimate source of pleasure. We value art because it is creative, he said, and therefore it shows how humans are made in God's image and can be co-creators with God. Modern secular art had lost much of this sense of pleasure and had become too agenda-driven, too "intellectual" to be great art. Schaeffer charged what little evangelical art that existed of falling into the same mistake: it did not allow the creative work of art to bring pleasure to human beings as they were created to be. "Too often we think that a work of art has value only if we reduce it to a tract," he wrote. "This too is to view art solely as a message for the intellect."[58]

Given his own penchant for seeking and finding purpose and message, Schaeffer had difficulty simply embracing the aesthetic pleasures of art. When he spoke of a particular work of art, especially if it were a secular, abstract piece, he almost always told his audience the exact intellectual content of the piece. He did this in the trilogy when he moved seamlessly from written texts to artistic works that he claimed conveyed the same message of secularity. He tended even toward this intellectual interpretation of art when he spoke of twentieth-century work that he was sure conveyed the meaninglessness of the modern dilemma. In other words, when he saw a piece of art that seemed incomprehensible and incoherent, he immediately related it to Kierkegaard's upper story/lower story separation. Theologian and jazz musician William Edgar parted with Schaeffer not only on Schaeffer's simplistic and one-dimensional understanding of how ideas develop in history, but also on art. Schaeffer's view of the arts, Edgar believes, was without complexity. Schaeffer believed that ideas always come before facts; the painter thinks something, then paints it. This ignores the possibility that consequences can produce ideas, and that social circumstances and the relationships can produce artistic expression.[59]

Schaeffer's view of art is confusing to say the least, for whereas he criticized artists for trying too hard to convey particular ideas, he also said that artists always convey a worldview, and a worldview, as he explained it, could only be conveyed in ideas. In short, he seemed to be telling artists to get away from conveying a message but also to be sure their art conveyed their worldview, which was a message of sorts. In *Art and the Bible,* for example, he called art without a message "art for art's sake" and said it was a recent and unhealthy development. The Renaissance artists did not do art this way, he wrote. Rather, artists from Cimabue in the thirteenth century through Michelangelo and Leonardo da Vinci in the sixteenth century worked either from a Christian point of view or from the point of view of Renaissance humanism, and even the Christian point of view was deficient from an evangelical perspective. Even a modern artist such as Picasso worked from a particular perspective or worldview and sought to convey this in his art. Since Picasso, however, artists had gotten away from this and were doing art with no purpose or worldview in mind, but even this turn reflected a worldview: they were rendering representations of meaninglessness, whether consciously or unconsciously.[60] Schaeffer believed that only in his own lifetime had the wheels come off western civilization, and the changes in art were indicative of the cultural decline.

Schaeffer believed it was possible for a non-Christian to do art that presented a Christian worldview. Conversely, he warned, a Christian artist could inadvertently express a non-Christian worldview if he or she adopted secular standards of art or failed to understand the total Christian worldview. Finally, it was even possible for some artists to be unaware that they were working from any worldview at all. Nevertheless, Schaeffer believed, some sort of worldview showed in virtually all art.[61] He would return to this idea in his book *How Should We Then Live?,* where he also argued that despite their fall into sin, human beings retained the image of God, the "mannishness of man," and could therefore create art even in their fallen, sinful state. "God is the great creator, and part of the unique mannishness of man . . . is creativity. Thus, man as man paints, shows creativity in science and engineering, and so on. Such activity does not require a special impulse from God, and it does not mean that people are not alienated from God and do not need the work of Christ to return to God. It does mean that man as man, in contrast to non-man, is creative."[62]

Schaeffer repeatedly returned to the *messages* in art. Its propositional content was, for Schaeffer, the most important thing about it. Try as he might to affirm the creativity of art and the value of art as an act of worship, both when authored and when experienced, in *Art and the Bible* Schaeffer could not get away from his notion that all art was to be evaluated according to the message or worldview it conveyed. As he said, an artist's work should be evaluated like a preacher's sermons. For him everything was message and worldview. He might attempt to discuss art aesthetically, but he almost always ended up evaluating art propositionally. Perhaps as a result, Schaeffer was much better at interpreting art than at telling Christian artists how to practice their craft.

In *How Should We Then Live?* he included a chapter entitled "Modern Art, Music, Literature, and Films," with an analysis of how modern art expresses the prevailing worldview of the modern era. As he had argued in the trilogy, the modern worldview separated truth into objective and subjective realms. Artistic expression was part of the upstairs realm of subjectivity, where there was meaning but no objectively true knowledge, not the downstairs realm, where science and objective truth resided. With Rookmaaker acting as an advisor for the film version of *How Should We Then Live?*, Schaeffer expanded considerably his knowledge of artists.

Schaeffer continued to believe that art was the second area in which the dichotomy between the objective and subjective was manifest, after philosophy but before music, general culture, and, last of all, theology. He believed the artistic breakthrough in this expression of the subjective came with the impressionists. He cited several, including Claude Monet (1840-1926), Pierre Auguste Renoir (1841-1919), Camille Pissarro (1830-1903), Alfred Sisley (1839-1899), and Edgar Degas (1834-1917). As interpreted by Schaeffer, the impressionists painted what came to them via their eyes, questioning whether there was any meaning or reality beyond the light waves and color. Monet, he said, carried this doubt about reality to its logical conclusion, and reality became only a dream.[63] In other words, the impressionists doubted the reality of the objects they painted and could be sure only that they were experiencing color and light.

Paul Cezanne (1839-1906), Vincent Van Gogh (1853-1890), Paul Gauguin (1848-1903), and Georges Seurat (1859-1891) all contributed to the further fragmentation of truth and life. "As philosophy had moved from unity [of truth] to fragmentation, this fragmentation was also carried into the field of painting," Schaeffer wrote.[64] With truth fragmented, ultimately there was only absurdity, which brought Schaeffer to a discussion of the early twentieth-century Dadaists, Marcel Duchamp (1887-1969) chief among them. "Duchamp realized that the absurdity of all things includes the absurdity of art itself," Schaeffer wrote.[65] Artists such as Duchamp, then the American Jackson Pollack (1912-1956), followed the philosophers just as the artists of the Renaissance had followed Thomas Aquinas's separation of faith and reason. The visual artists were then followed by musicians such as Claude Debussy (1862-1918) and eventually John Cage. Debussy moved from non-resolution to fragmentation, then Cage moved into absurdity and chance, flipping coins to determine what his music should be. The move from philosophy to art to music to general culture led to "an almost monolithic consensus, an almost unified voice shouting at us a fragmented concept of the universe and of life."[66] The shouting was difficult to resist, which is why he was so keen to impress upon Christian artists that their work should be different — that they should consciously attempt to counter the worldview of fragmentation and meaninglessness with propositional messages of the unity of truth under God.

In the visual arts, Schaeffer also analyzed films, and he found them rife with meaninglessness and fragmentation. In particular, he often mentioned Antonioni's *Blowup.*"[67] For Schaeffer this film was the expression of non-reason — that is, no certainties and no moral values. He saw a similar worldview in *Juliet of the Spirits, The Last Year at Marienbad, The Hour of the Wolf,* and *Belle de Jour.* Ingmar Bergman's film *The Silence* was of interest to Schaeffer because of Bergman's interview after the film in which he confessed that for him God was dead, so there was only silence in the universe. In 1979, in his pro-life film and book *Whatever Happened to the Human Race?* with C. Everett Koop, Schaeffer cited filmmaker Woody Allen, who like Bergman believed in no personal God and had the courage to express the meaninglessness of life in his films. Here was filmmaking with a clear worldview, and it fit Schaeffer's purposes perfectly. "If there is no personal God," Schaeffer wrote, ". . . then Woody Allen is right: life is both meaningless and terrifying."[68] Schaeffer quoted at length from an article Allen had written in *Esquire* magazine expressing the worldview that without God, all was "alienation, loneliness [and] emptiness verging on madness. The fundamental thing behind all motivation and all activity," according to Allen, "is the constant struggle against annihilation and against death. It's absolutely stupefying in its terror, and it renders anyone's accomplishments meaningless."[69]

Whatever the merits of Schaeffer's arguments, it is worth pointing out again how radical his brand of cultural engagement was for the evangelical world. To whatever extent evangelicals by the mid- to late 1970s were analyzing culture instead of rejecting it, Schaeffer was largely responsible. Much more common in Schaeffer's day were evangelical preachers who railed against culture and urged people to separate from its tainting influence rather than seriously consider its meaning and then engage its message. At about the same time Schaeffer tried to make sense of Woody Allen films and discussed the meaning of Beatles albums such as *Sergeant Pepper's Lonely Hearts Club Band* (1967), evangelists Jack Van Impe and Bob Larson, to name only two, urged evangelical young people to destroy their popular records and take a pledge to stop listening to the radio. Schaeffer was interested in why bands such as Cream, Jefferson Airplane, the Grateful Dead, Pink Floyd, and Jimi Hendrix, all of which he mentioned by name, sang about sex and hallucinogenic drugs.[70] He was convinced that the modern worldview of meaninglessness and relativity — what today would be called postmodernism — was the worldview behind art and culture, and that Christians needed to engage that message and answer it with the truth of Christianity.

Economics and Race

In the evangelical world of the mid-seventies, Schaeffer's discussions of art were anything but conservative, let alone fundamentalist. His was the radical, progressive message of engagement, and this approach spilled over into brief discussions here and there of economics and race. Although these were not major emphases of his published materials, he was consistently opposed to what he called the non-compassionate use of accumulated wealth, and those who knew him and studied at L'Abri recall his speaking regularly against the norms of middle-class affluence in America. In his address to the International Congress on World Evangelization at Lausanne in 1974, he said that if he were to write his early books again, he would change just one aspect: He would stress that when the Christian consensus prevailed in the West from the Reformation to the nineteenth century, Christians failed in the area of race and wealth. He spoke of a platonic tendency in evangelicalism to view giving money to missions as a spiritual good but using accumulated wealth to address social needs as non-spiritual. The New Testament, Schaeffer argued, made no such division between spiritual and social activism. While he stressed that there was no justification in the Bible for modern communism, he emphasized the early church's teaching that accumulated wealth should be used to address social needs. "We should add that we cannot hope to speak to the young people who have a Marxist Leninist ideology," Schaeffer wrote, "until we show by our teaching and our practice that we take seriously the question of that which is set forth in the Scripture, the compassionate use of accumulated wealth."[71] Likewise, the New Testament church was the model for racial reconciliation. Schaeffer told the Lausanne Congress in 1974 that the church at Antioch in the book of Acts was his favorite New Testament church, because there "Jewish Christians were no longer held back by racial thought and they told the Good News to their Gentile neighbors. . . . And that is, that at that time racial prejudice was destroyed."[72]

In a 1974 *Christianity Today* article entitled "Race and Economics," Schaeffer reiterated that if he were to write his early books again he would emphasize that even when a nation is built on a Christian base, as he believed America in its early years had been, there were still things that were sub-Christian — and in particular he cited America's history of racism and the failure of Christians to speak out against this national sin. In part he attributed the Christian slaveowners' inability to see African American slaves as fully human to the lack of belief in the historicity of a common ancestry for all humankind. He may have been referring implicitly to the "curse of Ham" theology, which set people of color apart from whites as a cursed race, but he did not say this explicitly. He did mention that when Christians told the story of the Good Samaritan, they usually avoided the racial issue inherent in the story: the Good Samaritan had rejected the notion that Jews were not supposed to be in contact with the hated Samaritans.[73]

In *How Should We Then Live?* (1976), Schaeffer once again attempted to make up for the absence of race and wealth as topics of consideration in his early works. While arguing that America had been founded on a Christian worldview, what he often called the "Christian base," he pointed out that slavery and then racial prejudice were glaring examples of specific areas where Americans did not follow the Bible, even as they worked from a general Christian base. After citing the horrendous conditions on the slave ships and the way that slave traders attempted to soften their moral failings by developing the view that Africans were not fully human, Schaeffer wrote, "Today's Christians, by identification with their forebears, must acknowledge these inconsistencies in regard to a twisted view of race. We can use no lesser word than sin to describe those instances where the practice was (or is) so far from what the Bible directs."[74] On the lack of compassionate use of wealth, he cited the Industrial Revolution's excesses and argued, "If industrialization had been accompanied by a strong emphasis on the compassionate use of accumulated wealth and on the dignity of each individual, the Industrial Revolution would have indeed been a revolution for good." Instead, the "noncompassionate use of accumulated wealth [during the Industrial Revolution] was particularly glaring."[75] Part of the problem in both slavery and the Industrial Revolution, Schaeffer believed, was that Christians bought into the worldview of utilitarianism; the greatest good for the greatest number justified clear violations of the biblical ethic concerning race and wealth.

While these attempts to address matters of race came later in Schaeffer's career, economics proved to be a more consistent focus. Indeed, even though race and poverty remained relatively minor themes for Schaeffer, before his Christian Right activism of the early 1980s many thought he was inclined toward a *progressive* view of politics, given his willingness to critique American materialism. Even in the late 1940s, in an article attacking liberal Christianity and socialism, he warned his fundamentalist brothers and sisters, "Worldliness is more than smoking, drinking and card playing. A far worse worldliness is keeping quiet when our nation breaks its promises; or sharing, through silence, in murder through mob violence; or by driving men to communism by squeezing them in any of the economic processes."[76]

By the mid-1970s, Schaeffer turned more of his attention to economics. In "Race and Economics," and in his book *No Little People,* which also appeared in 1974, he wrote at length about wealth and materialism. In the article he argued that the world would notice if Christian employers took less profit so that their employees could make appreciably more than the going rate for wages. He said this would be a greater witness than if the Christian business owner paid workers lower wages then donated increased profits to Christian schools and missions.[77] *No Little People* was a collection of six Schaeffer sermons, among them "Ash Heap Lives," the thesis of which was that "we spend most of our time and money for things that will end up in the city dump."[78] Such materialism existed among Christians because they were influenced by the spirit of the age and what Schaeffer called the "two core values of our culture" — personal peace and affluence. In 1976, two years after "Ash Heap Lives" appeared in *No Little People,* Schaeffer defined personal peace in *How Should We Then Live?* as "just to be let alone, not to be troubled by the troubles of other people, whether across the world or across the street." He then defined affluence as "an overwhelming and ever-increasing prosperity — a life made up of things, things, and more things — a success judged by an ever-higher level of material abundance."[79]

Schaeffer connected these distorted values to his larger intellectual project, arguing that once a society has jettisoned a Christian worldview and any notion of "true truth," as he called it, there was nothing left but personal peace and affluence. From time to time he said that the hippies of the 1960s looked at their parents' lives and saw only these two values instead of answers to the deep longings of humankind. With no hope of real meaning and only personal peace and affluence to look forward to, the hippies dropped out of mainstream middle-class culture and turned to drugs or joined the New Left in a violent revolt against mainstream society. As the turmoil of the sixties wound down, many people were relieved that the era was over, but Schaeffer said he could have wept. "The young people had been right in their analysis, though wrong in their solutions," he wrote. "How much worse when many gave up hope and simply accepted the same values as their parents — personal peace and affluence."[80]

Materialism posed a direct threat to community. In *No Little People* Schaeffer told of a missionary he knew in Spain who rented a luxurious apartment in the midst of poverty but bemoaned the fact that he seemed separated from the Spanish people, unable to evangelize effectively. Schaeffer related that when he first started L'Abri he felt sorry for the women of Huemoz who had to wash their clothes manually by the river, but over time he came to appreciate how this gave the women time to live in community with one another. He contrasted this to American housewives who had labor-saving machines but lived unfulfilled and desperate lives.[81]

In "Ash Heap Lives" Schaeffer argued that the world has two views of property. At the one extreme was the capitalist view that a person's private property was his or her own to be used however the owner wished. At the other extreme was socialism, in which the state owns everything. "The Christian has a third option," he wrote: "property acquired and used with compassion."[82] This was Schaeffer's watchword, "the compassionate use of accumulated wealth." He made clear he was not advocating that Christians despise wealth. There was nothing spiritual about such a view. "What is important is not despising acquired wealth; it is using all our money wisely before the face of God." He suggested that a suitable theme for a work of Christian art would be "Meditation on the Ash Heap" or "Ode on a City Dump."[83]

Schaeffer is one of few evangelicals to address the chief symbol of American affluence, the automobile. He wrote, "In our culture nothing has exhibited such folly more than our automobiles."[84] He then confessed to once buying a new car and being inordinately and sinfully proud of it until someone sideswiped him and left a long and ugly scratch. "That was one of the best things that ever happened," he recalled, "for suddenly I learned how much possessions stink if you look at them in the wrong perspective."[85]

In *How Should We Then Live?* Schaeffer argued very briefly that some modern philosophy, such as that of Herbert Spencer (1820-1903) and the ideas of Social Darwinism, opened the way for both racism and the non-compassionate use of accumulated wealth. In the name of science, Social Darwinism gave us the notion of "survival of the fittest," which became a justification for racial superiority and the idea that the weak and unfit should be allowed to die out in order for society to evolve progressively toward perfection. Later, Schaeffer said, such ideas would lead to Nazism.[86] Schaeffer did not, however, let Christians off the hook by laying at the feet of secular Social Darwinism all the blame for racism and the lack of compassion in the use of wealth. He consistently criticized evangelicals for adopting the two prevailing and impoverished values of twentieth-century American society — personal peace and affluence.

Such prophetic critiques of American materialism were popular with his younger audiences, but Schaeffer's tenure as a progressive would be short-lived. Evangelicals would soon be identified with more conservative politics centered on cultural issues, and just as Schaeffer had been one of the first evangelicals to sympathize with the 1960s counterculture, and one of the first to bless engagement with broader popular culture, here again he was ahead of the curve. By the time he wrote and filmed *How Should We Then Live?* in 1976, he was increasingly moving to the right in politics. His admonitions against racism and wealth would become muted, and his analysis of culture overshadowed by Christian Right political activism as he took up issues such as abortion and euthanasia. He was no less a prophet on these issues than on others, but the developing culture war over human life issues pulled him into the conservative camp, where he became much less of an independent voice. His move to the right would be mirrored by a strong reaffirmation of his fundamentalist militancy. The old separatism re-emerged as he waded into what would become known among evangelicals as the "battle for the Bible."

CHAPTER SIX

The Battle for the Bible

The trilogy established Francis Schaeffer as one of the most important evangelical voices of his time in relating Christianity to culture, and the books we examined in the previous chapter seemed to flow naturally from the concerns outlined in the trilogy. Taken together, his thought from the time of his first American lectures through the mid-1970s put Schaeffer on the cutting edge of evangelicalism. He had great appeal and popularity among young, intellectually engaged evangelicals interested in how faith intersected with everything from philosophy to the arts to the problems of urban life, race, and the environment. It appeared that Schaeffer had left the internecine warfare of his fundamentalist past thoroughly behind and had become something of a progressive evangelical, appealing especially to a maturing youth culture of the sixties and early seventies.

Perception was not necessarily reality, however, and in fact fundamentalist concerns were never far beneath the surface of Schaeffer's thought. In the early 1970s, even as books such as *Death in the City* and *Pollution and the Death of Man* rolled off the presses, Schaeffer produced other works that would reflect his fundamentalist instincts. He remained part of the conservative mainstream of evangelicalism in many ways, insisting on the necessity of a literal interpretation of Genesis and the inerrancy of the Bible in all matters, including history and science. He saw these as essential for the maintenance and preservation of evangelicalism, and when evangelical battles erupted in the 1970s, he viewed them in the context of his own earlier war on theological liberalism. The reemergence of his fundamentalist voice would serve as a transition to the Christian Right cultural engagement that would develop in the late seventies.

It should be noted that much of what we will see in this chapter appeared in conjunction with some of Schaeffer's more progressive positions on cultural engagement. It seemed that for a time he saw no inconsistency between defending conservative causes while at the same time calling for racial and economic justice. Like evangelicalism itself, however, he had difficulty maintaining the tension.

Genesis as Science and History

Schaeffer's first book in this more conservative genre was *Genesis in Space and Time,* which was published in 1972, the same year that *He Is There and Is Not Silent* rounded out the trilogy. After the trilogy was complete, Schaeffer wrote to British scholar Colin Duriez to say he was done with philosophy. He realized he had very little interest in theoretical apologetics and had no interest in ever writing another book like *He Is There and Is Not Silent.* He had said all that he had to say philosophically and believed God and the times were calling him to speak on other issues.[1]

Schaeffer intended *Genesis in Space and Time* for evangelical Christians who were tempted to agree with scholars interpreting the Genesis stories of the creation and fall as allegorical instead of literal. The book is something of a commentary on the first eleven chapters of Genesis. Its central thesis is that for Christianity to hold together, the creation stories and the fall of Adam and Eve into sin must be understood as historical events.

Schaeffer had used the phrase "space and time" as early as the late 1940s, when he wrote an article entitled "The Oneness of Unbelief" for the periodical *Biblical Missions,* in which he spoke of the resurrection as "a true event in space and time."[2] Now he sought to apply it to the beginning of the Bible. *Genesis in Space and Time* presents no sharp break with the trilogy, as Schaeffer argued once again that only the Christian faith can make sense of the world. Still, *Genesis in Space and Time* is a much more biblically focused book than the trilogy. It is a book written to gird Christians for apologetics, not a book directed to unbelievers to draw them into the faith.

Schaeffer believed that if the first eleven chapters of Genesis were not literal history, the whole Christian worldview that he had outlined in the trilogy would be in jeopardy. "Without a proper understanding of these chapters we have no answer to the problems of metaphysics, morals or epistemology, and furthermore the work of Christ becomes one more upper-story 'religious' answer," he stressed in the early pages of the book.[3] Schaeffer's insistence on recovering the unity between reason and objective reality on the one hand, and experience and meaning on the other, is the thread that runs from *Genesis in Space and Time* all the way back to his 1950 address on "The New Modernism," where he castigated modernists for letting go of the historicity of the Garden of Eden while trying to retain the significance of the fall.[4]

To make his case, Schaeffer referenced other places in the Bible where the creation is compared to historical events. He made much of the fact that these other passages seem to take the creation account literally; he argued that if the Bible itself treats the creation story as a literal space/time event, then it must be accepted as such. He cited Psalm 136, where the psalmist talks about God's activity in creation and then moves to God's activity in the Exodus. For Schaeffer this meant that if the biblical authors, inspired by the Holy Spirit, put the creation story in the same context as the historical Exodus, then the creation story had to be taken as history as well. "Give up creation as a space-time, historic reality," he wrote, "and all that is left is what Simone Weil called uncreatedness."[5] With respect to Adam and Eve, Schaeffer referenced Jesus' words about the creation in the same way he had cited the psalmist. It was simple for Schaeffer: since Jesus spoke of Adam and Eve as historical figures, Christians must do the same.

Schaeffer conceded that some scholars, even evangelical ones, viewed the Genesis creation story as a mythic parable because there are two creation stories in Genesis 1 and 2 that do not quite match up in their details. Nevertheless, he insisted that the mythic view was "not allowable" because Jesus treats the two stories as a unit. When Jesus answered the Pharisees about divorce and remarriage, he cited first from Genesis 1:27, then from Genesis 2:24 — "So Jesus puts the passages from Genesis 1 and Genesis 2 together as a unit."[6]

Though he did not address the form of the Old Testament stories in great detail, Schaeffer used Yale University scholar Erich Auerbach's 1952 book *Mimesis* to present another reason why we should accept the historicity of biblical stories. Auerbach argued that biblical stories have a different literary quality than other ancient myths. Homer's heroes, for example, arise each morning as if it were the first day the world began. In other words, the Greek myths often seem disconnected from history, or what Schaeffer would call space-time reality. By contrast, the Bible stories have the feel of real, historic individuals acting in history. "The form of the narrative gives the impression that something really occurred," Schaeffer commented. "It doesn't sound like a myth or a story."[7]

Such matters were really only details of a larger story, and Schaeffer was, as usual, more concerned with the big picture. As with the trilogy, Schaeffer wanted to present a Christian worldview that was coherent in its explanation of the human condition, and he believed that the Genesis creation account, taken literally, was the best explanation for the unity of the human race and the condition of humankind. Schaeffer tied the creation of Adam from dust and of Eve from Adam to the unity of the whole human race. He said that while everyone seems to be looking for a way to establish or explain such unity, the Christian answer is the best.

Among its other virtues, he said, the Christian story explains marriage better than the other theories. "[W]e can begin to understand something about marriage because God Himself ties the marriage bond into the relation of the unity of mankind," he wrote. "Hence, we can understand something of that particular union when the male and female constitute one whole, and become one flesh. Man, with a capital M, equals male and female, and the one-man, one-woman union reunites the unity."[8] Creation as a historic event, with Eve taken literally from Adam's rib, became necessary for explaining male and female differentiation as well as the desire of male and female to be one again. He delineated the sequence of creation as: 1) creation out of nothing; 2) differentiation in various forms; 3) differentiation of man from all other life forms; and 4) differentiation of Eve from Adam. "The whole sequence," he wrote, "testifies to Adam and Eve standing in space-time history."[9]

Like the creation, the fall of humankind into sin had to be acknowledged as a space-time event as well. Schaeffer insisted that this event caused man's separation from God, separation from himself, separation from other men, and separation from nature. Yet man was still man. "He has not lost those things which he intrinsically is as a man," Schaeffer wrote. "He has not become an animal or a machine." For this reason the painter can still paint, the lover can still love, and the thinker can still think.[10]

To deny the space-time nature of the fall — in other words, to view the story as myth that merely explains humankind's sinful condition — was to separate religious truth from objective historical truth and destroy the rational unity of the Christian worldview, and thereby diminish the explanatory superiority of the Christian faith over other ancient myths. Moreover, the apostle Paul in Romans 5:12 and other New Testament passages treated Adam and Eve as historical individuals, drawing parallels between Adam, through whom sin entered the human race, and Christ, through whom the human race is redeemed. It simply made no sense to Schaeffer to treat the fall as myth and the death and resurrection of Christ as historical. To deny the first as real history was to call into question the second.[11]

Here he presented two arguments, one from biblical authority and one from philosophical coherence. First, as we have already seen, if Jesus and Paul spoke of Adam and Eve as historic individuals, then we must also. Otherwise, we are denying biblical authority — we are saying that Jesus and Paul were wrong. Second, Schaeffer insisted that it would be philosophically incoherent to have a mythic fall remedied by a historic death and resurrection. In his 1975 book *No Final Conflict,* he called the fall "a brute fact" not subject to interpretation as to its historicity. "There is no room for hermeneutics, if by hermeneutics we mean explaining away the brute factness of the Fall."[12] The event was "not an upper-story statement — that is it is not in this sense a 'theological' or 'religious' statement."[13] He went so far as to say that if the historical parts of Genesis are not accepted as space-time events, the Christian worldview is altogether lost.

While Schaeffer insisted on the historicity of the first eleven chapters of Genesis, and by implication all of the Old Testament, he left room for interpretation as to some details of creation. He did not believe, for example, that the word "day" in the creation accounts had to be taken as a literal twenty-four-hour day; this was for him a matter of language. The Hebrew word for "day" has different uses, and does not have to be a twenty-four-hour period. He did not allow for the same latitude with the term "Adam," which some biblical scholars believe can be interpreted from the Hebrew as referring to humankind rather than a specific individual. Schaeffer approvingly cited nineteenth- and early-twentieth-century Princeton theologian B. B. Warfield's observation that "It is to theology, as such, a matter of entire indifference how long man has existed on earth."[14]

Schaeffer did not, however, leave the door open for theistic evolution, as did Warfield. In a quote Schaeffer did not reference, Warfield wrote, "Calvin's doctrine of creation is, if we have understood it aright, for all except the souls of men, an evolutionary one."[15] Schaeffer would not agree. He could allow for figurative days in Genesis that were actually long periods of time, but he believed that allowing for evolution would call into question the literal and historical nature of the creation and fall, which in turn would have jeopardized the unity of historic and religious truth found in scripture.

As he allowed for figurative "days" in Genesis, Schaeffer also acknowledged that the genealogies of the Old Testament were not literally accurate or complete. Individuals were left out, and sometimes the sequential listing of fathers and sons gives the appearance of chronology that is not correct. In a passage that came dangerously close to separating historic fact from religious meaning, Schaeffer wrote, "Consequently, the content of these various passages are accurate, but chronology was not what the authors had in mind."[16] He seemed to believe that there was little at stake in the consideration of the days of the Genesis creation account or the Old Testament genealogies. As long as the events of creation and fall were held as space-time events, objective history and religious truth were maintained in a unity that gave the Christian faith explanatory power.

Even though Schaeffer insisted on the space-time reality of the creation, he was of two minds as to whether the Bible was a scientific book. On the one hand, he wrote, "What the Bible tells us is propositional, factual and true truth. . . . It is a scientific textbook in the sense that where it touches the cosmos it is true, propositionally true." On the other hand, he continued, "The Bible is *not* a scientific textbook, if by that one means that its purpose is to give us exhaustive truth or that scientific fact is its central theme and purpose. . . . But all that does not change the fact that biblical revelation is propositional, to be handled on the basis of reason in relationship to science and coordinated with science."[17] Later, he even brought his analysis of Kierkegaard into his discussion of Joshua, saying that Joshua made a promise for the future that was based on a space-time past. "He did not ask the people to make a Kierkegaardian leap of faith."[18]

While not wanting to separate scientific knowledge from biblical truth, Schaeffer still recognized a difference between the two when he said that the creation account had no relationship to the big-bang theory. The creation tells us what was behind and before the origin of the universe. "Even if one accepts the big bang theory," he wrote, "Genesis 1:1 would then go beyond it by saying that God created out of nothing the primal stuff present at the big bang."[19] This line of reasoning could easily have led to an argument that while science tells us how the universe was created — in other words, the *facts* — scripture deals with the *meaning* of all reality. But Schaeffer would not go that far. Instead he simply concluded that scripture gives us "true truth" but not always "exhaustive truth."[20]

One might infer from this that if scripture does not give exhaustive truth, Christians should supplement and revise the truths found in scripture with truths found in science — in other words, interpret the Bible in light of science — but he never spelled out specifically whether it is acceptable to interpret scripture in light of science, which was something that orthodox Christian thinkers from Augustine in the fifth century through Galileo in the seventeenth to Charles Hodge in the nineteenth century had all affirmed. Hodge, who was from the same Reformed Presbyterian tradition as Schaeffer, argued explicitly that it is quite proper for Christians to read and interpret the Bible in light of science. "Nature is as truly a revelation of God as the Bible," Hodge wrote, "and we only interpret the Word of God by the Word of God when we interpret the Bible by science."[21] Of course, Hodge added that the "rule works both ways": if the Bible cannot contradict science, neither can science contradict the Bible, and he argued elsewhere that Darwinism was atheism because it excluded the supernatural in its reliance on natural selection.[22] When Schaeffer said that the Bible gives truth but not exhaustive truth, he did not say whether he considered it appropriate for Christians to find more exhaustive truth in science. Instead he simply said that the Bible gives us "adequate knowledge," and that information about the supernatural is brought in to help us understand the natural. He did not acknowledge the converse, as Hodge did, that knowledge derived from nature — that is, science — might help us understand the supernatural. It is hard to say whether Schaeffer had ever thought of this, or if it was simply beside the point that he wanted to make, which was that the Christian explanation for the condition of humankind was superior to other explanations, and that it was only coherent if Genesis 1–11 were taken as history.

Evangelicalism and the Inerrancy of the Bible

Schaeffer's subsequent books and addresses on the Bible were increasingly animated by the fundamentalist concerns of his early career. The battle against theological liberalism and the battle within evangelicalism for the inerrancy of scripture as a necessary fundamental of the faith were the same for him. The latter erupted in the mid-1970s, and Schaeffer was ready for battle when it happened.

Fuller Seminary in Pasadena, California, was at the center of this evangelical inerrancy battle of the 1970s. Harold Lindsell had been one of the founding faculty members at Fuller before moving on to become editor at *Christianity Today* in the 1960s, then to pastoral work and finally retirement. His book *The Battle for the Bible* became a centerpiece of the inerrancy wars, and in it he spent an entire chapter criticizing Fuller's drift away from the inerrancy position. Just before the book appeared in 1976, Lindsell gave a copy of the book proofs to Schaeffer when the two met at a meeting in Washington, D.C. Schaeffer said he read the book and gave its publisher the right to quote his approval of the book.[23] Some of Schaeffer's books from the mid-seventies, including *Joshua and the Flow of Biblical History* and *No Final Conflict,* both published in 1975, fell into the same genre of intra-evangelical apologetics as Lindsell's *Battle for the Bible.*

In *Joshua and the Flow of Biblical History,* Schaeffer framed the issue as a need to refute the liberal biblical scholarship that was creeping into evangelical circles. Then he proceeded with a basic commentary on the book of Joshua, repeatedly bringing the discussion back to the propositional truth of the Bible in relationship to modern culture. He criticized the documentary hypothesis, which held that the Pentateuch was oral tradition passed down for centuries prior to its being written. This theory, he maintained, contradicted scripture itself, for example Deuteronomy 31:9, which reads, "And Moses wrote this law, and delivered it unto the priests, the sons of Levi."[24] Schaeffer's gloss on this verse was that Moses not only spoke the oral tradition, but also wrote. "He gave propositional, verbalized communication from God to man in written as well as spoken form."[25]

Of course, the irony of Schaeffer arguing for the necessity of literal Mosaic authorship, given that Schaeffer's own books were largely taped lectures that were transcribed by students and then edited together by James Sire, is worth noting. Still, it must be pointed out that Schaeffer's process had many more guarantees of accurate reproduction than the so-called documentary hypothesis could claim. Little time passed between Schaeffer's talks and his words appearing in written form. Also, he signed off on the final form his writings took after others had transcribed and Sire had edited. Perhaps what really rankled Schaeffer about the documentary hypothesis was its assertion that so much time passed between the first circulation of biblical stories and their being put into written form. This, it would seem, would weaken their reliability.

Whatever the exact nature of his concerns about what he considered liberal scholarship, he was convinced that the nature of the Bible was the central issue for evangelicals in the seventies. He opened *No Final Conflict* with these words: "It is my conviction that the crucial area of discussion for evangelicalism in the next years will be the Scriptures. At stake is whether evangelicalism will remain evangelical."[26] The issue, he declared, was whether the Bible was God's verbalized communication to humankind, not only where it touches on religion, but in matters of history and the cosmos as well. The attack on this inerrantist view of the Bible came from two sources: 1) theologians who say that biblical revelation is limited to those areas that touch on things not open to empirical research, such as history and the cosmos; and 2) scientists who are Christians who argue that "the Bible teaches us little or nothing where it touches on that in which science has an interest." In both cases, he argued, "we are left with the Bible as an authority only in religious matters."[27] Unlike in the thirties and forties, however, he did not draw a line between fundamentalists and modernists. This time he, like Lindsell and others, called for a line that would exclude many evangelicals from evangelicalism. Clark Pinnock, one of the most influential young scholars in the evangelical camp, argued for the infallibility of scripture only in matters of theology. This rankled Schaeffer, in part because Pinnock had studied at L'Abri. If a product of L'Abri could adopt such views, evangelicalism was in serious danger. Because of Pinnock's views, Schaeffer said, "I personally could no longer advise anybody to study at Regent [College]," where Pinnock taught.[28]

Schaeffer was not eager for a personal fight; he told Hans Rookmaaker that he still lamented the kind of ugliness that transpired in the McIntire movement of the 1930s. But if inerrancy were not maintained, he said, the ground would be cut from beneath the next generation of evangelicals.[29] To critics who believed he was dividing the evangelical community, he said, "The people who are taking a weak view of Scripture are the ones who are troubling evangelicalism today. I say this with gentleness and love toward these people. The people who are making the difficulty are the people who have demoted Scripture from what it has been understood to be in the evangelical world until the fairly recent past."[30]

Parts of *No Final Conflict* were excerpted from Schaeffer's address to the International Congress on World Evangelization that met in Lausanne in July 1974. In that address he lamented that some who go by the name "evangelical," both individuals and institutions, no longer held to a "full view of scripture," and he called for recognition of the clear difference between those who were inerrantists and those who were not. "[E]vangelicalism is not consistently evangelical," he said, "unless there is a line drawn between those who take a full view of Scripture and those who do not."[31] The issue was the infallibility or inerrancy of the Bible in all matters on which scripture touches, including history and the cosmos. Many evangelicals, in his view, had actually gone over to the "neo-orthodox, existential" idea that the Bible is a "quarry" from which we can get religious experience, but that it is not infallible in matters of history and science. He quoted Martin Luther: "If I profess with the loudest voice and clearest exposition every portion of the truth of God except precisely that little point which the world and the devil are at that moment attacking, I am not confessing Christ, however boldly I may be professing Christ."[32] For Schaeffer the battle over scripture was the "watershed" issue, a term also used by Lindsell and others.

Schaeffer took partial credit for getting the Lausanne Congress to strengthen its statement on the Bible, but he still lamented that the final Lausanne Covenant said that the Bible was "without error in all that it affirms." He worried that the phrase "in all that it affirms" would be used as a loophole by those who believed scripture is not inerrant in matters of history and science. Those who used what he called the "existential methodology," including Pinnock, could say in their minds that "all that it affirms" means only matters of faith and salvation and not matters of history and science.[33] While at the Congress, Schaeffer contemplated pressing the issue even further, but others convinced him that "in all that it affirms" was a phrase necessary to eliminate out-of-context biblical quotations someone might use — such as "there is no God" without the preface "the fool has said in his heart" — and to make a distinction between what the Bible actually affirms and the projections that people make from scripture. Still, Schaeffer recalled, eighteen months after the Congress, "I knew in myself [the clause 'in all that it affirms'] would be used as an escape hatch and am convinced that it was by hundreds."[34] Advocating a stronger statement for the North American Presbyterian and Reformed Council, he told his friend Robert Rayburn at Covenant Seminary, "Frankly, I don't think the words infallible, inerrant or without error have any meaning in the present theological climate unless some phrase is included as: 'infallible not only where it speaks of religious matters but where it speaks of history and the cosmos.'"[35]

In 1978, Schaeffer was among more than three hundred signers of the Chicago Statement on Inerrancy. In its "Summary Statement" the Chicago document, like the Lausanne Covenant, included the affirmation that scripture was "divine authority in all matters upon which it touches" and "is without error or fault in all its teaching," both qualifications that caused Schaeffer concern at Lausanne in 1974. The Chicago Statement, however, also said that scripture was without error or fault "no less in what it states about God's acts in creation, about the events of world history, and about its own literary origins under God, than in its witness to God's saving grace in individual lives." Moreover, Article XII clearly stated, "We deny that Biblical infallibility and inerrancy are limited to spiritual, religious, or redemptive themes, exclusive of assertions in the fields of history and science."[36] Schaeffer must have been pleased by this affirmation that the Bible was inerrant not only in matters of salvation but with regard to history and the origins of the universe as well.[37]

At L'Abri Schaeffer was free to fashion an inerrancy statement that would be as strong as he thought necessary, and this is exactly what he did. How could he travel America insisting on inerrancy statements as tests of fellowship for evangelicals if his own community failed to adhere to such a statement? Unfortunately, Schaeffer's own son-in-law John Sandri refused to sign the statement and was barred from teaching at L'Abri thereafter. With the hindsight of thirty years, Schaeffer's son Franky saw Sandri's silencing as a true L'Abri tragedy. "If L'Abri produced one true saint, . . . one real biblical scholar, it was John Sandri," Franky wrote. Franky also remembers his sister Priscilla, Sandri's wife, "aghast" that her father was returning to the fundamentalist fights of the 1940s. She believed that Franky was largely responsible for this direction of their father's later career, and she resented him for it.[38]

Fundamentalist Separatism Revisited

In tying the evangelical battle for the Bible of the 1970s to the fundamentalist-modernist wars in the 1930s, Schaeffer warned in his Lausanne address against any blurring of the line between liberal and evangelical theology. He claimed that the Bible forbade evangelical cooperation with liberals and that evangelicals lose their credibility when they say they believe the Bible but then cooperate with liberals who do not.[39] Still, Schaeffer recognized a difference between the seventies and the thirties. This time, those who were soft on inerrancy were evangelical brothers who were orthodox in theology, and this made the new battle even more difficult than before. Schaeffer wanted to avoid the ugliness of fundamentalism and maintain a spirit of love as he took his stand once again for scripture. At the same time, however, there was significant continuity between his fundamentalist years before L'Abri and his efforts to defend inerrancy in the 1970s.

The question of whether to keep fellowship with those on the other side was a delicate one, and sometimes Schaeffer seemed to contradict himself. He told evangelical scholar Kenneth Kantzer that he had made a plea "for not breaking off fellowship with those who are clearly brothers in Christ." At Lausanne, however, Schaeffer had strongly implied that those who were soft on inerrancy were not evangelicals. This made it difficult to tell whether Schaeffer believed they were still brothers in Christ. While somehow not breaking fellowship, the inerrantists needed to continue to do three things: 1) publicly attack the non-inerrantist position, 2) refuse leadership positions to those who were soft on inerrancy, and 3) inform young people that they should not study at any institution that takes the non-inerrantist view.[40] Unless Schaeffer was implying that inerrantists could worship with non-inerrantists but not study with them or allow them to serve as missionaries, it is not clear how this was anything other than a call for breaking fellowship with evangelicals who did not believe the Bible was inerrant in matters of history and science. He wrote to Kantzer, "If on the basis of fellowship with these our brothers in Christ who I believe are destroying the Scripture and condemning the next generation to liberal positions . . . we fail to make a distinction between fellowship and these three points I have just named, then I would say that under the name of love we are unfaithful to the Lord and it is not really love, but it is a poor timidity or even compromise." Then, in a vague allusion to the past, he continued, "If there can be a new alignment perhaps even the pieces can be picked up all the way back to the 30's."[41]

This "new alignment" may well have been a reference to Trinity Evangelical Divinity School, Covenant Seminary in St. Louis, and Westminster in Philadelphia, all of which Schaeffer listed as schools remaining faithful to scripture, over against Fuller and other schools that were moving away from the position that the Bible was inerrant in matters of history and science. Three weeks after writing to Kantzer, Schaeffer followed Lindsell's lead when he told Hans Rookmaaker that Fuller Seminary was at the forefront of the view that the Bible was inerrant only in matters of faith and not history and once again clearly implied that such a view was not evangelical: "While insisting on using the word 'evangelical' [Fuller's] position has clearly become that the Bible is authoritative when it speaks of 'salvation matters' but not when it speaks of history and the things which interest science."[42] Such a position made fellowship difficult for Schaeffer. At Lausanne he had said, "The first direction in which we must face is to say most lovingly but clearly: evangelicalism is not consistently evangelical unless there is a line drawn between those who take a full view of Scripture and those who do not."[43]

Science and Evolution

Schaeffer's concern about the Bible's authority in matters of history and science led him into a brief discussion of evolution reminiscent of his argument in *Genesis in Space and Time*. In *No Final Conflict* he said that even if he were still an agnostic he would not believe in evolution from molecule to man in an unbroken line, because the theory was weak and had not been proven. He cited Murray Eden of the Massachusetts Institute of Technology as saying that it was impossible that pure chance and any amount of time could have produced the universe's complexity. A belief in macroevolution of this sort, Schaeffer added, was a faith statement, pure and simple. Schaeffer said, however, that while he did not believe in theistic evolution, "it must be said that there is a certain possible range of freedom for discussion in the area of cosmogony bowing to what God has affirmed."[44]

God had affirmed two absolutes about Genesis, Schaeffer believed. First, there was discontinuity between the creation of conscious life and the creation of man. In other words, humankind did not evolve from lower forms of animals. Second, as he had argued already in a theological sense, Adam was a historic individual, and Eve was created from Adam. He said that he had never heard of a theistic evolutionist who held to these two absolutes, but he seemed to leave open the possibility that such a theistic evolutionist might exist.[45]

Schaeffer believed that theistic evolution was but one of several unnecessary concessions Christians made to science. He complained that there was a tendency among some Christian scientists to insist that the Bible must be understood in light of science but not the converse, that science should be understood in light of the Bible. Such individuals, while professing to believe the Bible was true, exhibited that in fact they believed science was more true than scripture.[46] He

149

insisted, nevertheless, that there was "no final conflict" between science and the Bible if the study of each was undertaken properly.

In addition to Schaeffer's concern for the authority of scripture, his working-class populism and anti-elitism can be detected in his discussion of science, just as these were at play in the trilogy, where he was relatively uninterested in what scholars had to say about the great thinkers of western history. As we will see in chapter eight, he did not defer to scholars, not even in complex matters of science, and he seemed to believe that any ordinary person of reasonable intelligence could critique scientists and reinterpret scientific data. For example, he mentioned in passing that he was not at all convinced that dinosaurs were already extinct when humans appeared on earth, and he accused scientists of ignoring the fossilized footprints of humans alongside those of dinosaurs in Paluxy, Texas. "[O]ne can ask," he wrote, "whether scientists would not have used this as evidence that man lived at the same time as dinosaurs, were it not for the fact it contradicts their own theory."[47] He made one brief reference to Creation Science when he listed as one of his seven freedoms in interpreting Genesis the possibility that the flood affected geological strata.[48] Creation Science taught that the earth was very young (roughly ten thousand years) and that fossilized geological formations from Noah's flood gave the earth the appearance of being much older, and it was growing in popularity among fundamentalists and evangelicals. By the 1980s some evangelicals and fundamentalists offered Creation Science as an alternative to evolution, and some states such as Arkansas and Louisiana even passed laws, later struck down by the courts, giving Creation Science equal time with evolution in public school classrooms.[49]

Schaeffer was not ready to commit to Creation Science's insistence on a relatively young earth, but he questioned whether scientific measurements of the age of the earth were reliable. "Scientists accept the uniformity of the emission of radiological material; but they accept this, I think, by faith," he wrote in *No Final Conflict*.[50] There was simply no way, Schaeffer believed, that we could be sure that the regularity of radiocarbon emissions over a short time could be projected back over billions of years. Schaeffer already suspected scientists' ability to consider evidence that conflicted with their theories; here Schaeffer believed they were too quick to accept evidence that was inconclusive. On the other hand, he criticized Creation Scientists in a similar way for their unwillingness to be open to discussion regarding the age of the earth. He complained to Kantzer that some of those who held to a strong view of scripture contributed to an unnecessary polarization within the evangelical community by holding a young earth as non-negotiable and insisting that the geological strata could have been formed only by a flood.[51] While Schaeffer may not have been the first evangelical to believe the worst about secular scientific thinking, and although he was not ready to commit to Creation Science, he was an important figure in promoting suspicion about secular science, and this suspicion would grow steadily among evangelicals in the last two decades of the twentieth century.

Schaeffer's discussion of the relationship between science and scripture notwithstanding, his real concern was to promote biblical inerrancy in the face of challenges from within the evangelical camp. He stressed two reasons for holding to a strong view of scripture. First, it reflects what the Bible itself teaches and the way Jesus approached scripture. This should be reason enough, Schaeffer thought, but "today there is a second reason. . . . There may be hard days ahead of us — for ourselves and for our spiritual and our physical children. And without a strong view of Scripture as a foundation, we will not be ready for the hard days to come."[52] As was so often the case, Schaeffer was maddeningly obscure here, but taken in light of the corpus of his writings, especially his forthcoming *How Should We Then Live?,* he seemed to be alluding to the evangelical battle against secular forces that would become increasingly hostile to the faith. Because this battle loomed on the horizon, he seemed to be saying, it was important for evangelicals to keep their house in order by shoring up the foundation of their faith: the inerrancy of the Bible.

By the mid-1970s, Schaeffer was convinced that just the opposite was happening. "[E]vangelicalism today," he wrote, "although growing in numbers as far as the name is concerned . . . is not unitedly standing for a strong view of Scripture. The *existential methodology* has infiltrated that which is called evangelicalism."[53] He again referenced unnamed evangelicals who believed that scripture was authoritative primarily or only in matters of faith and theology. This softness on scripture started in matters of history and science, but it was already moving into moral issues, Schaeffer argued, where certain moral absolutes taught by the Bible were viewed as culturally condi-tioned and not authoritative for today.[54]

Schaeffer's Critique of Charismatic Experience

Schaeffer's concern about the integrity of evangelicalism extended from the inerrancy question to the issue of spiritual gifts, especially as practiced by Pentecostals and charismatics. In the late 1960s and early 1970s, the "Jesus People" movement emerged as a significant re-ligious dimension of the counterculture. It included an emphasis on neo-Pentecostal or charismatic views of the gifts of the Spirit such as healing, speaking in tongues, and the gift of prophecy. This con-cerned Schaeffer because he saw it as an irrational expression of Christianity, one in which the test of orthodoxy and community was religious experience instead of doctrine. He addressed this in a little 1972 pamphlet called *The New Super-Spirituality,* where he also dis-cussed new, non-Christian religious movements many young people found attractive.[55] The old Pentecostalism, he argued, emphasized external signs, but theological content was still the basis for fellow-ship. The new Pentecostalism, by contrast, often put an emphasis on the external signs themselves as the test of fellowship and accep-tance. This kind of Pentecostalism paralleled liberalism by placing an emphasis on experience over doctrinal content.[56]

Schaeffer tied this to an explanation for how heresy entered the church. He told his readers to imagine that the whole of orthodoxy consisted of one hundred points of doctrine. Heresy happens when the church stops teaching, for example, points forty through fifty. Then, someone begins to overemphasize those very points, and be-cause the church has ignored them, people are hungry for them and begin to buy into the overemphasis. The overemphasis is heresy. When another group sees the heretical overemphasis, it starts preach-ing those points even less than before, even ignoring or attempting to refute them. The proper response, Schaeffer pointed out, is not for the church to ignore points forty through fifty, but to attempt to bring them back into their proper place in the doctrinal system.[57]

As always, the threat that religious experience might eclipse bibli-cal doctrine alarmed Schaeffer. He had a twofold reason for concern:

first, his belief in biblical inerrancy, and second, his commitment to Enlightenment rationalism. Religious experience threatened biblical inerrancy because experience might become authoritative over scripture, as it had in theological liberalism. Religious experience threatened Enlightenment rationalism because it opened the way for a religion that could not be explained reasonably — in other words making religion a *wholly* upper-story experience cut off from lower-story rationality. Biblical inerrancy and Enlightenment reason went hand in hand for Schaeffer, as they did for many conservative Christians throughout the twentieth century.

While emphasizing inerrancy and other correct evangelical doctrines, however, Schaeffer often emphasized that the true mark of the Christian was a twofold love — love for all of humanity and love for other Christians. This was a delicate balance, because love is not a propositional doctrine and is not readily subject to rational analysis and proof. Schaeffer acknowledged this delicate balance, but he nevertheless believed that love was absolutely essential for the church to bear witness to the watching world.[58]

The Great Evangelical Disaster

Schaeffer returned to the inerrancy theme in his last book, *The Great Evangelical Disaster,* which was published in 1984. There he attempted to tie together the intellectual themes of the trilogy and the cultural themes of his political activism (which we will see in chapter eight) with the issue of inerrancy at the center of the argument. By the time he wrote *The Great Evangelical Disaster,* Schaeffer had been involved in Christian Right politics for several years, where his activism was dominated by the abortion issue, and he was dying of cancer. He wanted to bring his cultural and political analysis together with the great fundamentalist concern for the Bible that had animated his ministry since his years in the fundamentalist battles of the thirties and forties. He argued that without a belief in the inerrancy of the Bible, the entire program he had outlined throughout his more than twenty books would fall apart.

Chapter two of *The Great Evangelical Disaster* was entitled "Marking the Watershed," and much of the chapter reiterated his earlier arguments and even contained direct excerpts from Schaeffer's 1974 Lausanne address that had already been published in *No Final Conflict*. There was a ridge of rock, he began, that formed a watershed high in the Swiss Alps, not far from L'Abri. Melted snow on one side of the rock flowed down one valley to the Rhine River, then north through Germany before emptying into the North Sea. The snowmelt on the other side of the ridge flowed into the Rhone Valley, southward through France, and into the Mediterranean. He used this watershed as an analogy to discuss one last time in his life the great issue of evangelical Christianity — the inerrancy of the Bible. "Evangelicals today are facing a watershed concerning the nature of biblical inspiration and authority. It is a watershed issue in very much the same sense as described in the illustration," Schaeffer argued. He said that evangelicals who do not hold to inerrancy may start out close to those who do, but the two groups will end up a thousand miles apart, as far apart as the North Sea from the Mediterranean. Schaeffer was convinced that compromising the authority of scripture alters the very theological meaning of Christianity.

This was a new problem in the history of Christianity, because from ancient times through the Reformation and into the late eighteenth century nearly all Christians took the inerrancy of scripture for granted. Even the medieval Catholic church, Schaeffer argued, believed in the inerrancy of the Bible. The problem, as he saw it, was that Roman Catholicism compromised by adding church tradition to scripture and attempting to make church teaching as authoritative as the Bible itself. Until recently, he said, belief in inerrancy and claiming to be a Christian always went hand in hand. Only in the past two centuries did people begin to say, "I am a Christian, but at the same time I believe the Bible to be full of errors."[59] Just as he had called Karl Barth's Neo-orthodoxy the "the new modernism," so now he called evangelicalism that does not hold to inerrancy "the New Neo-orthodoxy." He continued to hammer Fuller Seminary, though not by name, instead referring obliquely to seminaries that went by the name "evangelical" but did not adhere to inerrancy any longer. He quoted at length from a friend studying at Tyndale House in Cambridge, who wrote to Schaeffer, "I am studying at Tyndale House for a few days. And down the corridor from me is a very amiable professor from a prominent seminary in California which calls itself evangelical, who calls himself an 'open evangelical.' He has stated publicly in theological debate that he believes the Bible 'despite all the mistakes in it.'"[60]

In calling out unnamed evangelicals who had become like liberals in their compromise on scripture, Schaeffer told of a 1982 appearance on Milt Rosenberg's Chicago radio program *Extension 720*, where he debated a young liberal pastor. As Rosenberg pressed the young pastor as to the differences between himself and Schaeffer, the young pastor finally acknowledged that he knew the truth primarily by an inward experience of Jesus — a characteristically liberal response. Schaeffer connected this admission to a discussion he had a few years before with an evangelical who did not believe in inerrancy, but nevertheless claimed he knew the truth of the resurrection of Christ "because of the inward witness." "[N]ote that the liberal pastor and the leader with the weakened view of Scripture who calls himself an evangelical both end up in the same place — with no other final plea than 'an inner witness,'" Schaeffer wrote. "They have no final, objective authority."[61] This was the infiltration of existentialism into Christian thought, and it left Christians with no answers to a culture that was now based totally on the subjective decisions of autonomous individuals. The Bible was divided into the part that was true and the part that referred to history and science that was not necessarily true. "In other words," Schaeffer wrote, "the Bible is divided into halves. To someone like myself this is all very familiar — in the writings of Jean-Paul Sartre, of Albert Camus, of Martin Heidegger, of Karl Jaspers, and in the case of thousands of modern people who have accepted the existential methodology."[62]

Schaeffer traced the problem within the evangelical world not only to the modern liberal spirit of existential infiltration but also to the loophole that had been put in the Lausanne Covenant a decade before, the words "without error in all that it affirms." Schaeffer mentioned again that he had not fully supported this clause in the Covenant and now believed that in the ten years since the Lausanne Congress, many evangelicals had used the loophole to separate the objective and verifiable from the subjective religious values taught in scripture. As he had been saying for a decade, an additional statement was needed, an affirmation that "the Bible is without error not only when it speaks of values, the meaning system, and religious things, but it is also without error when it speaks of history and the cosmos."[63] Oddly, he did not reference the Chicago Statement, which affirmed what Schaeffer believed was missing from the Lausanne Covenant.

How were evangelicals to be a force in the culture war if they had allowed the values of the culture to so infiltrate their thinking that they were actually adjusting their views of scripture to fit modern ways of thinking? "Or to say it another way," he pleaded, "the culture is to be constantly judged by the Bible, rather than the Bible being bent to conform to the surrounding culture." The early church had succeeded in doing this with regard to the culture of the Roman Empire; the Reformation leaders had judged all things by the Bible at the end of the Middle Ages; and the early modern revivalists had done the same in the eighteenth and nineteenth centuries. But American evangelicals in the late twentieth century were failing. This was the "great evangelical disaster."

As some evangelicals argued that the historical or scientific parts of scripture were culturally conditioned by their ancient context, they slid easily into saying that even some moral matters were culturally conditioned. Among these, Schaeffer mentioned two: easy divorce, and order in the home and the church. He believed evangelicals had become too accepting of divorce, again as a result of bending the Bible to fit culture. When speaking of order, Schaeffer seemed to be speaking of gender roles, but he was less than clear and did not elaborate in detail.

He also tied this great evangelical disaster to abortion and authoritarian politics, arguing very briefly that both were made possible wherever the existential methodology of the modern world created an atmosphere devoid of absolutes. Abortion, even for the mere happiness of the mother, was legal because all was relative, and what could restrain the power of the state once an absolute moral standard was removed? One was left with the prospects of another Mao or Stalin. Evangelicals who did not hold to the inerrancy of scripture had nothing with which to battle such forces. "Here then is the watershed of the evangelical world," he wrote before repeating an exact quote from his writings in the mid-seventies: "evangelicalism is not consistently evangelical unless there is a line drawn between those who take a full view of Scripture and those who do not."[64] As he had said a decade earlier, if evangelicals were to battle the forces of culture, they needed to get their own house in order by shoring up their views of scripture.

Schaeffer's Battle for the Bible

Schaeffer, Lindsell, and others in the 1970s and 1980s overstated their case when they warned that institutions that failed to maintain the strict inerrantist position would soon slide into liberalism. Fuller Seminary, among others, remains evangelical in its belief statement a generation later despite taking the softer view that scripture is infallible or inerrant only in matters of theology but not necessarily in history and science. Of course, Schaeffer blurred important distinctions. There are key differences between inerrancy-soft evangelicals in the 1980s and the modernists or liberals of the early twentieth century. The liberals had very nearly rejected supernaturalism altogether, which swept away fundamentals of the faith such as the deity and virgin birth of Christ, the incarnation, bodily resurrection, and miracles. Moreover, they accepted a model of evolutionary development that relegated the teachings of the Bible to an inferior status when contrasted to modern religious experience. Evangelicals in the seventies and eighties, even those who were soft on inerrancy, did not say this. They were still evangelicals in the content of their faith. They argued that there was a transcendent standard of morality that was articulated by an authoritative scripture, and they claimed that Christianity was a religion centered on the supernatural events of the incarnation, resurrection, and life-transforming work of a risen Christ. There was, as it turns out, more to the rise of theological modernism than a mere rejection of inerrancy.

Even Karl Barth at mid-century did not relinquish supernaturalism or fundamentals such as the incarnation and resurrection, but Schaeffer still treated him like a rank heretic because Barth believed the Bible could be true in what it teaches theologically without necessarily being inerrant in all its historical details. In 1950, Schaeffer called this approach "the existential method"; he used the same term for the way some evangelicals in the seventies and eighties would not affirm the inerrancy of the Bible in matters of history and science. This "existential method" reflected Kierkegaard's separation of upper-story experience from lower-story fact.

Throughout his career, when locked in battle, Schaeffer fought hardest against those who were comparatively close to him in belief — Karl Barth rather than Rudolf Bultmann, Clark Pinnock more than

Paul Tillich, Fuller Seminary rather than the University of Chicago. This was the legacy of fundamentalism. Some fundamentalists from the first half of the twentieth century, Carl McIntire chief among them, were far more adept at heresy hunting within the evangelical camp than at consistently battling the hostile forces in the larger culture. Douglas Sweeney has argued compellingly that even the evangelicals who emerged in the 1950s to downplay infighting in order to champion positive engagement with culture still retained a good bit of the old fundamentalist defense of the faith. There can be no doubt that this was true for Schaeffer.[65]

Schaeffer's analysis of how Barth and evangelicals developed their beliefs about scripture was substantially correct. They had applied the tools of modern criticism to scripture, and they were willing to judge the historical statements and scientific implications of scripture using those tools. But Schaeffer failed to acknowledge the important difference between using these tools while believing that the Bible was God's special revelation and doing so on the assumption that the Bible was more or less like any other piece of ancient literature.[66] The evangelicals Schaeffer attacked in the 1980s stood much closer to him on any continuum of belief than to Camus, Jaspers, and Sartre, and in retrospect it is difficult indeed to believe that these evangelicals had lost their ability to judge culture by scripture just because they had appropriated some historical and scientific tools to better understand the Bible.

On the other hand, there are those today who would point to Pinnock and the "open theism" debate and say that Schaeffer was correct. In this debate, evangelicals are now squaring off with each other over the question of whether God at all times knows the future completely. On one side are mostly Reformed evangelicals, who believe that any notion that God is not fully omniscient weakens God's sovereignty. On the other side are more Arminian theologians, including Pinnock, who point to Old Testament texts where God is said to have changed his mind as history unfolded in ways God had not foreseen. There can be little doubt that Schaeffer would have sided with the Reformed camp against open theism, but it is not clear how he interpreted texts that say literally that God changed his mind. Nor is it altogether clear how holding the line on inerrancy would have helped in keeping those in the open theism camp within what Schaeffer believed were the parameters of evangelicalism, given the presence of such texts. Inerrancy may not have been a watershed after all.

Schaeffer's time at L'Abri, and his cultural engagement in the trilogy, turns out not to have been a dramatic watershed for Schaeffer's thinking, either. It seems clear that he viewed the fundamentalist fight against liberalism in the 1930s and the battle for the Bible in the 1970s as two theaters of the same war. He sometimes recognized the difference between the two fronts, but for him the stakes were just as high in the fight against non-inerrantist evangelicals as in the fight against the liberals. It appears that L'Abri and the trilogy were more of an interlude in Schaeffer's fundamentalism, rather than a dramatic turning point for his thought. Once his campus lectures and the trilogy drew him back to the United States, he jumped into the new fundamentalist battles as if he had never been gone.

CHAPTER SEVEN

Filmmaker

Francis Schaeffer, like almost all significant leaders, was a complex person, a bundle of contradictions. One view popular with some of Schaeffer's own followers from the sixties and early seventies, including people who lived at L'Abri, holds that Schaeffer's life can be divided into three periods: the fundamentalist early years, the evangelical prophet years, and the Christian Right activism of his later career. There is something to this interpretation, though only as long as one allows for considerable overlap in the periods. That said, however, Schaeffer's thought was fundamentally consistent. He took on new emphases throughout his life without ever completely letting go of previous concerns. Even when he was the progressive prophet of culture at L'Abri, the fundamentalist insistence on correct theology and the battle against theological liberalism were never far from the surface. There is no need to divorce the evangelical prophet from the fundamentalist warrior, because Schaeffer never separated them himself. He saw no inconsistency and little tension between these two roles. Rather, he saw himself as both a product and critic of fundamentalism and evangelicalism. And he saw only continuity in the course of his activities.

Still, there were indeed different emphases, and those who divide his career into three periods are correct that the most important themes changed over time. From the founding of L'Abri in 1955 until the beginning of the 1970s, Schaeffer was most concerned about the state of western intellectual life and culture and how Christians should understand and resist modern trends. In the early seventies this concern continued but was accompanied by a renewed fundamentalist emphasis on the battle for inerrancy. His regular trips to America beginning in the mid-sixties put him back into the intramural debates within American evangelicalism, to which he had paid less attention from 1948 until 1965. Then, in the late seventies, his concerns about western intellectual life and culture translated into conservative Christian activism, and he began to advocate cultural warfare. His son loomed large in the transition.

Franky

In 1973, Edith and Francis embarked on what was supposed to be semi-retirement. They moved out of Chalet les Melezes and into Chalet le Chardonnet and planned to spend more time at L'Abri after nearly a decade of travels to the United States and around the world.[1] The next year, however, Schaeffer returned from the Lausanne Congress of 1974 and entered one of his blackest periods of personal depression. Many of those who knew him say Schaeffer was prone to periods of depression, and in such cases it is not necessarily profitable to assign causes. He may have been in despair about the state of evangelicalism, as we saw in chapter five, or he may have been experiencing something that was purely biochemical and therefore unattached to any external cause. Franky, then twenty-two years old, was alarmed and decided he would postpone his own career goal as an artist and filmmaker so he could dedicate the next ten years to promoting his father. As it turned out, Franky's desire to pump up his father's career would dovetail nicely with his own dream of making films. Franky would be intimately involved in Francis's career from that point on, directing the films and inspiring many of Francis's later activities and ideas.[2]

Franky was not a L'Abri member at the time, which meant he was not part of the decision-making apparatus of the community. Prior to the films, decisions were made by consensus among the members. Most of the members disagreed with the film idea, but the family overrode the members and started the first film project anyway. *How Should We Then Live?* was the first major decision made at L'Abri that was not unanimous. Because the Schaeffer family decided against the wishes of the other members to go ahead with the film, many members left. Of course, others flooded in, so L'Abri continued to prosper.[3]

That the films were Franky's idea was bad news from the perspective of many who had lived and studied at L'Abri. Franky was a problem for the Schaeffers. He was the family's only male child, born eight years after his next youngest sibling and seventeen years after the family's eldest child. He suffered polio as a youngster and grew up in a house full of people, many of them women who doted on him. He had no chance for anything resembling a normal childhood. Who would be surprised that his parents and sisters took this all into consideration and indulged him? Moreover, Francis and Edith were simply too busy with L'Abri to keep track of Franky. He ran unsupervised for most of his childhood, much of the time not even attending school. As he wrote in his 2007 autobiography, "On any given day, from the time I was about seven on, you could have asked my parents where I was and they would have had no idea."[4]

Friends remember Edith and Francis being unable to say no to young Franky. He would burst into the middle of the room to ask a question as his father was attempting to lead a discussion or Bible study. Rather than being disciplined for interrupting the session or told to wait patiently until the meeting was over, Franky would bring everything to a halt and receive undivided attention.

Eventually Franky was packed off to a boarding school in England. When told that Franky had run away from school, some who were living at L'Abri at the time recall Francis saying something like, "Good for Franky. He's a Bolshevik, and we want our young people to be Bolsheviks for the Lord." In fact, though, Franky was not a Bolshevik rebel; he was simply undisciplined. Those who heard this exchange recall thinking that Franky needed a good spanking. When old enough to travel with the Schaeffers once the speaking tours in America began, Franky ran wild on Christian college campuses, attempting to seduce the coeds, wracking up huge long-distance phone bills at homes where the Schaeffers stayed, and at least once throwing pies across a ballroom like they were Frisbees.

Everyone agrees, however, that Franky was very talented, perhaps even brilliant. As some L'Abri members put it, he was an untutored genius. Because of his deep interest in art, the Schaeffers hired a very fine art tutor to work with Franky, but Franky was too undisciplined to follow through with his lessons, and he eventually dropped out of English boarding school at the age of fourteen.[5]

As an adult, long after his father's death, Franky wrote his own trilogy, which would become a source of great embarrassment and heartache for Edith and the Schaeffer sisters. Published in 1992, *Portofino* is a thinly disguised exposé of the family's worst side. The father figure, Ralph Becker, is a fundamentalist Presbyterian missionary who along with his wife, Elsa, operates a retreat center in Switzerland called L'Arche. Ralph broods in dark depressive moods most of the time and verbally abuses Elsa routinely, often causing ugly family scenes in the resort restaurant in Portofino, Italy, where the real Schaeffers and fictional Beckers spent their summer vacations. While the mother tries to keep the family mood happy, Ralph keeps his nose stuck in Christian magazines and grumbles about liberals. The novel also has its lighter moments. In one scene Elsa is intent on giving young Calvin, the character who clearly represents Franky, a sex talk that the fourteen-year-old has heard many times before and dreads hearing again. In the book's most shocking scene, the boy catches his mother about to physically consummate an emotional affair she is having with one of the coworkers from the mission back in Switzerland. When Ralph learns of the quasi-affair, he throws a tantrum and leaves, only to return remorsefully, admitting that his own boorish behavior has driven his wife to the brink of infidelity. Running throughout *Portofino* and the other novels is Calvin's adolescent coming of age and his love for Jennifer, his best friend from England whose family also vacations in Portofino.[6]

Five years after *Portofino,* Franky published *Saving Grandma,* again a barely fictionalized novel, this one about Ralph's mother who came to L'Arche in her old age, just as Schaeffer's mother came to L'Abri in real life in the early 1960s. The unsaved, foul-mouthed Mother Becker thinks her son is a useless "poop" of a missionary who ought to get a real job. Grandma hates her daughter-in-law, because she's convinced that Elsa and her genteel, snooty ways had pushed Ralph away from engineering (real work) and into the useless ministry. Everyone tries to humor the cantankerous Mother Becker as she grumbles about everything at L'Arche in a moody display of elderly misbehavior. Most shocking is one of the final scenes, in which Calvin is accused of sexual deviance with one of the neighboring cerebral palsy victims, whom everyone calls "spastics." To turn the tables on his parents, Calvin runs to his father's secret drawer and pulls out for everyone to see the hardcore pornography Ralph keeps hidden and locked away.[7]

The third book in the Calvin Becker trilogy is *Zermatt,* published in 2003. Zermatt was the location of the family's annual ski vacation. As winter is to summer, *Zermatt* is a colder, darker version of *Portofino.* The family's idiosyncrasies, mild dysfunctions, and occasional dark moments become disturbing lapses in morality, temporary dementia, and extreme narcissism. In the central event of the book, the fourteen-year-old Calvin is seduced, quite willingly, by Eva, a waitress and maid in her thirties at the Hotel Riffelberg, just up the mountain from Zermatt. The event causes the family to spin out of control, leading to Elsa's return to L'Arche with younger daughter Rachael while Calvin and the eldest Becker girl, Janet, stay behind with their father, who decides he has been under the control of Elsa long enough and will now backslide into his sinful ways. Meanwhile, Calvin's attempt to have sex again with Eva results in his inadvertently leading her to conversion — much to his disappointment. Eventually, the family reunites at L'Arche, where Ralph resubmits his life not to God, but to Elsa, who turns out to be so narcissistic that she distorts the whole event into a story about Calvin's conversion. She tells her story to all the young people in a Bible study, and it brings her the attention and control she craves. *Zermatt* ends with Calvin hating his mother, whom he now sees as a liar and manipulator, and believing that his dad may be redeemable after all.[8]

In addition to Calvin's obsession with sex, the other thread running through all three books is that he hates his family and wishes he could be raised with normal parents and sisters. Were the books more fictional in nature and perhaps more loving in their critique, they might constitute an engaging and bitingly satirical look into the idiosyncrasies of evangelicalism. Given that they are a thinly disguised exposé of the dark side of one of the leading families of evangelicalism, written by a son who seems determined to savage his family publicly, they are much more troubling to read.

It appears that Franky was in search of independence. His turn against his family was preceded by his vitriolic non-fiction attacks on evangelicals, with such memorable titles as *Addicted to Mediocrity* and *Sham Pearls for Real Swine*.[9] But perhaps the ultimate act of independence for Franky was his conversion to Eastern Orthodox Christianity. He has said his father would have had no trouble with his conversion, even implying that Francis was moving in a similar direction before his death.[10]

How Should We Then Live?

Franky was largely responsible for the last phase of Francis's career. Schaeffer himself attributed the films to Franky. When asked in an interview how the idea for the first film developed, he replied, "My son, Franky, is an artist." Franky approached his father one day and said, "Dad, I have two little children, and if what you say is right, and I believe you're right, then we have a responsibility to try and change the flow."[11] Turning Francis's lectures into a film series had been the brainchild of Franky and Billy Zeoli, who ran a company called Gospel Films. Zeoli was the son of evangelist Anthony Zeoli, under whose preaching Francis had been converted back in the late twenties. Franky served at first as producer of *How Should We Then Live?*, with Zeoli as executive producer, Wendy Collins as associate producer, and John Gonser as scriptwriter and director (he would be replaced by Franky). The budget for the first film was over a million dollars, much of it coming from Rich DeVos, one of the co-founders of Amway.[12]

In making the films, the Schaeffers enlisted the help of several Christian scholars as consultants. Among them were Hans Rookmaaker and John Walford on art and William Edgar on music history. Franky wrote to Rookmaaker in August 1974 asking for help in making a film called "The Rise and Decline of Western Thought and Culture," the original title of *How Should We Then Live?* Franky offered 1500 dollars for one month's work. Franky told Rookmaaker that "large portions of important research and work must be done by experts in their own fields which are touched by the script."[13] Edgar, who was teaching at a private New England prep school when the films were being made, says the project appeared to be a fiasco at times, and he wonders how the film ever came to completion.[14] Walford's role was to go to Italy and scout out the sites for the segments on the Italian Renaissance. Gonser wrote the film script and then sent all the material having to do with art history to Walford, who was supposed to ensure that Schaeffer was not saying anything inaccurate.

Walford found a lot of things that were troublesome from an art history point of view, statements that would not make Schaeffer look good. The classic example concerned Michelangelo's *David*. In the film Schaeffer talks about the long gallery that leads to the sculpture. Down the side of the gallery are variants of Michelangelo's captives or slaves, which were done for the tomb of Pope Julius II. The sculptured captives are in various stages of completion, from rough stone to nearly finished. Schaeffer describes these as man tearing himself from the rock and implies that the *David* was the culmination, a progression through the unfinished captives to the exaltation of humankind autonomous from God. In reality, however, the *David* was done first, and the captives much later. Presenting the *David* as the climax of those figures was inaccurate, but the Schaeffers did not want to hear it. They liked their own version of the story and thought it made good film drama. Walford sent endless critiques to Gonser, but he eventually concluded that the Schaeffers viewed him as a gadfly standing in the way of the progress of the film.[15]

Of course, on the big stage, the temptation to fudge a bit on detail to make an overarching point can be overwhelming. And in fact, this is precisely what Schaeffer had been doing with ideas throughout his career. He was not, as we have seen, a master of detail — he was far more interested in the big picture. But he was also rarely accountable to anyone, so his ideas and arguments were only rarely challenged. Apart from two workers in their fifties, the oldest people at L'Abri for many of the years leading up to the film projects were in their mid-thirties, and most at L'Abri were much younger than that. While they would debate Schaeffer occasionally, he was *the* authority in most of his contexts. Perhaps as a result he was unprepared to take the kind of criticism offered by Walford and others. His son, in any case, certainly was.

With the inexperienced twenty-two-year-old Franky at the helm, *How Should We Then Live?* was indeed, as Edgar says, a fiasco. Francis decided Franky would take over as director after Gonser, for reasons unknown, was unable to continue. Franky had no experience in filmmaking, so others had to show him what to do — very carefully, of course, because he was Francis's son. Such amateurish leadership led to carelessness, which resulted in poor production values and sometimes even anachronism, as in one scene with Roman women in 1970s hairstyles.[16] In one segment Schaeffer refers to Samuel Rutherford's book *Lex Rex* as "the *Rex Lex* tradition," which would change the phrase "the law is king" to "the king is law" — the exact opposite of what Rutherford and Schaeffer meant.[17] *How Should We Then Live?* was originally supposed to be thirteen episodes but was shortened to only ten because there was not enough footage for the longer version. Francis blamed Gonser.[18]

However problematic the film version, *How Should We Then Live?* was Schaeffer's best book. The books accompanying the films *How Should We Then Live?* and *Whatever Happened to the Human Race?* were virtually the only ones before *Christian Manifesto* that were actually written as books, rather than edited into book form by James Sire from transcribed lectures. As such, *How Should We Then Live?* was in much better shape than usual when Sire received the manuscript; he suspects that someone had already done substantial editing by the time he saw the work.[19]

How Should We Then Live? appeared in print in 1976 and brought together Schaeffer's entire intellectual and cultural project. The title was taken from Ezekiel 33:10, "Thus ye speak, saying, If our transgressions and our sins be upon us, and we pine away in them, how should we then live?"[20] Schaeffer recapped the argument of the trilogy in much tighter prose than in those three early books, and he displayed much better command of the great philosophers and artists of the western intellectual and cultural tradition, even though he made many of the same errors of detail as in the trilogy. The sharper focus and better examples were no doubt the product of several more years of reading and reflection on Schaeffer's part, but they also reflect the use of expert advisors for the film version of the book. Anyone wanting to understand Schaeffer's overarching argument about how western culture moved from a Christian worldview at the time of Aquinas to the relativistic secularism, or what he calls simply secular humanism, of the late twentieth century, need read only *How Should We Then Live?*

The first words of the version of the book published in *The Complete Works of Francis A. Schaeffer* reflect the criticism Schaeffer had received for his errors of detail in the trilogy and other works. The book begins with an "Author's Note" — a disclaimer: "In no way does this book make a pretense of being a complete chronological history of Western culture. It is questionable if such a book could even be written. This book is, however, an analysis of the key moments in history which have formed our present culture, and the thinking of people who brought those moments to pass."[21]

One major difference between *How Should We Then Live?* and the trilogy is that here Schaeffer pushed his argument back to the ancient Greeks and Romans, in an attempt to show that individuals and societies usually have a prevailing worldview, and that their lives usually exhibit consistently the presuppositions of that worldview. By this time Schaeffer was well known for this type of worldview thinking, and his attempt to alert Christians to the need for intentionally and self-consciously forming a Christian worldview based on solid Christian presuppositions was the central part of his intellectual project. The ancient Greeks and Romans, he said, did not have presuppositions on which to build a worldview that could answer the questions most basic to humankind, questions of metaphysics and morals. They tried, therefore, to supplement their worldview with belief in their gods. But their gods were finite and therefore not big enough to answer the questions about unity, diversity, finite and particular human personality, and infinite time and space. Without an adequate base of objective, transcendent morality, the Roman state degenerated from a republic to an authoritarian dictatorship, then fell of its own weight. "Rome did not fall because of external forces such as the invasion of the barbarians," Schaeffer wrote. "Rome had no sufficient inward base; the barbarians only completed the breakdown — and Rome gradually became a ruin."[22]

After speeding through ancient Rome in seven pages, Schaeffer moved to the Middle Ages. There he tried to show how the pristine Christianity of the New Testament was distorted, as a humanistic element was added in the form of church authority that became equal to the Bible. This reference to church authority being equal to the Bible was one of Schaeffer's frequent swipes at Roman Catholicism, but he also showed correctly that medieval Christianity had absorbed Greek and Roman ideas and even some pagan superstition. "It would be a mistake to suppose that the overall structure of thought and life was not Christian," he wrote. "Yet it would be equally mistaken to deny that into this structure were fitted alien or half-alien features — some of Greek and Roman origin, others of local pagan ancestry — which at times actually obscured the outlines of the Christianity underneath."[23] For anyone who has read Schaeffer's earlier works, it is not difficult to see where the argument is heading. Early Christianity was pure and biblical; medieval Roman Catholic Christianity became increasingly corrupt; the Renaissance introduced humanism; then the Reformation recaptured true Christianity and held humanism at bay until the twentieth century. It was a jeremiad — that is, a sermon in the tradition of Jeremiah, who often preached about decline. As in the trilogy, things really began to get off track for the biblical worldview when Aquinas integrated the thinking of Aristotle into Christian theology and separated nature and grace. Then the Renaissance moved toward humanism, but the Protestant Reformation staved off full-blown secularism by reconstituting the Christian base in northern European countries.

In *How Should We Then Live?* there is much less emphasis on antithesis and synthesis than in the trilogy, and many more references to autonomy. Autonomy, as Schaeffer used the term, denies that human beings find meaning in reference to anything outside themselves, including their creator. By this time he realized that the modern view of the autonomy of the individual was the crux of the modern problem.

Still, a central part of the western intellectual problem remained Aquinas's attempt to synthesize secular Greek thought with the Christian faith. The Reformers, of course, had avoided this pitfall. "Because the Reformers did not mix humanism with their position, but took instead a serious view of the Bible, they had no nature-versus-grace problem," Schaeffer wrote in an almost exact replication of the trilogy's argument.

Schaeffer's desire to keep the Reformation free from the intellectual forces that shaped the Renaissance was the most consistent point of contact between *How Should We Then Live?* and the trilogy. "One could say that the Renaissance centered in autonomous man, while the Reformation centered in the infinite-personal God who had spoken in the Bible," he wrote.[24] Again he cited nineteenth-century historian Jacob Burckhardt's *The Civilization of the Renaissance in Italy* to buttress this view that the Renaissance and Reformation were opposed to one another. But as if to soften the point, and perhaps to address criticism he had received, Schaeffer offered a vague disclaimer that the Reformation was not a golden age.

In the book's chapter on the Reformation the new element was the connection between the Reformation and American democracy. It was to be a foreshadowing of Schaeffer's Christian Right activism. Here he brought seventeenth-century Scottish thinker Samuel Rutherford (1600-1661) into the discussion, especially Rutherford's book *Lex Rex,* "Law is King." This was the first mention in print of what would become Schaeffer's view that the American Revolution and the U.S. Constitution were profoundly influenced by Rutherford — a notion shared by few if any American historians. Schaeffer traced Rutherford's influence in America through Presbyterian preacher and scholar John Witherspoon (1723-1794), president of Princeton College and the only ordained preacher to sign the Declaration of Independence, and through the writings of John Locke (1632-1704). Locke, Schaeffer claimed, appropriated much of *Lex Rex* even though he did not share Rutherford's or Witherspoon's Christian foundation. Schaeffer concluded from the Rutherford influence that the American founders, even those who were not Christians, were working from a "Christian base." (He took up this argument more forcefully in *A Christian Manifesto,* as we will see in the next chapter.) While Schaeffer was quick to criticize how the Christian Aquinas unhelpfully appropriated non-Christian thinking, he was just as quick to praise non-Christians, such as Jefferson, who worked from a "Christian base." It seems that for Schaeffer, when a Christian utilized non-Christian thinking, the product was sub-Christian, but when a non-Christian used Christian influences, the product was thoroughly Christian.

In *How Should We Then Live?* Schaeffer stressed the Enlightenment more than in his earlier works. When he did, he interpreted the Enlightenment as Renaissance humanism and individual autonomy at floodtide. The Reformation could only temporarily stave off full-blown humanism, and the Enlightenment then took it up with a vengeance.

Having attributed the American Revolution and subsequent U.S. Constitution primarily to the Reformation base, he argued that the

French Revolution, by contrast, was purely a product of the humanistic Renaissance-cum-Enlightenment. "Sometimes the French Revolution is likened to what occurred in the United States at a slightly earlier date," he wrote. "This is incorrect."[25] Schaeffer believed that the American Revolution, with its Reformation base, was related to the Glorious Revolution in England in 1688, where the people's representatives in Parliament proved supreme over the king. He connected the Enlightenment-based French Revolution to the Russian Revolution of 1917, led by the atheist Lenin. Both the French and Russian Revolutions included wholesale massacres led by elite leaders with no adequate base of transcendent morality, while in England and America the violence was nearly non-existent or confined to the battlefields. His chapter on the Reformation was followed by one tellingly entitled "The Reformation Continued," which was almost entirely on the American Revolution and formation of the U.S. Constitution, while the chapter on the Enlightenment dealt primarily with the French and Russian Revolutions. The message was clear: The Reformation, with its Christian base, leads to democracy; the Enlightenment, with its humanistic and secular base, leads to dictatorship and communism.

In addition to this connection between the Reformation and American democracy, another new element in *How Should We Then Live?* was Schaeffer's emphasis on science. While he had discussed the relationship of biblical creation and science in *Genesis in Space and Time,* in *How Should We Then Live?* he devoted an entire chapter in the book and a full episode in the film to the rise of modern science. The basic argument was that modern science, like democracy, can be attributed primarily to Christianity. The Christian base gave the West the notion that there was an objective universe, created by God and external to humankind, that can be known through reason. By contrast, Schaeffer said, the East, with its pantheistic idea of reality, was incapable of developing modern science. Nearly all the great thinkers of the Scientific Revolution — Bacon, Descartes, Galileo, Kepler, and Newton — were either practicing Christians or had a Christian worldview. As was so often the case, Schaeffer got the big picture substantially correct, at least in regard to the West, but he stretched things in attempting to head off any criticism that Christianity actually resisted science. In a strained passage he argued that when the

Roman Catholic Church attacked Copernicus and Galileo, "it was not because their teaching actually contained anything contrary to the Bible. The church authorities thought it did, but that was because Aristotelian elements had become part of church orthodoxy, and Galileo's notions clearly conflicted with them."[26] In other words, the error of Aquinas in integrating Aristotle with Catholic Christianity was responsible for the church's resistance to modern science.

In the film version, Schaeffer refuted the idea that Isaac Newton was interested in how the universe worked but not the deeper question of why things are the way they are. He stressed Newton's writings on scripture and his frank acknowledgment that God was the prime mover behind the universe's laws of nature. Likewise, Francis Bacon, the great scientific philosopher, took the Bible seriously, Schaeffer argued. "To these founders of modern science," Schaeffer opines on camera, "man, including his science, is not on his own. He is to take seriously the teaching of the Bible concerning history and the cosmos."[27]

In a chapter entitled "The Breakdown in Philosophy and Science," Schaeffer tried to show what happened to Christian-based science and Reformation-based philosophy that led to modern secular humanism. There were three shifts, he said. First, in science there was a shift from modern science to what Schaeffer called "modern modern science," which was essentially the shift from "the uniformity of natural causes in an open system to the concept of uniformity of natural causes in a closed system."[28] By "open system" he meant a universe open to the supernatural intervention of God; a closed system was self-contained, naturalistic, and materialistic. The closed system left no room for God and turned humankind into a machine. In science, Darwin was of course the primary player in the development of the naturalistic, materialistic closed system. In the film, there is a segment in episode six on Nazism whose basic argument is that the naturalistic science of Darwin was translated into the philosophy of the survival of the fittest, which turned science into a sanction for the racism of Hitler's Nazi party. In addressing the behaviorist science of B. F. Skinner, Schaeffer argued that "science has become our new religion."[29] Anticipating the postmodern critique of modernity, he argued that twentieth-century people are conditioned to believe that science gives objective answers without realizing that the views of scientists are often shaped by their naturalistic and materialistic worldview.

This modern scientific worldview was a result of the shift in philosophy brought about by four crucial thinkers: Rousseau, Kant, Hegel, and Kierkegaard. As covered in the trilogy and chapter four of *How Should We Then Live?*, in Schaeffer's schema these men completed the separation of reason from faith that had started with Aquinas. The result was that western intellectual life was left with the upstairs/downstairs dichotomy that was central to Schaeffer's analysis. As Schaeffer had been arguing since the early sixties, meaning, emotion, and values resided upstairs, completely detached from reason, while downstairs one found reason and objective knowledge of the universe. Interestingly, in *How Should We Then Live?* Schaeffer stressed the role of the romantic Rousseau more than the existentialist Kierkegaard. Episode seven in the film, "The Age of Non Reason," begins with Rousseau and his concept of autonomous freedom for humankind, in which the ultimate ideal was that each individual be completely free from restraint to experience and intuit the truth apart from rationality. This line of thinking seemed to replace Schaeffer's earlier argument in the trilogy that Hegel's synthesis and Kierkegaard's leap of faith were the most important components leading to relativistic secular humanism and the modern dilemma. One wonders if Schaeffer had discovered C. S. Lewis's argument that romanticism was the key to understanding the shift from a Christian worldview to modern relativism. Philip Yancey pointed out in 1979 that C. S. Lewis "startled the intellectual world with his premise that the Romantic movement (not Hegel's synthesis or the Renaissance) caused the most profound shift in recent history, yet Schaeffer seems to sidestep that area entirely."[30] Schaeffer may have sidestepped the Romantic movement in the trilogy, but not in *How Should We Then Live?*

Schaeffer's second shift in philosophy and science concerned the shift to an impersonal view of the origins of the universe and humankind. Schaeffer believed there were only three possible explanations of origins: 1) everything came from nothing; 2) everything was made by a personality that created the universe; and 3) some form of the impersonal has existed forever. Obviously, the second is the Christian, or at least theistic, view, while the first and the third are modern secular views. The third goes beyond pantheism to what Schaeffer called "pan-everythingism." "In modern thought," he wrote, "all begins with the impersonality of the atom or the molecule or the energy particle, and then everything — including life and man — comes forth by chance from that."[31] Schaeffer summarized his argument to this point by writing, "Now having traveled from the pride of man in the High Renaissance and the Enlightenment down to the present despair, we can understand where modern people are. They have no place for a personal God. But equally they have no place for man as man. . . . Beginning only from man himself, people affirm that man is only a machine."[32]

The third and final shift was toward a relativistic worldview, with the upstairs/downstairs dichotomy that worked its way into the general culture and then into theology. Here Schaeffer's argument was identical to the one he put forth in the trilogy, with most of the same examples thrown in from music and the visual arts, a few new references to theologian Paul Tillich (1886-1965) and philosopher Friedrich Nietzsche (1844-1900), and many of the same references to Karl Barth as had appeared in Schaeffer's thought since 1950. He also included an improved discussion of the fragmentation of knowledge and brief critiques of positivism and linguistic analysis. In short, he was grappling with what today would be called postmodernism — the belief that, rather than meaning being drawn from "the God who is there," there is nothing transcendent, and subsequently all we are left with is power to will our own meaning out of nothing. Postmodernism has been defined more simply as the belief that there is no bottom line, anywhere. Schaeffer was acutely aware that this was the dilemma facing the West, and that Christians had to develop a response.

Schaeffer continued in the film version of *How Should We Then Live?* to critique existentialism, particularly the thought of Jean-Paul Sartre, as he had since the trilogy. In one scene Schaeffer tells of Sartre's view that meaning comes only through an act of the will, so that there is no moral difference between helping an elderly woman across the street and in running her down with a car. Both are equally self-authenticating acts of the will. On screen, as Schaeffer narrates, there is a scene of a man stopping his car to help an elderly woman, followed by another scene where a car bears down on the woman as she screams for her life. Citing Sartre's signing of the Algerian Manifesto declaring that France's war in Algeria was unjust, Schaeffer argued that Sartre could not live consistently with his own relativistic worldview. Instead Sartre had smuggled a standard of judgment into his worldview after all. Schaeffer also argued that the counterculture's turn to drugs and Eastern religions in the 1960s was an existentialist attempt to achieve the authentication of the self in the area of non-reason. But human beings, as Sartre demonstrated, cannot live consistently with this worldview. Eventually, Schaeffer pointed out, people stopped taking drugs as an effort to self-authenticate and instead took drugs out of despair.[33]

A Call to Culture War

The final new aspect in Schaeffer's thinking in *How Should We Then Live?* was the answer to his title. Christians could either sell out to culture by adopting the two core values discussed in chapter five, personal peace and affluence, or they could do battle with the culture. The last three chapters of the book and a significant segment of the film constituted a call to culture war, and the 1973 *Roe v. Wade* Supreme Court decision legalizing abortion was central to this call.

Here again, Franky's influence was crucial. Schaeffer's career to this point had been thoroughly apolitical. Through his years as a fundamentalist warrior, his work as pop evangelical intellectual, even as an evangelical prophet of culture, Schaeffer had uttered scarcely a word about political involvement. As Franky tells the story, however, Franky's absolutist stand against abortion "goaded my father into taking political positions far more extreme than came naturally to him."[34] Schaeffer initially resisted taking on the pro-life cause, partly because he saw it as a Catholic issue. Franky overcame these objections, persuading his father that a call to activism was the logical extension of his critique of the decline of western intellectual and moral life.

Schaeffer argued in the film that the U.S. Supreme Court had begun to make the Constitution say whatever the justices wanted it to say. This meant the justices were acting as if they were above the law. Law was no longer king. Schaeffer saw this as part of humankind's desire to be autonomous from God's revelation. "Sociologically, *law is king* (Samuel Rutherford's *Lex Rex*) was no longer the base whereby one could be ruled by law rather than by arbitrary judgments of men and whereby there could be wide freedoms without chaos," he wrote.[35] Democracy continued to function only through inertia; American society was simply borrowing on past principles that it no longer had a philosophical basis for holding.

Schaeffer saw several things worth noting about the legalizing of abortion. He found the decision to be arbitrary both medically and legally. The decision was arbitrary medically because while a fertilized egg has all the genetic potential of a fully developed human being, there was no consensus in the medical and philosophical communities as to what constitutes a person. Disregarding this lack of consensus, the Supreme Court made an arbitrary decision that the fetus was not a person. On the legal side, Schaeffer cited University of Texas law professor Joseph Witherspoon's argument that the Thirteenth and Fourteenth Amendments were intended to ensure that states could never again consider any class of human beings as less than persons, as had happened in the *Dred Scott* decision of 1857 deeming slaves as permanent property. Schaeffer argued that the Court's decision to consider the fetus as less than a person was an arbitrary decision that ignored precedent.

On a larger scale, the abortion decision was arbitrary because it ignored the Christian consensus of America's past. Early Christians, Schaeffer argued, were unique within the Roman Empire for their stand against abortion. The Council of Ancyra barred people from the Lord's Supper for practicing or even promoting the practice of abortion, and the Synod of Elvira (305-306) specified excommunication. Schaeffer said that the arbitrary decision of the Supreme Court was accepted against this former consensus because modern people had no absolutes.

He then tied the acceptance of the abortion decision to the potential for authoritarian government in the United States: "if this arbitrary absolute by law is accepted by most modern people, bred with the concept of no absolutes but rather relativity, why wouldn't arbitrary absolutes in regard to such matters as authoritarian limitations on freedom be equally accepted as long as they were thought to be sociologically helpful?"[36] His reference to authoritarian government was especially significant in light of his two-and-a-half-page discussion of Communism that had preceded his argument on abortion. He said that Communism was "a leap into the area of nonreason. It is its own kind of Nietzsche game plan."[37]

As Schaeffer issued a call for Christians to resist the slide toward authoritarianism, he changed his rhetoric about secular humanism. Previously, he had characterized humanism as a worldview in competition with the Christian worldview. In *How Should We Then Live?* he moved beyond secular humanism as a valueless, unfortunate, and dangerous worldview, to secular humanism as a concerted effort, a plot, and a war, carried out against Christian values. Humanism as an ideology gave way to humanists as real people conspiring against the faith. "Humanists," he stated flatly, "have been determined to beat to death the knowledge of God and the knowledge that God has not been silent, but has spoken in the Bible and through Christ." More and more, from this time forward, Schaeffer spoke of "humanists" as an organized group of persons and even as agents of anti-Christian activity, whereas before he had spoken of "humanism" as a worldview that had developed slowly over time, often through the thought of well-meaning individuals such as Kierkegaard.

This call to arms against a flesh and blood army of humanists was a bold, and in some ways risky, turn for Schaeffer. With it he began to alienate Christian scholars and others who had been drawn to his apolitical philosophical critique of western intellectual history. In their place, Schaeffer began to solidify a popular constituency more inclined toward activism — and thus better suited for culture war. Schaeffer had learned from his fundamentalist heritage that a war against a visible army embodied by real people was much more energizing for populist foot soldiers than abstract arguments against dangerous, yet disembodied, ideas.

Consistent with his belief in a humanist conspiracy against the faith, Schaeffer argued that the loss of values leading to moral degeneracy could usher in a much more ominous threat: a small cadre of elite leaders who would arbitrarily decide what absolutes would replace the Christian consensus. "Some group or some person will fill the vacuum," he prophesied darkly. "An elite will offer us arbitrary absolutes, and who will stand in its way?"[38]

The shift in tone from the trilogy could hardly have been more stark. In the trilogy he had offered an apolitical analysis of ideas that had been developed by people who were for the most part long dead. In *How Should We Then Live?*, by contrast, he called Christians to actively resist an elite of living secular humanists who were forcefully replacing the Christian consensus with arbitrary absolutes. Yet this new approach was not very different from Schaeffer's earlier fundamentalist battles, which had always been directed not just against ideologies, but against living people and contemporary institutions, from Karl Barth in the 1950s to Clark Pinnock and Fuller Seminary in the battle for the Bible in the 1970s. Here again, there was continuity to Schaeffer's life along with apparent change.

In this latest battle, the only hope for America against the secular humanist elite was the "silent majority," which President Richard Nixon had named in his campaign for reelection in 1972. In the face of the counterculture that protested the Vietnam War, the president had said there was a silent majority of Americans who supported law and order and were patriotic defenders of their nation. But even this majority was problematic; Schaeffer saw it as divided into the Christian minority, who had a real basis for absolute values, and a majority who had only the two values of personal peace and affluence to guide them. The majority of the silent majority, Schaeffer believed, would give in to the loss of their liberties without a fight as long as their own lifestyle was not threatened. This left the Christians as the only real hope for resistance against the secular humanist elite.[39] Schaeffer saw only two alternatives for American culture: either society would return to its Christian base, or there would be an imposed order.

While he often talked about the threat of Communist authoritarianism around the world, his analysis seemed to suggest the threat of fascism, although he never used the term. "If further economic recessions come," he warned, "if fear of the loss of personal peace and prosperity increases, if wars and threats of wars intensify, if violence and terrorism spread, if food and other resources in the world become ever scarcer, . . . then the trend is speeded up."[40] This would seem to suggest the acceptance of an authoritarian government that would restore order and protect personal peace and affluence, not a Communist state that would deny people their private property through state ownership of the means of production. In the film, Schaeffer acknowledged that this type of elite authoritarian government would not be modeled after brutal dictators such as Hitler or Stalin; rather, American authoritarianism would be less overt and more subtly manipulative.[41] He almost seemed to be anticipating what one scholar in 1980 called "Friendly Fascism," an authoritarian regime that would seem as American as baseball and apple pie.[42]

While not naming clearly the type of authoritarianism America would experience, Schaeffer cited science and social science as part of the problem. His analysis was often consistent with George Orwell's *1984,* in which elite scientists, operating without the checks of a system of absolute values, attempt to use scientific advances to engineer utopia. Schaeffer spent an entire chapter of *How Should We Then Live?* citing everything from scientist Francis Crick's call for genetic engineering to Arthur Koestler's suggestion that a chemical be developed to rid humankind of aggression, to subliminal advertising aimed at controlling people's purchasing habits. In the absence of the absolute values necessary to support human freedom and dignity, all types of scientific manipulation would be considered by various elites. Having argued that modern science had been built on a Christian base, Schaeffer was now showing that modern science had gone wrong in the absence of Christian parameters that had sustained its beginning. Even in the absence of an authoritarian government such as Hitler's Nazi regime or Stalin's Soviet Union, the elites might control the masses through the unprincipled application of science.

Schaeffer saw a kind of non-conspiratorial conspiracy. "[T]o be looking only for the possibility of a clandestine plot opens the way for failing to see a much greater danger," he warned: "that many of those who are in the most prominent places of influence and many of those who decide what is news do have the common, modern, humanist worldview we have described at length in this book."[43] In other words, even if there is no intentional conspiracy of elites to inculcate the secular humanist worldview, since so many people in positions of influence and authority hold this worldview, their separate actions work in concert just as if they were conspiring intentionally.

In the end, Schaeffer had only general suggestions in *How Should We Then Live?* for how the silent majority should resist the secular humanist elite; a more specific program of resistance would have to wait until he wrote *A Christian Manifesto*. Rather, in *How Should We Then Live?* he urged Christians to do just three things, all of them quite vague: first, pay attention to their values to ensure that they were not sucked into the modern worldview with its existentialist methodology; second, act upon the correct Christian worldview; and third, look back to Christians during slavery and the Industrial Revolution such as Elizabeth Fry, Lord Shaftesbury, William Wilberforce, and John Wesley, all of whom spoke and acted against slavery and the non-compassionate use of accumulated wealth. In like fashion, Schaeffer suggested, Christians must speak out against the threat of authoritarian government and not be content to keep silent: "The danger in regard to the rise of authoritarian government is that Christians will be still as long as their own religious activities, evangelism, and lifestyles are not disturbed."[44] He ended the film by reiterating that the choices are between a biblical worldview and an order imposed by an authoritarian elite. Once again he emphasized that people act according to the ideas they have, according to their worldview. "The problem is not outward things," he said in closing. "The problem is having the right worldview and acting upon it — the worldview that gives men and women the truth of what is."[45]

Whatever Happened to the Human Race?

The second film and its companion book, both entitled *Whatever Happened to the Human Race?,* appeared in 1979. The film and book were done with C. Everett Koop, who was at the time surgeon-in-chief at Philadelphia Children's Hospital. Schaeffer and Koop had known each other since Koop had treated Priscilla more than thirty years before, but by 1977 they had not seen each other for fifteen years. They reconnected that year when Koop was speaking about abortion, infanticide, and euthanasia at York University in Canada and learned that Schaeffer was at the other end of the campus addressing the same issues. Koop completed his lecture and went over to the auditorium where Schaeffer was speaking, met Schaeffer with a mutual embrace, and suggested that the two get together soon. In June Koop went to L'Abri and met with Francis and Franky, whom he had treated for polio in the mid-fifties. Franky clearly had the next film in mind when he told Koop, "If you can talk as well as you can write, I think there are some things we can do together."[46] Koop gave a lecture to the L'Abri students, then he and Franky took a mountain walk, discussing ideas for a major project on human life issues. That evening they sketched out plans for a five-episode film series and book. Edith remembers Franky arriving early the next morning at the Schaeffer's chalet and excitedly telling Francis about Koop's lecture and the idea Franky and Koop had hatched. "Look — we have to do something, before it's too late," Edith recalls Franky telling his father. "We have to make a movie, combined with biblical answers."[47] As Koop put it, "Together, the Schaeffers — father and son — and I determined to awaken the evangelical world — and anyone else who would listen — to the Christian imperative to do something to reverse the perilous realignment of American values on these life-and-death issues."[48]

Franky and a partner, Jim Buchfuehrer, formed a new non-profit production company called Franky Schaeffer V (FSV) Productions. Filming started in August 1978. The first scene was shot at the Philadelphia city dump, followed by other scenes in the U.S., including several in Washington, D.C., then some in Europe and the Middle East, before the film wrapped up at L'Abri. Filming ended in early October; editing and production would take nearly a year.

The film opened in 1979 at the Academy of Music in Philadelphia, where Edith and Francis had attended their first orchestra concert together in 1933. The film tour was a four-month, twenty-city affair that finished in Nashville's Grand Ole Opry House in December. Typically, the film and seminars would last two to three days in each city, with Koop and Schaeffer lecturing and leading discussions after each episode.

The film begins with Koop doing surgery on an infant and Schaeffer's voice in the background saying that the value of human life that was based on the Judeo-Christian consensus was rapidly giving way to a humanist worldview. "The consensus of our society no longer rests on a Christian base, but upon a humanistic one," Schaeffer said in a familiar refrain. [49] The film and book graphically describe the abortion process to make clear that euphemisms like "ending a pregnancy" were merely a cover for the killing of human beings. While Koop describes the three basic abortion techniques, the film shows hundreds of dolls lying in what first appears to be melting snow. As the camera pans away, Koop is standing on a rock in the midst of the shallows of the Dead Sea. What appeared to be snow is actually salt, and viewers learn that Koop is standing where the ancient city of Sodom once stood.

At a time when evangelicals had not yet been energized about abortion, this was clearly an attempt to shock the audience into the realization of the gravity of the situation. And it seemed to work. Few Protestant denominations had taken a stand against abortion before 1980, as it was generally considered a Roman Catholic issue. Throughout the seventies, for example, America's largest Protestant denomination, the Southern Baptist Convention, issued a series of resolutions at yearly meetings that were so equivocating that they could be interpreted as moderately pro-life or moderately pro-choice. These resolutions deplored abortion on demand while maintaining that abortion should nevertheless be legal. In 1980, however, conservatives in the SBC engineered a clearly pro-life resolution that called for legal measures to stop abortion, including a constitutional amendment if necessary. Some of the key leaders of the SBC conservative movement had read Schaeffer and attest to his influence on their cultural and political activism.[50] Some Southern Baptist conservative leaders used the film in their churches.[51] That such a resolution by the largest Protestant denomination in America followed on the heels of the film version of *Whatever Happened to the Human Race?* does not prove a causal relationship, but his push against abortion certainly helped fuel the evangelical pro-life movement. Once again Schaeffer found himself on the leading edge of evangelicalism.

The book, like the film, offers as a common notion the idea that nations are judged historically by how they treat their most vulnerable people. The authors said that the reason they wrote the book was because "we feel strongly that we stand today on the edge of a great abyss."[52] The abyss was abortion and what it symbolized — the wholesale devaluation of human life. After three decades of surgery on children, many of them severely deformed at birth, Koop spoke with authority on the issue of the value of human life, even life with severe physical deformity.

The first half of the book was authored largely by Koop. He argued that the decline in value of life was the result of the worldview shift to relativistic humanism that Schaeffer had outlined in his earlier books. Unthinkable decisions to take human life had become thinkable, Koop said. Children, in particular, were subject to arbitrary decisions about the value of their lives. From child abuse to abortion to decisions to allow deformed babies to die, the trend was ominously toward a situation where the elites of science would decide who was fit to live and who should die.[53] Koop graphically depicted abortion as a new holocaust, one that would open the door for others: "The wide-open door of abortion-on-demand leads naturally to infanticide which leads naturally to euthanasia."[54]

In the movie Schaeffer and Koop argued from the assumption that America had previously rejected abortion from a broadly shared Christian consensus.[55] Research published since their film, however, seems to challenge their assumption. For two hundred years prior to the mid-nineteenth century — a period when, Schaeffer believed, America had operated on a Christian base — abortion had been legal in America. Early-term abortions during this period were considered of little moral consequence until "quickening," which was when the woman could feel the fetus move within her womb. Before the Civil War (1861-1865) many states outlawed only abortions after quickening, and most such laws deemed the post-quickening abortion to be merely a misdemeanor. There seems to have been no widespread Christian resistance to such lax laws against abortion. Only after 1860 did states begin passing more stringent anti-abortion laws.[56]

It may be that this post-1860 era was the Christian consensus to which Schaeffer and Koop referred, but as we will see in chapter eight, Schaeffer believed American was operating on a "Christian base" in its earliest days and beginning to *lose* that base by 1860. It is at least ironic that the most stringent laws against abortion were enacted when, according to Schaeffer's larger argument, America was losing its Christian base. One explanation may be that lax abortion laws were the result of inattention, not willful acceptance of the practice, and that the Christian consensus emerged as Americans became sensitized to the issue after the Civil War. The inattention could be explained by the fact that abortion in the nineteenth century was usually an induced miscarriage. While the moral gravity of an induced miscarriage may be the same as the dilation and extraction methods Koop described in the film, the explicitness of the latter method may well have alerted Christians to a moral problem that went previously unacknowledged. Whether there is evidence for such an explanation is unclear, but Koop and Schaeffer never made this argument. They seem rather to have assumed that strong anti-abortion laws exist wherever one finds a Christian consensus, which is nearly as problematic as assuming that strong anti-slavery laws have existed wherever there has been a Christian consensus.

That said, the logic of the argument that the legalization of abortion would lead to infanticide and euthanasia was not without persuasive evidence. Koop used his medical experience and research to show that already in the 1960s and 1970s doctors and hospital teams were making decisions to allow severely deformed newborn babies to die. Conversely, he told of many instances in which newborns with deformities were saved through heroic measures and multiple surgeries, eventually leading full lives. In one particularly poignant scene, Koop sat in his living room with several grown patients, all of whom had severe deformities at birth and would have been, in his view, candidates for infanticide. Koop said that the best way to determine if life is worth living for those with disabilities is to ask them. All, of course, were glad they were alive, and that their handicaps were addressed by Koop's surgery and their parents' care. Some were married, and all were highly functioning; some had visible deformities, while some looked normal and whole. Koop said that the young people all had serious problems at birth — one born without a rectum, another with no esophagus, some with cancer, lupus, short bowel, or other serious conditions. He said that there had been a shift from an emphasis on saving lives and alleviating the suffering of patients to, in some cases, the view that the doctor should alleviate the suffering of the other family members by ridding them of the burden of caring for the handicapped.[57]

In an arresting passage of the book, Koop quoted from a letter to *Newsweek* magazine. The letter was a response to a quote by a Yale University Medical School professor that had appeared in a previous issue. The quote read, "The public has got to decide what to do with vegetated individuals who have no human potential."[58] The response began, "I'll wager my entire root system and as much fertilizer as it would take to fill Yale University that you have never received a letter from a vegetable before this one, but, much as I resent the term, I must confess that I fit the description of a 'vegetable' as defined in the article 'Shall This Child Die?'"[59] The author of the letter had suffered severe brain damage at birth and had never been able to dress herself, toilet herself, or physically write; her secretary had typed the letter to *Newsweek*. Doctors had told her parents that there was no chance she would ever live a meaningful life, yet through extensive and expensive rehabilitation and education the physically vegetative woman had become a psychologist.[60] In both the film and book, Koop argued that it is not the prerogative of medical professionals to decide which lives can be meaningful. In the film, he said that he has known many patients with severe handicaps and deformities who are much happier than many normal individuals he has known. Physical wholeness, he said, is not a good predictor of happiness. The medical doctor's sole prerogative, therefore, was to do everything possible to preserve life.

In arguing that euthanasia would quickly follow infanticide, Koop and Schaeffer cited the famous Karen Quinlan case. In 1975 Quinlan was taken to a hospital by friends after she passed out from alcohol and drug consumption. She lapsed into a coma and was placed on a respirator. Believing Quinlan was in what today is called a persistent vegetative state, her parents requested that a judge allow them to take their daughter off the respirator so she could die. The New Jersey Supreme Court granted their request, and she was taken off the respirator in May 1976. But at the request of her father, Quinlan's feeding and hydration tubes remained intact. She lived for ten more years.[61] At the time of the Quinlan court battles, Koop had four young patients who matched some of the criteria used to judge Quinlan a vegetable. All these children, Koop said, went home well.[62]

In another segment from the film, a young man named Craig is shown walking on the beach, where he eventually meets up with Schaeffer and sits for a chat. Craig, the viewers learn, is a philosophy graduate from California State University, and at the time of the film was attending Covenant Theological Seminary. He was born with no left leg, dwarfed arms, and no hands. Craig said that when his dad saw him at birth, he said to his mother, "This one needs our love more." Craig was a poignant walking argument for choosing love over death for the handicapped.

The call to arms that Schaeffer had issued in *How Should We Then Live?* echoed in *Whatever Happened to the Human Race?* The authors' message was that the church must take a stand: "Those in the church who have not made these questions a burning issue have forgotten the church's centuries-old tradition of social action on behalf of the weak and the unwanted," Schaeffer and Koop wrote. As Schaeffer had in *How Should We Then Live?*, the authors again cited the nineteenth-century English anti-slavery agitator William Wilberforce as an exemplar of Christian resistance to dehumanization.[63] The lack of such resistance from twentieth-century Christians would allow the logical development to continue from abortion to infanticide to euthanasia. When the first German elderly, infirm, and retarded were killed in the gas chambers by the Nazis in the 1930s, there was no outcry from the medical profession or the people of Germany, and it was "not far from there to Auschwitz."[64] In Nazi-occupied Holland, by contrast, the Dutch often distinguished themselves by defending their Jewish countrymen: "The Dutch resistance movement, armed only with great courage and a few typewriters, stood against the evil of its day."[65] In the final segment of the second tape, Schaeffer stands in front of the Capitol in Washington, D.C., tying abortion, infanticide, and euthanasia together, warning, "This final step of the carrying out of this low view of the human life may be closer than we think."

In the book version of *Whatever Happened to the Human Race?* Schaeffer used L'Abri as an example of a community that valued all human life, where unwed mothers were taken in and children cared for. In a scene that would be parodied by Franky in his novel *Saving Grandma,* Schaeffer recounted briefly how his mother had moved to L'Abri and eventually needed constant attention and care. Students and others there took turns playing checkers with her, reading to her, and caring for her in other ways (and, as Franky tells it, listening to her disparage Francis). Koop and Schaeffer challenged their readers and viewers first to resist the practice of abortion and infanticide, then to be willing to offer Christian hospitality and care for others who might be tempted to abort fetuses or allow severely deformed infants to perish.

In the film, Schaeffer attempted to tie the issues of abortion, infanticide, and euthanasia to slavery. One scene shows slaves walking up the steps of the modern Supreme Court building, while Schaeffer's voiceover says that slavery was based on economics. Blacks were viewed as non-human for economic reasons. "Apparently, in every age, there's always someone branded as sub-human," he intoned. "It once was the black; later the Jew; today it is the unborn and the child."[66] He referred again to the *Dred Scott* decision to show that the Supreme Court is sometimes wrong, and he reminded viewers that many churches were passive in the face of slavery, and that some even supported it. Likewise, in our own time, he said, some segments of the church favor infanticide. He then cited a task force of the Anglican Church in Canada that concluded it could be morally right to allow a newborn to die if he or she has serious brain damage. "This is humanism bringing forth inhumanity," he said. It should remind viewers of those who defended slavery by arguing that Africans were not human.[67]

The second half of the book version of *Whatever Happened to the Human Race?* was written mostly by Schaeffer and consisted of his basic worldview argument tied to human-life issues. Abortion, infanticide, and euthanasia were the natural consequences of a culture that had lost its Christian base and no longer had any justification for the dignity of human beings. The corresponding segment of the film begins with a cartoon version of the Broadway show tune "Anything Goes." Schaeffer said that the inhumanities explored in the previous episodes came about because of the worldview of philosophic materialism, which he defined as everything being made up of matter, nothing more. Sometimes it is called naturalism, he continued, because it says no supernatural exists, while at other times this worldview is called humanism, because it puts man at the center. Whatever one calls it, he concluded, this worldview is the basis for society today.

In both the book and the film Schaeffer argued that in a materialistic and relativistic worldview, human beings are machines with no innate dignity. "It was the materialistic world-view that brought in the inhumanity," he wrote in the book; "it must be a different world-view that drives it out."[68] Here, as in the trilogy and *How Should We Then Live?*, we see again Schaeffer's tendency to interpret the actions of human beings as direct products of their thinking. Human beings are rational creatures, according to this view, and they act according to the ideas in their minds. This is a surprising emphasis for a Calvinist such as Schaeffer, who generally believed that even when human beings had the correct worldview they would still be prone to selfishness that could lead to decisions inconsistent with their moral standards, such as abortion for convenience. Moreover, the historical example of slavery, which he used repeatedly, should have alerted him to the fact that even when people have a Christian worldview — even a Calvinist worldview — they can engage in grotesquely dehumanizing activities. Some of the best southern Reformed preachers and theologians, such as Robert Lewis Dabney, defended slavery. Still, as presented in *Whatever Happened to the Human Race?*, the problem was a worldview shift to materialistic and relativistic secular humanism, and the remedy was the reestablishment of the Christian base that had been lost in the twentieth century as a result of the ideas of the Enlightenment that had spread throughout the culture.

By the time Schaeffer wrote and filmed *Whatever Happened to the Human Race?* he had nearly stopped talking about the Renaissance, instead attributing the disastrous worldview shift solely to the Enlightenment. The Enlightenment enthroned reason and created a false optimism about what humankind could achieve through science, he now argued. The emphasis on autonomous human reason led to relativity, then to the abandonment of reason for the existential method. The existential method located meaning in experience, with no concern for whether there was anything real behind it. It was experience for experience's sake. This had come into the church, Schaeffer argued, as even evangelical theology more and more emphasized religious experience instead of truth articulated in propositions.

While Schaeffer had argued throughout his career that Christianity was the only worldview that answered adequately all the big questions, in the book version of *Whatever Happened to the Human Race?* he went so far as to say that this was the reason people should choose the Bible and the Christian worldview. In a remarkable passage, Schaeffer outlined briefly how the scientist considers various hypotheses as possible answers to a particular scientific question, then advocated that people do the same with worldviews. When a particular hypothesis is proven true by the scientific method, the hypothesis becomes a scientific law. "The same principle applies, so Christians maintain, when we consider the big questions. Here are the phenomena. What key unlocks their meaning? What explanation is correct?"[69] The only alternatives to the Christian worldview, he said, are materialistic humanism and the pantheism of Eastern religions, but neither can answer all the big questions. He even said that Christians believe scripture to be objectively true "*because* we have found that it does give answers both in knowledge and in life."[70]

Was Schaeffer suggesting that Christians begin with no assumption that the Bible is true, instead testing the Bible against the important questions to see if it were in fact a viable explanation? When he was discussing the explanatory power of the Christian faith, he often implied, and in this instance actually said, that Christians believe the Bible is absolutely true because it best explains the phenomena before us. Philip Yancey of *Christianity Today,* among others, found this rational and scientific way of arriving at the Christian worldview odd. "One puzzling aspect of Schaeffer's work is the downplaying of the nonrational (not irrational) aspects of the gospel," Yancey wrote the same year that *Whatever Happened to the Human Race?* appeared. "Schaeffer seems to rely on the power of reasoning, as if the only way a person could come to Christ is by arguing himself into the Kingdom. After all, many of the gospel's most salient features — unearned grace and unmerited sacrifice, for example — would not be arrived at on the basis of logic from natural revelation."[71] Yancey asked where in Schaeffer's thought was the sense of longing that had led C. S. Lewis to the Christian faith.

Perhaps in an effort to balance out his statement that Christians accept the Christian worldview because it best explains the phenomena before them, later in the book Schaeffer warned against accepting the Christian worldview for utilitarian reasons — because, say, it would improve society. He said that while true Christianity could indeed stop the cultural drift toward social degeneracy and authoritarian government, it would not do so if Christianity were only being promoted as useful by those who do not really believe the faith. As was so often the case, the key to interpreting Schaeffer was to keep in mind what point he was trying to make at any given time. He often became so narrowly focused on a single issue that he failed to hear the broader implications of what he said or wrote.

Much of Schaeffer's section of *Whatever Happened to the Human Race?* was a brief condensation of his basic argument for how the worldview of the West came to be humanistic. The end result of humanism was the "meaninglessness of all things and the relativity of morals."[72] Although evolution was not prominent in Schaeffer's argument in either the book or the film, he worked it in where he could, saying that evolution made human beings feel superior to other forms of life and gave an illusion of progress. Since it was part of the materialistic worldview, however, evolution really offered no basis on which to judge human beings as a higher form of life. "Higher" and "lower" have no meaning when there is no transcendent standard by which to make an evaluation. Moreover, "No one has offered to explain, let alone demonstrate it to be feasible, how the impersonal plus time plus chance can give personality. We are distracted by a flourish of words — and, lo, personality has appeared out of a hat."[73] In the film he stressed that evolution cannot explain the "mannishness of man," the creativity and ability to verbalize that make human beings qualitatively different from other forms of animal life.

Only in the last few pages of *Whatever Happened to the Human Race?* did Schaeffer and Koop reiterate the call to action Schaeffer had put forward in *How Should We Then Live?* Together they urged Christians to stand firm in the faith, even if it meant career sacrifice. In the business world one must be ethical, and in the academy the sociology professor must refuse to teach social determinism, even if it meant missing a promotion. The pastor must be willing to lose the pulpit rather than cave in to liberal theology. In a reference to political action that foreshadowed Schaeffer's next book, *A Christian Manifesto*, Schaeffer and Koop wrote, "Faithfulness to the Lordship of Christ means using the constitutional processes while we still have them. . . . The Lordship of Christ means using these processes to speak and to act on the basis of the principles set forth in the Bible."[74] Human-life issues presented Christians with their greatest moral test of the twentieth century, and they must not fail, the authors said. Schaeffer and Koop hoped that in the future people would look back at the end of the twentieth century and see that in the midst of the decline of respect for human life, one group stood in resistance.[75]

Whatever Happened to the Human Race?, in both film and book versions, was among Schaeffer's final projects, and it was in many ways a deep disappointment for him. A reviewer wrote in *Christianity Today*, "Not that the Schaeffers' popularity has waned — their books are selling as well as ever. But the new film seminar series, *Whatever Happened to the Human Race?*, has fallen flat when compared with the first series, *How Should We Then Live?*"[76] According to the review, only seven hundred people attended the seminars held at Madison Square Garden, fifteen hundred in Chicago, and seven hundred in Houston. Noting the twenty-eight-dollar price for the two-day series, the reviewer asked, "Do Christians really want to know that much about euthanasia, infanticide, or abortion?"[77] Low turnout meant financial problems, as auditorium rental costs outstripped revenue from ticket sales. In separate accounts, Edith and Francis attributed the low interest level to apathy among Christians and even opposition from Christian leaders who did not want their comfortable status in society jeopardized by the film's radical message.[78] Still, the Schaeffers were cheered by the effect the film seemed to have on those who did attend. Both believed that the enthusiasm for the film eclipsed anything they had ever seen in their forty-five years of ministry together. Moreover, they were pleasantly surprised when the film was shown across England and venues were filled to capacity.[79]

Koop was optimistic about the success of the film. He noted that the book had sold fifty thousand copies by 1991 when his memoirs appeared, and that thousands had seen the film and subsequent video series. He estimated that about 45,000 people attended the initial tour in 1979 alone, and he also said that for many years thereafter people frequently came up to him and said something like, "I never understood the sanctity of life until you made it clear in those seminars built around *Whatever Happened to the Human Race?*"[80]

For his part, Schaeffer would only live five more years after the film's appearance, so he did not have the benefit of Koop's longer view of the impact of the film. But in retrospect, there is little doubt that Koop is correct. Evangelicals in the first decade of the twenty-first century have been among the most solidly pro-life constituencies in America, rivaled only by the Roman Catholic Church, and Schaeffer deserves much of the credit for mobilization of evangelicals on this issue.[81]

With *How Then Should We Live?* and *Whatever Happened to the Human Race?* Schaeffer had come a long way from his engagement with the counterculture. He was no longer perceived primarily as an intellectual leader and politically independent prophet of culture; now he was becoming a full-blown Christian Right activist. The final step in that public journey would be *A Christian Manifesto*.

CHAPTER EIGHT

A Manifesto for
Christian Right Activism

During the filming of *Whatever Happened to the Human Race?* Schaeffer was exhausted much of the time. In the film he appears to be out of breath frequently as he speaks on camera. Film crew and family members attributed the fatigue to the strain of the work and the heat, especially in the scenes filmed in the Middle East. Back in Switzerland for the final segment, Schaeffer donned a jacket that was much too large for him. Franky was puzzled because it was the same jacket his father had used at the beginning of the film. Schaeffer stepped onto the scales to find he had lost twenty-five pounds. Alarmed, he went to Swiss doctors, who sent him to the Mayo Clinic in Rochester, Minnesota. A week of medical tests in mid-October 1978 determined that he had cancer of the lymph system, a tumor the size of a football, and cancer cells in 30 percent of his bone structure.[1] The Schaeffers moved into an apartment in Rochester, and Francis began chemotherapy immediately. The cancer went into remission periodically, and Schaeffer would live an active life for nearly six more years.

Throughout his life, according to his son, Francis had been easily annoyed and given to complaining. But while cancer now ravaged his body, it seemed to strengthen his spirit. He faced the disease with great courage, stopped complaining, became less prone to bouts of depression, and generally seemed thankful for the life he had left to live.[2] Now he would tie up any remaining disconnect between his fundamentalist militancy and his intellectual critique of western culture. The result was a distinct form of Christian activism.

192

John Whitehead and Francis Schaeffer

The films and accompanying books set the stage for Schaeffer's book *A Christian Manifesto,* his call for Christian Right activism. The story of how the book came into existence includes Rutherford Institute founder John Whitehead. Originally from Tennessee, Whitehead grew up in Peoria, Illinois, then attended the University of Arkansas for his undergraduate and law degrees. A hard-partying drug user and by his own account an anti-establishment quasi-hippy, Whitehead had a dramatic conversion to Christianity in the early 1970s after reading a copy of Hal Lindsey's *The Late Great Planet Earth,* which Whitehead had purchased because he thought it was science fiction.[3] After becoming a Christian, he continued to fight the establishment by taking cases representing Christians who had experienced discrimination for their faith. This would be Whitehead's legal niche.

In 1976, while living in California, Whitehead met Rousas John Rushdoony, the father of Christian Reconstructionism. While all Reformed Calvinists and virtually all traditional Christians believe that the moral law of the Old Testament is still binding for Christians under the New Covenant, Reconstructionists believe that Old Testament civil law is the norm as well. Simply put, they believe that the goal of politics is the eventual reinstitution of Old Testament law as the legal system of the United States. Their agenda includes the death penalty for homosexuals, adulterers, and even incorrigible children. To be fair, most Reconstructionists do not believe that the Old Testament can or should be imposed by force in America. Instead, they believe that over time Americans will become so disenchanted with their permissive society that they will turn away from big government toward local communities and families as the foundation for society. This decentralization will set the stage for a widely embraced political system based on biblical law.[4]

Schaeffer was enamored with Rushdoony's writings in the 1960s, and it is quite likely that Schaeffer's belief that the United States was founded on a Christian base came in part from Rushdoony. People who lived at L'Abri recall Schaeffer talking about Rushdoony and being very excited about his books.[5] Schaeffer eventually lost interest in Reconstructionism because Rushdoony was a postmillennialist — that is, he believed that the kingdom of God will be built on earth before Christ's second coming. Schaeffer, like virtually all fundamentalists, was a premillennialist. Schaeffer also believed Rushdoony's Reconstructionism would necessitate the merger of church and state, which Schaeffer opposed. Specifically, Schaeffer believed that only the principles, not the actual details, of Old Testament civil law were applicable under the New Covenant, which meant that specific laws, such as the one requiring the stoning of adulterers, were not applicable in America. "The moral law [of the Old Testament], of course, is constant, but the civil law only was operative for the Old Testament theocracy," he wrote in 1981. "I do not think there is any indication of a theocracy in the New Testament until Christ returns as king."[6]

Rushdoony lived three hours north of Los Angeles in Vallecito, where he headed an organization called the Chalcedon Institute. He drove to Los Angeles every Sunday to preach to a congregation that met at the Westwood Chapel Mortuary, the famous resting place of actress Marilyn Monroe, among others. Rushdoony wrote prolifically and had an impressive library of books in his home, many of them pertaining to theology, philosophy, and the American founding. In the late seventies, Whitehead began attending Rushdoony's Westwood Chapel church and at the same time began to read Schaeffer's views concerning the relationship of Christianity to the American founding. Like Schaeffer, Whitehead also became fascinated by this issue and started traveling to Rushdoony's institute to do research of his own. He never took Rushdoony's ideas about the establishment of Old Testament law seriously, especially capital punishment for homosexuals and incorrigible children, but he did come to believe with Rushdoony that the American founding had much deeper Christian influence than secular academics and media figures believed. Whitehead would eventually use the material he discovered at Rushdoony's home as the basis for his own first book.

Whitehead came to the notice of Christian activists when he won a case in San Francisco in 1980. The tiny First Orthodox Presbyterian Church had dismissed its organist on the basis of his sexual orientation. The organist sued the church on the basis of the city's ordinance outlawing discrimination against homosexuals. A judge agreed with Whitehead that the church had a First Amendment right to hire the organist of its choice based on the moral and theological views the church espoused. The judge ruled that the anti-discrimination ordinance could not, therefore, be applied against churches.[7]

Shortly after the case, Franky called. Whitehead was shocked. He had moved from California to Washington, D.C., and was renting a small nondescript office from the National Association of Evangelicals, barely making a living. He could scarcely believe that Franky would call him on the phone.[8] According to Whitehead, Franky said, "Hey, man. It's good to talk to you. I read your brief in the San Francisco case and tracked you down. I want you to work with my dad and me."[9] Whitehead was intrigued, to say the least. Franky then told Whitehead, "You've gotta write a book on this, John. You could call it *The Second American Civil War*. My dad and I will help you get it published."[10] Whitehead and Franky met in Washington, and Franky invited Whitehead to an April 1981 meeting of the Christian Legal Society at Notre Dame, where Francis gave an address to about five hundred lawyers, urging them to get involved in abortion and church-state issues. In the speech, he mentioned Whitehead and the San Francisco case prominently. Whitehead and Schaeffer met afterward, and Schaeffer invited Whitehead to his hotel room to discuss their work together. This sort of attention was all new to Whitehead, who had not yet made much of a name for himself in evangelical circles.[11] The result of these conversations with Franky and Francis would be Whitehead's *The Second American Revolution* (a title he liked better than the one Franky suggested). Before that book came out, however, Whitehead had another book to work on: he would play a major role in Schaeffer's *A Christian Manifesto*.

Whitehead completed the manuscript for *The Second American Revolution* in 1981 and sent a copy to the Schaeffers. Franky wrote back and said his dad loved it and even cried when he read it. Eventually Franky asked Whitehead if he would like to help Francis write his next book in exchange for an advance and a portion of the royalties. Whitehead would do the research for *A Christian Manifesto,* then let the Schaeffers work the material into book form. During the process, Whitehead told Schaeffer he wanted to adapt some of his material from *The Second American Revolution* manuscript and put it into *A Christian Manifesto* so that *Manifesto* would be a precursor to Whitehead's as-yet-unpublished manuscript. Schaeffer thought this was a good idea, so Whitehead developed about 130 pages of research and sent it off to the Schaeffers. Once Schaeffer received the material, he wrote to Whitehead requesting further assistance in tracking down citations for some of the quotations.[12] Schaeffer incorporated Whitehead's material into a revised version of the speech he had given to the Christian Legal Society at Notre Dame.

Because Schaeffer was so well known, *A Christian Manifesto* appeared a few months before Whitehead's book, even though *The Second American Revolution* was completed before *A Christian Manifesto* was even an idea. Whitehead was shocked at how quickly the whole process moved once the Schaeffers got on board. Schaeffer hoped that the two books and Franky's film version of *The Second American Revolution* would form a "triad that the Lord can use as a unit."[13]

A Christian Manifesto

Schaeffer saw *Manifesto* as a continuation of *How Should We Then Live?* and *Whatever Happened to the Human Race?*, the three forming a second Schaeffer trilogy. He saw *How Should We Then Live?* as carrying his analysis of western thought into a discussion of how the worldview shift during the modern era had transformed society, government, and law. *Whatever Happened to the Human Race?* was the next step, showing how the worldview shift to modern arbitrary law and humanistic medicine came together on human-life issues. Schaeffer said that *Manifesto* was the logical third step: "What is the Christian's relationship to government, law, and civil disobedience?"[14] Like all of Schaeffer's books dealing with ideas, *Manifesto* was a worldview book. He emphasized again that Christians must see things whole, not in bits and pieces. He surveyed the two competing worldviews, the Christian and humanistic, and said once again that there was no way to blend them.

A brief but new element in this argument was his mention of Philip Jacob Spener's seventeenth-century Christian pietism. Pietism emphasizes the heartfelt, experiential nature of the Christian faith, sometimes to the detriment of doctrinal and intellectual elements. While Schaeffer acknowledged that pietism began as a healthy protest against a dead orthodoxy, he believed that the movement played into the divorce of ideas from experience that he had been critiquing since the trilogy.[15] In other words, much like modern secular philosophy from Kierkegaard forward, pietism put experience "upstairs," separated from the arena of facts, ideas, and science, which were "downstairs" in Schaeffer's schema. The result was that many Christians meant something quite different from Schaeffer when they used the word "Christianity." Pietistic evangelicals meant "experience" when they spoke of the Christian faith; Schaeffer meant "worldview," and he believed that thinking of Christianity as merely an experience played into the hands of humanists, because pietism relegated the Christian faith to the realm of the private and subjective.

Schaeffer criticized Martin Marty, a leading historian of Christianity in America, and himself a professing Christian, for playing on this confusion. Schaeffer cited an open letter Marty had published in *The Christian Century* magazine in which Marty argued for the multiple meanings of the term "humanist" against Schaeffer's and others' more simplistic use of the term. Marty believed that there could be such a thing as Christian humanism, but Schaeffer would have none of this. He accused Marty of deliberately eradicating the stark distinction between Christianity as propositional and rational and the humanistic worldview that was subjective and non-rational. In so doing, Schaeffer wrote, "Dr. Marty has come down on the nonreligious humanist side, by confusing the issues so totally."[16]

As he had in *How Should We Then Live?*, once again in *Manifesto* Schaeffer attributed American democracy to the Reformation, and here again he stressed the work of the seventeenth-century author Samuel Rutherford and his book *Lex Rex*. The Reformation, Schaeffer argued, reasserted the Christian base, paving the way for what he called "form and freedom" — individual freedom within a society that maintained order. He was convinced that this was a contribution attributable solely to the Reformation. Only with a Christian worldview, Schaeffer believed, could freedom be kept from degenerating into chaos. Thus the replacement of the Christian base of American government with the humanist worldview would lead either to chaos — the lack of form — or to authoritarian government — the lack of freedom.

Schaeffer took Rutherford's belief that in a just society "law is king" and traced this idea through American founder John Witherspoon, like Rutherford a Scots Calvinist. "John Witherspoon knew and stood consciously in the stream of Samuel Rutherford," Schaeffer wrote. Schaeffer believed that the Christian influence of Rutherford was crucial, as it shaped Witherspoon's work on the Declaration of Independence and influenced various committees of the founders. As Schaeffer put it, "This linkage of Christian thinking and the concepts of government were [*sic*] not incidental but fundamental."[17]

Nowhere in any of his works does Schaeffer give the Enlightenment credit for the development of democracy. Even when Schaeffer mentioned John Locke, the greatest of the Enlightenment thinkers, he attributed the positive aspects of Locke's thinking to his having drawn heavily from Rutherford's *Lex Rex*. Because the deist Thomas Jefferson was a disciple of Locke, Schaeffer credited much of Jefferson's thinking to Rutherford through Locke. When the founders wrote of "certain inalienable rights," they knew those rights were created by God, which to Schaeffer was proof of the Christian influence in the founding that was attributable to Rutherford.[18]

This Christian influence of the founding era was in no way eclipsed by the First Amendment. Schaeffer said the amendment had two primary purposes. First, it ensured there would be no established national church, and second, it stated that the government should not interfere with the free exercise of religion. In the late twentieth century, Schaeffer argued, the First Amendment was being used by humanists to do exactly the opposite of what its second purpose was. "Today the separation of church and state in America is used to silence the church," he wrote. "To have suggested the state separated from religion and religious influence would have amazed the Founding Fathers."[19]

The influence of Whitehead and Rushdoony is unmistakable here. Schaeffer acknowledged freely that not all the founders were Christians, but he believed they worked from Christian concepts and values nevertheless. One also hears clearly the influence of Franky, who was an absolutist on these issues, especially on abortion, the issue that drove the increasingly activist Francis.[20] In one of his more stark passages, he ended chapter two with these words: "And until the takeover of our government and law by this other entity, the materialistic, humanistic, chance world view, these things remained the base of government and law."[21]

It is not clear where Schaeffer first latched onto Rutherford, but

Whitehead learned about Rutherford from Schaeffer, and then Whitehead read Rutherford for himself and fed the material back to Schaeffer in the research for *Manifesto*.[22] Significantly, virtually no professional historian, Christian or secular, believes that Rutherford had significant influence on the American founding. Schaeffer's emphasis on Rutherford, therefore, is highly idiosyncratic, and it would probably be safe to say that whenever one sees a Christian author discussing Rutherford, the author probably has been influenced by Schaeffer and/or Whitehead. As we will see, a number of Christian scholars quickly took issue with Schaeffer's emphasis on Rutherford.

Having laid out briefly the Christian base of the original American form of government, Schaeffer then traced its demise. He began chapter three with the words, "And now it is all gone." Schaeffer saw two major steps in the eradication of the Christian base. First, in the nineteenth century there was an influx of non-Protestants. "After about 1848," he wrote, "the great influx of immigrants to the United States meant a sharp increase in viewpoints not shaped by the Reformation Christianity."[23] This was the beginning of Christian pluralism.

It should be pointed out that Schaeffer said that religious freedom means freedom for all people, not simply Protestants or even all Christians. Still, the anti-Catholicism that had always been just below the surface in many of Schaeffer's writings did not go unnoticed. Writing in *Newsweek,* religion correspondent Kenneth Woodward referred to this section of *Manifesto* and commented, "Schaeffer's note of rankled Protestant nativism reveals more about the emotional underpinnings of the modern fundamentalist movement than do any of the more polished position papers of the new religious right."[24]

But Schaeffer was not focusing on ethnic differences. He was more concerned that this greater mix of religions in America had led to a new understanding of pluralism, one that lays all options before people and urges them simply to choose whichever worldview they prefer. "Pluralism has come to mean that everything is acceptable," he wrote.[25] This new vision of pluralism eventually pervaded all aspects of personal ethics, social ethics, and law. As he had since *How Should We Then Live?*, Schaeffer referred to "sociological law," by which he meant law that was grounded merely in what was convenient for society rather than in a transcendent morality. As he had argued strenuously in *Whatever Happened to the Human Race?* and the film version of *How Should We Then Live?*, the Supreme Court's stance on abortion was the clearest example of sociological law.

The second major step in the move away from the Christian base of the American government, and by far the more important of the two, was the development of secular humanism. Schaeffer called this the "humanist religion," and he traced its development from Humanist Manifesto I (1933) through Humanist Manifesto II (1973). He quoted extensively from those documents to show that the authors and signatories believed their humanist worldview was a religion. He cited an example that would become ubiquitous in Christian Right literature throughout the 1980s and 1990s, and one that probably came from Whitehead's research: the Supreme Court case *Torcaso v. Watkins* (1961), which declared that secular humanism was a religion. *Torcaso* struck down a Maryland law requiring that state officeholders believe in God. A footnote appears in the majority opinion that lists secular humanism among several other non-theistic religions. The majority considered requiring belief in God an unconstitutional establishment of theism that would discriminate against believers in non-theistic faiths. Once in Christian Right literature via Whitehead and Schaeffer, this example has been widely used, often described erroneously as a Supreme Court decision holding that secular humanism is a religion, rather than as a mere footnote grouping secular humanism with other non-theistic faiths. The gist of Schaeffer's larger argument is that secular humanism is not one footnoted possibility among many, but rather the established religion of the state. "Ironically," he wrote, "it is the *humanist religion* which the government and courts in the United States favor over all others."[26]

The "Open Window" of Ronald Reagan and the Religious Right

The election of Ronald Reagan to the U.S. presidency in 1980, and the conservative swing that election signaled, provided what Schaeffer called an "open window" for the reassertion of the Christian worldview over humanism. Schaeffer's unabashed support for conservatives and the Republican Party seemed a marked departure for him. The progressive social and cultural causes we saw earlier, combined with his pro-life leanings, seemed to position Schaeffer as independent in his political leanings. In a less public way, however, the groundwork for Schaeffer's identification with the Republican Party had been laid in the early 1970s. Joanne Kemp, wife of prominent Republican congressman Jack Kemp, asked Edith Schaeffer to speak to a group of Washington wives of senators and congressmen sometime in the early seventies. Joanne then started a weekly class in which she taught Schaeffer's ideas to a group of twenty-five women. Through their wives, Jack Kemp and Francis became friends, and the congressman invited Schaeffer to speak at luncheons of representatives and senators. The Schaeffers were also hosted in the White House by Gerald and Betty Ford during the Ford presidency in the mid-seventies, and Edith and Betty subsequently became friends.[27] At about the same time that *Manifesto* appeared, Schaeffer attended a dinner party in suburban Washington, where he met with Jack Kemp and Senator Paul Laxalt of Nevada, like Kemp part of the conservative wing of the Republican Party that was asserting its power under Reagan's leadership. According to Woodward of *Newsweek,* Schaeffer talked to Kemp and Laxalt about the possibility of Christians having to someday rise up in civil disobedience against the American state.[28]

When conservatives took control of the party with the nomination of Reagan in 1980 and inserted the pro-life plank into the party platform, Schaeffer's support for the party strengthened. Still, even as he implied that the new Republican ascendancy was good news for Christians, Schaeffer warned that Christians must oppose humanists, whether liberal or conservative. "As Christians we must stand absolutely and totally opposed to the whole humanist system," he wrote, *"whether it is controlled by conservative or liberal elements.* Thus Christians must not become officially aligned with either group just on the basis of the name it uses."[29]

Maintaining such independence would be easier said than done, especially when the abortion issue increasingly drew evangelicals into the conservative Republican camp. Schaeffer was loath to criticize even the most vocal and visible Christian Republican group, the Moral Majority, led by the Reverend Jerry Falwell. The Moral Majority had been founded in 1979 for the express purpose of getting conservative Christians and their allies involved in Republican politics. It was the first highly visible and influential organization of what came to be known as the Christian Right. In two passages in *Manifesto* Schaeffer vigorously defended the Moral Majority, implying that criticism of the organization was attributable to the liberal, secular media. "Some of us may perhaps have some questions about the Moral Majority and some of the things they [*sic*] have said," he wrote. "But I would say one thing we certainly must do is get our information about anything like the Moral Majority not from the secular media, which so largely have the same humanistic perspective as the rest of culture has today."[30] A few pages later he returned again to the Moral Majority, saying that whether readers agree or disagree with all the organization does, Falwell and the Moral Majority "have certainly done one thing right: they have used the freedom we still have in the political arena to stand against the other total entity. They have carried the fact that law is king, law is above the lawmakers, and God is above the law into this area of life where it always should have been. And this is part of true spirituality." Critics, he said, should try to "do it better."[31]

While publicly defending the organization, however, in private Schaeffer expressed his own reservations about Falwell and the Moral Majority. In late 1980 or early 1981, when Schaeffer was in the U.S., Falwell picked him up in his private jet, and the two spent about five hours together, during which time Schaeffer told Falwell of his concerns about the Moral Majority. First, he was worried about style: Falwell and the Moral Majority came on too forcefully, which Schaeffer believed would be used by critics to divert attention away from the issues and toward Falwell's fundamentalist style. This warning to Falwell was in keeping with Schaeffer's concern for three decades that Christians not exhibit the kind of public persona that Carl McIntire and others often had — an alienating factor for Schaeffer in his earlier break with fundamentalists. Second, Schaeffer was concerned that Falwell was getting into too many issues, thus diluting the Christian cause. Schaeffer believed that all Christians should be able to agree on human-life issues such as abortion, infanticide, and euthanasia; things that weaken the family; and government regulation of churches and Christian schools. Falwell, by contrast, spoke on many issues over which Schaeffer believed Christians could legitimately disagree. Schaeffer mentioned specifically the Strategic Arms Limitation Treaty (SALT) and gun control; he may have had taxes and economic policies in mind as well.[32]

Falwell vigorously defended the belief in a Christian America in ways that made even Schaeffer uncomfortable. A singing ensemble from Falwell's Liberty Baptist University toured the country in the early 1980s putting on programs emphasizing love of God and country, and Falwell held "Honor America" rallies that routinely wrapped the cross in the American flag. Schaeffer was concerned that such activities failed to make clear the difference between the use of Christian principles in government and the actual establishment of religion. He feared that Falwell's approach would lead to the charge that the Moral Majority wanted a theocracy. Privately, Schaeffer told Whitehead that Falwell had left himself vulnerable on this issue because he had not made clear enough distinctions between the American nation and the Christian faith.[33]

Without naming names, Schaeffer pressed his point in *Manifesto:* "[W]e must be definite that we are in no way talking about any kind of a theocracy. Let me say that with great emphasis. Witherspoon, Jefferson, the American Founders had no idea of a theocracy. That is made plain by the First Amendment, and we must continually emphasize the fact that we are not talking about some kind, or any kind, of a theocracy." Schaeffer went on to say that there is no basis for linking church and state in the New Testament; church-state union did not begin until the fourth century, under Emperor Constantine. "The whole 'Constantine mentality' from the fourth century up to our day was a mistake. . . . To say it another way: 'We should not wrap Christianity in our national flag.'"[34]

Such private and public disclaimers notwithstanding, Schaeffer's public defense of the Moral Majority in *Manifesto* and his open support for Reagan's "window" gave the appearance that he was part of the Christian Right, and many of his longtime followers shared this assessment. William Edgar believed Schaeffer was being drawn back into his fundamentalist past when Schaeffer got involved with Jerry Falwell. Edgar tried to explain to Schaeffer that Falwell and the others did not have the big-picture Christian worldview that Schaeffer advocated, and that their fundamentalism could not hold such a worldview. Edgar recalls Schaeffer responding that while the word "fundamentalist" was not popular, that was exactly what he was going to call himself. Schaeffer believed that he had a ministry to Falwell and could help him broaden his outlook and message. Edgar, however, saw the situation differently. He recalls, "A lot of us worried about this because it seemed as though he was falling into a default American right-wing conservatism, which we didn't recognize as the Schaeffer we had met in the sixties."[35] Edgar believes that the allure of politics and invitations to the White House and to other functions held by powerful political elites was heady stuff for Schaeffer. He believed he had a ministry to those in power, to be sure, but Schaeffer's path during this period was nevertheless worrisome for Edgar and others who had known Schaeffer at L'Abri.

There were at least two important trends to note regarding Schaeffer and the Christian Right. First, as we now know, there was developing a polarized political situation in which it was difficult for public figures to stand in the middle or outside the fray. As James Davison Hunter has argued concerning culture war in America, the middle voices tend to be lost as the extremes on the left and the right dominate the media.[36] As a very public figure, Schaeffer was pushed perhaps further to the right than he desired. Second, however, Schaeffer's own approach to issues, shaped as it was by his early fundamentalism, meant that he saw things in sharply contrasting either/or categories. He had been saying since at least *How Should We Then Live?* that there was a battle going on between two clearly identifiable camps, Christianity and humanism. And there was no question which camp he would join. By training, experience, or temperament, he was unaccustomed to taking mediating positions — all the more so when pushed by Franky, as he was during the rise of the Religious Right. Try as he might to distinguish himself from Falwell, the Moral Majority, and theocracy, he did not succeed in carving out a political stance that was distinct from the Christian Right. Rather, he became the movement's intellectual guru.

Civil Disobedience?

When Reagan was elected, no one could be sure that the "window of opportunity," as Schaeffer called it, would stay open. "What happens in this country if the window does not stay open?" Schaeffer asked. "What then?"[37] The answer was civil disobedience. Schaeffer cited a column by George Will in which the conservative columnist argued that Reagan's 1980 mandate was probably composed of roughly 20 percent ideological conservatives and 80 percent voting for an improved economy regardless of how the improvement was achieved. This dovetailed nicely with Schaeffer's sermon "Ash Heap Lives" and his book *How Should We Then Live?* where he argued that the supreme values of the majority of the silent majority were personal peace and affluence. In *Manifesto* he asked what might happen if an economic downturn, such as took place in the seventies, denied people these two cherished values. He answered: "I do not think there will be a return to the old liberalism of the last fifty years. Rather, my guess is that there will be some form of an elite authoritarianism."[38] As in *How Should We Then Live?*, Schaeffer here seemed to be suggesting the prospect of fascism. He alluded to the first century B.C. transition from the Roman Republic to the Roman Empire under Caesar Augustus — which, he noted, took place under the guise of constitutionalism. On the next page Schaeffer suggested that the elite authoritarian power in his own time might be the U.S. Supreme Court. The Court was already ruling under the guise of arbitrary sociological law; justices were making law themselves, and they had come to dominate the other two branches of government. (He hedged his prediction by adding that his main point was not to name the elite authoritarians but to warn of the possibility that the masses might embrace an authoritarian government if affluence were threatened.)[39]

In discussing civil disobedience, Schaeffer stressed how many times in history Christians had said "no" to the state. He cited the early Christians in the Roman Empire and then included several examples of Protestants who resisted the tyranny of Catholic states during the Reformation era. Among these he was especially taken with Scottish Reformer John Knox, one of Rutherford's forerunners in Scotland. As he had with Rutherford, Schaeffer got much of his material on Knox from Whitehead.[40] Knox was converted to Protestantism in Catholic Scotland before taking a church in England during the Reformation there in the 1540s. When Queen Mary I came to power in 1553, she attempted to turn England back to Catholicism. Highly visible Protestants such as Knox were the targets of Mary's repression of Protestantism, and many went into exile on the Continent. Knox left England for Geneva, where he studied with John Calvin. When Mary died and Queen Elizabeth I (1558-1603) came to power, many Marian exiles, as the Protestants in exile were called, returned to England, but not Knox. He had written a book entitled *The First Blast of the Trumpet against the Monstrous Regiment of Women*. Even though his primary target in the book was what he called the "evil trinity of Marys" — Mary I of England, Mary Queen of Scots, and the Virgin Mary — Knox had offended Elizabeth by his argument that a woman was not fit to be monarch. Unwelcome in England, Knox returned to Scotland and became the pastor of a burgeoning Calvinist revolutionary party that eventually overthrew Mary Queen of Scots and the Catholic party and instituted a Reformed government.[41] Schaeffer drew the connection between Knox and Rutherford: "And it was John Knox, an exponent of godly resistance in the face of tyranny, who planted the seeds that were later nurtured by such men as Samuel Rutherford." Schaeffer concluded this section on Reformation resistance by saying that wherever the Reformation flourished, there was civil disobedience.[42] The case was now clear: Knox influenced Rutherford, who in turn was responsible for much of what the American founding fathers believed about resistance to England. This reinforced and restated Schaeffer's basic argument that the American Revolution and subsequent U.S. Constitution were built on a Christian and Reformation base.

Since humanism had taken over and was subverting the Christian base of the American government, resistance was once again required of Christians, as had been the case during the Reformation. Rutherford had taught that since tyranny was satanic, failure to resist tyranny was disobedience to God. While Christians were always to be subject to the office of the magistrate, they were also required to resist the officeholder if the officeholder were tyrannical. "That is exactly what we are facing today," Schaeffer wrote. "The whole structure of our society is being attacked and destroyed."[43]

For Rutherford, there were three possible forms of civil disobedience. First, a citizen must use legal means of protest. If that failed, flight was an option. Otherwise, citizens may have to resort to force. While flight may have been an option in Rutherford's day, because of the reach of the modern state, it was unlikely to be effective in the twentieth century. There simply was nowhere a group of Christians could go that would be beyond the arm of the state. For Schaeffer, this left Christians as a corporate body with two alternatives: legal protest and armed defense. Legal protest was the most viable — at least at the moment. Schaeffer's primary object of protest by this time was legalized abortion, and the form of protest Schaeffer suggested was the withholding of tax payments that might be used to fund abortions. Schaeffer also suggested that the regulation of Christian schools that led to undue entanglement with the state might justify civil disobedience, although he did not suggest exactly what form this type of protest might take.

At the time Schaeffer wrote *Manifesto* the first Creation Science court case was taking place in Arkansas. The state had passed a law requiring that public schools give equal time to the teaching of Creation Science wherever evolution was taught. The Arkansas chapter of the American Civil Liberties Union (ACLU) sued in United States District Court, claiming that because Creation Science was derived from a literal reading of the book of Genesis by a small number of sectarian fundamentalists, it was actually religion masquerading as science. Schaeffer's main point in citing the Arkansas Creation Science case in *Manifesto,* however, was to argue that the lower magistrates — government officials in Arkansas — were being subject to the tyranny of the U.S. courts. "If there was ever a clearer example of the lower 'magistrates' being treated with tyranny, it would be hard to find," he wrote. He then suggested that if the federal courts ruled against Arkansas, this would be an occasion "for the state government to protest and refuse to submit." Comparing the case to the events that led to the Boston Tea Party in 1773, Schaeffer argued that the founders would have considered the case tyranny.[44] This brief discussion of lower and higher magistrates was part of the Calvinist right of resistance theory that had been developed by Theodore Beza and other associates of John Calvin in the context of the French Wars of Religion (1562-1598), when Huguenot Calvinist lower magistrates resisted the tyranny of the French Catholic monarchy.

Arkansas not only declined Schaeffer's suggestion that the state take the route of sixteenth-century Huguenots and resist the federal courts; the state did not even appeal the decision, largely because the Arkansas attorney general botched the case so badly. Louisiana, however, passed a Creation Science equal treatment law at about the same time as Arkansas. The Louisiana case eventually reached the Supreme Court, where the law was struck down as an unconstitutional advancement of religion — the same decision reached at the lower level in the Arkansas case. The Supreme Court ruled that the Louisiana legislature had passed the law specifically to advance religion.[45] In discussing the Arkansas Creation Science case, Schaeffer made the now-familiar Christian Right charge: "In the United States the materialistic, humanistic world view is being taught exclusively in most state schools."[46] He also identified federalism with the Reformation, saying that a major element of moving back to the Reformation base would be the curtailing of the power of the national government and empowering state and local governments.[47]

Following his discussion of the Arkansas case, in *Manifesto* Schaeffer asked, What if legal protest and civil disobedience did not work? When is it appropriate to use force? Again, Schaeffer turned to the issue of abortion, but he was reluctant to advocate force. On the abortion issue Christians should first support human-life legislation or a constitutional amendment that would protect the unborn; second, they should pursue the issue in the courts in an effort to overturn *Roe v. Wade;* third, they should engage in legal and political action against hospitals and clinics that perform abortions; and fourth, Christians should bring pressure to bear on the state through sit-ins and marches at legislative halls and the Supreme Court.[48] Indeed, Schaeffer never actually identified the point at which Christians in the 1980s should use force. Instead, he shifted again to a discussion of the American Revolution in an effort to show how Rutherford's principles proved that religion was a major influence in the Revolution and helped shape American founders who eventually resorted to violence. It was much safer to talk about eighteenth-century Americans resorting to force than to instruct Christians in the 1980s to take up arms. In making his case, Schaeffer cited Perry Miller, who had argued forcefully that religion was crucial in getting American colonists to endorse the Revolution. The closest Schaeffer would come to suggesting when Christians were to move beyond civil disobedience to defensive violence was to say, *"If there is no final place for civil disobedience, then the government has been made autonomous, and as such, it has been put in the place of the Living God."*[49] Still, Schaeffer admitted, "I really am not sure all that it means to us in practice at this moment." After all, he reminded his readers, the Reagan window was still open.[50]

Schaeffer's Break with Evangelical Scholars

Many mainline Christians and even some evangelicals testified in the Arkansas and Louisiana Creation Science cases on the side of the ACLU, saying that Creation Science was indeed more closely akin to a religious doctrine than a scientific theory. Among those who testified was evangelical historian George Marsden, whose testimony would rankle Schaeffer and prompt an anti-evangelical screed from Franky. Franky also wrote to an acquaintance, "It really does not matter what Mr. Marsden's motivation was for working with the ACLU. Like sin, motivation is to be judged by God. However, as human beings we are free to judge actions and issues. . . . There is no nice way to say that Marsden worked with the ACLU, given where the ACLU is currently coming from."[51] Marsden wrote to Schaeffer after reading *Manifesto,* commending Schaeffer for writing an important attack on secular humanism but also pointing out what Marsden believed were Schaeffer's historical errors in the book. Schaeffer, for example, had said incorrectly that the Arkansas law "allowed" the teaching of Creation Science, when in fact the law *required* the teaching of Creation Science wherever evolution was taught. For Marsden, this turned the case from free exercise, as Schaeffer saw it, to one of "establishment of the views of a rather small group of Christians."[52] Schaeffer wrote back to Marsden: "I must say, I think you were mistaken in taking an active part on the side of those who are tyrannically shutting out the possible freedom of Christians to speak in our public school system."[53] Schaeffer used the word "tyranny" four more times on that page of his letter to Marsden and even said that the tyranny of the public schools in America "is just as tyrannical in regard to Christian teaching as are the Soviet schools."[54]

For his part, Marsden could not reconcile the inconsistency between Schaeffer's professed aversion to theocracy and the establishment of religion on the one hand, and Schaeffer's belief that the Reformation had gotten things just about right on the other. Marsden reminded Schaeffer that the Calvinist version of the Reformation had sought a theocracy — or at least the establishment of Calvinism. "As it turns out," wrote Marsden, "you seem to favor not so much the Calvinist Reformation political views as the secularization of these in Locke and the American Declaration of Independence and Constitution, where the God-given moral principles are based on an appeal to natural law."[55] Marsden must have known that telling Schaeffer that he preferred the secularization of Reformation thought would pique Schaeffer's interest, to say the least. Marsden had corresponded with Schaeffer in the past and seemed to have an older letter at hand when he wrote to Schaeffer. From this older letter, Marsden anticipated that Schaeffer would accuse him, and by extension other scholars, of quibbling over fine points rather than standing together for the cause of evangelical Christianity against a hostile humanist culture. In anticipation of such an argument, Marsden told Schaeffer that the role of the scholar is different from that of the evangelist, and that one thing Christian scholars needed to do was to establish "complete credibility academically and intellectually, as Christians had done before the twentieth century."[56] Marsden was trying to persuade Schaeffer that quibbling over facts was necessary for Christian scholars to get the story straight and to be taken seriously in the academic community. Marsden held up Schaeffer's fundamentalist hero J. Gresham Machen as one who was a model of such scholarly accuracy.

Right on cue, Schaeffer responded exactly as Marsden had anticipated. He told of being criticized for speaking at a conference of dispensationalists in San Diego. Although Schaeffer was not a dispensationalist, he told Marsden, he was willing to stand shoulder-to-shoulder with dispensationalists for the cause of Christ and culture. The implication was that Christian historians like Marsden should stop quibbling and get on board with Schaeffer and the Christian Right. This, after all, was what Schaeffer had done with Falwell and the Moral Majority. Moving to the specifics of Marsden's letter, Schaeffer insisted that America's founding fathers did hold to a Reformation base, because they acknowledged God and His creation. Schaeffer went so far as to say that even men such as Benjamin Franklin were working more from a Reformation base than from the secularized views of Locke.[57]

A Christian Manifesto was putting Schaeffer at odds not only with Marsden but with several other Christian scholars who had been influenced by his earlier engagement with culture. The dialogue between Schaeffer and Marsden, and soon other Christian scholars as well, heated up in November 1982 after Woodward wrote a one-page article on Schaeffer in *Newsweek* entitled "Guru of Fundamentalism."

In the article Woodward quoted philosopher Arthur Holmes of Wheaton College as saying, "Many of our students arrive here with some exposure to Schaeffer. We then use Schaeffer as an example how not to do philosophy."[58] Holmes had said many positive things about Schaeffer also, none of which were quoted.[59] Wheaton professor and historian Mark Noll was also quoted in the *Newsweek* article as saying, "The danger is that people will take [Schaeffer] for a scholar, which he is not. Evangelical historians are especially bothered by his simplified myth of America's Christian past."[60] Like Holmes, Noll had also told Woodward much that was positive about Schaeffer's influence, but Woodward quoted only the negative.[61]

After the article appeared, Noll wrote to Schaeffer, "I apologize if my comment on your work in a recent NEWSWEEK did you unintended harm. I was quoted correctly but also very incompletely." Noll had told Woodward that Schaeffer was a very effective evangelist and a beneficial influence in the recent history of conservative Protestantism, and that Schaeffer had pioneered in fundamentalist-evangelical circles an interest in the importance of the history of ideas and in taking the arts more seriously.[62] Noll explained to Schaeffer why he told Woodward that Schaeffer was not a scholar: "[Y]our work does not take advantage of the crucial technical studies (often by Christians) which illuminate the past." Indeed, *Manifesto* was based on the research of Whitehead, a lawyer with little training in history, rather than the findings of professional historians. Noll told Schaeffer that after ten years of study on the American founding era he had concluded that "it is very difficult to see explicit biblical influence on the founding documents of the United States or in the political thinking of even the evangelical Founders like John Witherspoon." Noll pointed out that Witherspoon based his lectures at Princeton on Scottish thinker Francis Hutcheson, "whom [Reformed theologian Jonathan] Edwards rightly opposed for letting ideas of natural capacities become more important than convictions concerning regenerate righteousness."[63] In other words, even the thought of an evangelical Calvinist such as Witherspoon was based more on nature than on the Bible. Moreover, with regard to Rutherford, whom Schaeffer had held up as the key influence on the founders, Noll told Schaeffer that Rutherford and *Lex Rex* had no influence on Witherspoon, and by implication on any other founder as well. Noll also sent an essay entitled

"The Bible in Revolutionary America," which fleshed out his ideas on the subject.

The same day that Noll wrote to Schaeffer, he also fired off a letter to Woodward in which he lamented that the *Newsweek* religion editor had used none of the positive comments Noll had made about Schaeffer: "I wish your article on Francis Schaeffer could have quoted some of my positive estimates of his overall values. I would also have appreciated a stronger awareness of Schaeffer's beneficial place in the history of fundamentalists and evangelicals." Noll acknowledged, however, that he did not find Woodward's article offensive. "And," he wrote, "I think you are exactly right on the way in which the Far Right is co-opting Schaeffer. It might interest you to know that during the 1960s, Schaeffer was an inspiration to some evangelicals on the political left."[64]

Noll's letter to Schaeffer, meanwhile, touched off a yearlong round of correspondence among Noll, Marsden, and Schaeffer largely about the Christian influence on America's founding. Schaeffer responded to Noll in a twelve-page, double-spaced, typed letter. Schaeffer thought Noll had been naïve to think Woodward would not use the quotes the way he did, and he did not hesitate to tell him so. Schaeffer then responded primarily to Noll's essay on "The Bible in Revolutionary America." Schaeffer believed that Noll was demanding proof texts from the American founding fathers — in other words, passages in which the founders cited chapter and verse from the scriptures that influenced them. By way of analogy, Schaeffer said that while he often does not cite chapter and verse from the Bible in his writings, Noll would surely acknowledge that Schaeffer's work was biblically based. Similarly, the founders' writings could be biblical without explicit references to the Bible. Schaeffer said there were two errors to avoid: 1) to baptize the founders as wholly Christian, and 2) to insist on finding proof texts instead of broad biblical knowledge on the part of the founders in order to dismiss them as unbiblical. Schaeffer believed he avoided the first, but that Noll had slipped into the second error. Schaeffer insisted that America's founding fathers "showed more biblical influence politically than today's 'evangelicals' are showing in comprehension and leadership in today's cultural and political situation."[65] Slipped into the argument was Schaeffer's query as to why Noll could not acknowledge the biblical influence in the founders' work, especially when the stakes were so high in the cultural battles of the time. The idea of writing history without a political agenda — that is, merely to get the story correct — was difficult for Schaeffer to appreciate.

Noll rejected Schaeffer's analogy about proof texts, saying that he did not need to see proof texts to know that Schaeffer's commentary about the arts was biblically informed. Noll knew that Schaeffer had spent his life trying to bring his thinking under the authority of scripture. The situation with founders such as Jefferson and Franklin, however, was different, because they had spent their lives trying to *evade* the authority of scripture. James Madison was at best ambiguous about biblical authority in his thinking, while Witherspoon and other explicitly evangelical founders deliberately set aside the Bible and the whole category of revelation when they entered the political arena.[66]

Evidence of Christian thinking that Noll looked for but did not find in the founders included: "(a) the conviction that human groups, even those in the 'new world,' are crippled by sin and need to feel the effects of redemption, and (b) the conviction that it is God's specific and gracious providence which undergirds political life of whatever kind, and that it is not simply nature or human nature by itself that is the basis of politics."[67] Again, Noll emphasized that even the evangelical founders such as Witherspoon did not share these convictions. Instead their approach made it possible for nature to eat up grace, which "(as I have learned from you) is a recurring evil in western civilization."[68] Noll acknowledged that of course there was much biblical influence in early America, much more than in the late twentieth century, but simply no explicitly or even substantively Christian thinking about politics.

Knowing of Schaeffer's affinity for Abraham Kuyper, Noll contrasted the American situation in the nineteenth century with Kuyper's in the Netherlands. Noll believed that the tendency of Americans in the nineteenth century to see their culture and politics as based on Christianity had made it difficult for them to view America critically and to develop a thoroughly Christian approach to politics. Kuyper, by contrast, did not start with the view that his culture was basically Christian. He was, therefore, better able to develop a distinctly Christian center to fight for the truth against non-Christian presuppositions.[69] Kuyper founded a university and a political party based on Christian values; he did not assume that his culture needed only to shore up a Christian base that already existed.

In a passage that must have sent Schaeffer over the edge in his view that Noll, Marsden, and other Christian scholars were suspect in their views, Noll told Schaeffer that he did not see how Christians "who took the Bible seriously and who understood the course of events in the 1760's and 1770's as they really were, could have supported the American Revolution."[70] From Noll's perspective, Britain had demonstrated no tyranny over fundamental rights. "In this regard," he wrote, "the series of charges against George III in the Declaration of Independence constituted propaganda of the most irresponsible kind."[71] Noll then argued that, rather than looking to America's past for the answer to current moral dilemmas, it would be more helpful to look for continuity between the sins and omissions of America's founding and present realities. Whereas Schaeffer argued that *Roe v. Wade* showed that an America based on secular humanism had resulted in dehumanization, Noll pointed out the similarities between *Roe v. Wade* and the *Dred Scott* decision of 1857, where the Supreme Court ruled that slaves were property and thus could not gain freedom merely by escaping to free territory. After *Dred Scott,* no state or territory could outlaw slavery; after *Roe v. Wade,* no state could outlaw abortion. Noll also cited America's treatment of Native Americans as showing continuity between dehumanization in the past and present United States. "Early America was more theistic than popular culture today," he acknowledged, "but so inconsistently and with so many lapses is [*sic*] very difficult to regard it as a proper guide."[72]

Noll's wholesale refutation of the core argument of *Manifesto* created a kind of obsession in Schaeffer. Schaeffer would check the mail each day to see if there was a letter from Noll. If there was, he would immediately become absorbed in Noll's argument, then immediately write a response. He would read his response to others at L'Abri to see what they thought. He wanted the entire community to be engaged in the conversation. Some who were staying at L'Abri at the time worried that Schaeffer was too absorbed in the question of the Christian nature of America's founding and the criticism he was receiving from Christian scholars.[73]

Schaeffer's thin skin for criticism and his view that there was a culture war in which Christians must stand together revealed themselves in letters he wrote to Whitehead at the same time he was corresponding with Noll and Marsden. Schaeffer sent Whitehead a copy of a 20 November 1982 letter he had sent to Noll. In the cover letter to Whitehead Schaeffer referenced the *Newsweek* article, a letter Noll had sent to Schaeffer, and Noll's essay "The Bible in Revolutionary America." Schaeffer told Whitehead, "[Noll's] view of history and toning down the Christian influences in the early founding of the country is, unhappily, a rather prevalent one among a number of 'weak Christians' and does influence definitely in colleges like Wheaton and Calvin. Of course, if this view prevailed it would wipe out *A Christian Manifesto* and the book and film *The Second American Revolution* — happily his is not correct historically but it is one more threat in any kind of a clear stand today."[74]

A few months later Schaeffer began lumping Christian historians who did not believe in America's Christian-based founding with evangelicals who were weak on the inerrancy of scripture and with political liberals:

> I think with Noll and others like Ronald Wells at Calvin, however, that it is something deeper. I am convinced that they really wish to flatten out the difference between what the country was and what it is. If this is not conscious at least it seems to be an obsession. I am increasingly convinced that this stream of 'Christian historians' is one more element, along with those who devaluate the Scripture and those who confuse the socialistic program with the kingdom of God, who really must be challenged. This is not only a necessary thing if there is going to be a battle fought that needs to be fought against the collapse of our generation, but especially if the students in these Christian schools are really going to be any help at all in trying to turn around the sad situation which we face.[75]

Gone was Schaeffer's concern from the 1940s that fundamentalists such as McIntire focused too much on attacking other Christians and not enough on defending the faith against liberalism. As he had in the battle for the Bible a decade before, Schaeffer was again willing to divide evangelicalism in an effort to defend views he believed essential. Schaeffer was not saying anything about Christian scholars he would not tell them directly; in April 1983, he asked Noll outright, "I am curious — I have wondered whether you also hold this weakened view of Scripture?"[76] While Schaeffer said that there was no necessary connection between a weak view of scripture and a weak view of the Christian base of America's founding, the latter clearly made him suspicious about the former, and Schaeffer at times accused Noll of unwittingly joining the anti-Christian side of the culture war. "And to seem to join the deliberate debunkers who mean to cause the U.S., including the Christians, to be anesthetized as to the present consensus of all nature and no grace in the stream of life, is negative and not a positive contribution," he wrote to Noll. "In summary, I am sorry but I do think unless you change the direction of your writing toward the direction I have suggested above that you will prove to be as destructive in the midst of the severe needs of our day as you did in not realizing how Ken Woodward would use you as he did."[77]

Schaeffer's words revealed just how far apart he was from Noll, Marsden, and other Christian scholars. He had written *Manifesto* not as a dispassionate historical treatise, but as a tract in the culture wars. His agenda was to mobilize evangelicals politically. Noll and Marsden were far less concerned than Schaeffer about the immediate political consequences of their interpretation of the past. They wanted almost the opposite of what Schaeffer hoped to accomplish. Rather than inspiring evangelicals to act, Noll and Marsden wanted evangelicals to engage in sober reflection.

Even after having been accused essentially of siding with secularists against Christians, Noll continued to try to reach Schaeffer. He highlighted what they believed in common: that Christians err "when they divide life artificially into a sphere of nature and a sphere of grace"; that Kuyper and his party in the Netherlands were exemplary, but not errorless, in their effort to live all of life under the sovereignty of God; that late twentieth-century evangelicals were "woefully weak" largely because they had bifurcated their lives into a private religious realm and a public realm that seemed devoid of Christian thinking; and that the Enlightenment's emphasis on the autonomy of individuals and the autonomy of human reason was pernicious to the type of Christian living to which evangelicals aspired. Still, this left plenty of room for disagreement, which Noll summarized as his own view that the Christian founders were the first ones to blame for the nature/

grace compartmentalization; that the American Revolution was very different from the Reformation — in fact, that the American Revolution was closer to the French Revolution than to the Reformation in finding its ground of authority in nature, not scripture; that it was not helpful to compare the courage of the founders with the "spinelessness" of contemporary American evangelicals, because the question was not whether the founders were courageous, but whether they were biblical; and that the thinking of evangelical Christians had become nearly useless largely because of the privatization of their faith. The disagreement on this last point had to do with why evangelical thinking was so ineffective in political matters. Noll believed it was because evangelicals were "not self-critical about a political tradition which, for all its exemplary aspects, has never been a distinctly or particularly Christian one." By implication Noll included Schaeffer in this error. He replied to Schaeffer's charge that he was undermining Christian efforts: "In return, I would say that you should not undermine what you are trying to do by an unduly favorable opinion of the nation's founding."[78] This was the Noll-Schaeffer exchange at its hottest.

The very same day that Noll wrote those words, Marsden jumped back into the fray with his own letter to Schaeffer. Noll had been sending copies of the Noll-Schaeffer correspondence to Marsden, so the latter was privy to the discussion. He assured Schaeffer that while it was possible that anti-Christian forces might use Marsden's and Noll's scholarship for ill ends, this was certainly not their motive — nor was it something they could control. He reminded Schaeffer that there were super-patriotic evangelists in the Christian Right who were using Schaeffer's *Manifesto* in ways he did not intend, specifically to mix Christian faith and patriotism. Like Noll, Marsden again tried to explain the task of the Christian scholar as he saw it. The first goal is to be accurate, not to fashion a story that is useful for an agenda, however just that agenda might be. In a more critical vein, Marsden charged Schaeffer with his own inconsistency: throughout his career as a Christian author, Schaeffer had argued that Aquinas and theological liberals were similarly guilty of creating a nature/grace dualism, yet America's founding fathers seemed to get a free pass when they engaged in the same type of thinking. Elaborating on Noll's arguments, Marsden insisted that at no time in the history of Christianity had the nature/grace dichotomy that Schaeffer had criticized for two decades been more prevalent than in Britain and its colonies in the eighteenth century. The acceptance of this as broadly Christian simply because it was not militantly anti-Christian like the French Revolution was in Marsden's view precisely what had opened the door for the twentieth-century secular revolution that he, Noll, and Schaeffer all lamented.[79]

Given that Schaeffer held logic and argument in such high esteem, it was fitting that Marsden offered Schaeffer a syllogism. If America's founding was, as Schaeffer had begun to admit in his letters, merely a mixture of Christian and non-Christian themes, and if Schaeffer designated that mixture as "Biblical, Biblically-based, Judeo-Christian, Reformation-based, Christian, and the like" (all of which Schaeffer had), then "You are appearing to (even if you do not intend to) attribute the authority of God's Word to what is in reality a compromise between Biblical and extra-Biblical influences." Marsden added a "corollary": "It is such confusions, i.e. designating large sections of the American heritage as more-or-less Christian, that have helped lower the guard of Christians in distinguishing what is truly Biblical from what is merely part of their cultural heritage."[80] The result, therefore, was that Christians in twentieth-century America had actually facilitated the development of secularism by failing to recognize the absence of Christian influence in much of America's founding or by confusing what is secular or natural with what is Christian.

Editor Lane Dennis of Crossway Books, which had published *Manifesto,* was also privy to the correspondence among Noll, Marsden, and Schaeffer. Dennis tried to play the role of mediator, suggesting that Noll did not give enough credit to the influence of the Christian ethos in America's founding, while Schaeffer did not give enough credit to the non-Christian Enlightenment influences. Dennis believed that the delicate balance or harmony between the Christian and Enlightenment influences in the nation's founding was lost as the Enlightenment began to take over. He compared Schaeffer's analysis to that of sociologist Max Weber, who had argued for the Calvinist influence in the rise of capitalism. Weber had not tried to show how Calvinists applied specific points of their Calvinism to economics; rather he argued that an ethos developed by Calvinism contributed to the rise of capitalism. Likewise, the founders had a Christian ethos that influenced their work.[81] Dennis also took Noll to task for his comment to *Newsweek,* saying that the quote was unfortunate and that Woodward was not interested in being fair to Schaeffer but rather wanted to distort his views to achieve his own agenda. "But I think the quote was also unfortunate because it was untrue," Dennis wrote. Using Webster's dictionary definition of a scholar as being a learned man, Dennis argued that Schaeffer was indeed a scholar: "The effect of the *Newsweek* quote was to leave the impression that since Dr. Schaeffer is not a 'scholar' he is therefore a charlatan." Dennis also rejected Noll's view that Schaeffer held to a myth of a Christian America.[82]

Such criticisms notwithstanding, Noll thanked Dennis for his analysis, commending him for stating the case well. Seemingly weary after three months of letters on this topic, Noll also wrote, "I am regretting more and more the preemptive strike in Newsweek." Acknowledging that he should have known what Woodward would do with his quote, Noll continued, "In sum, I am afraid that the Newsweek piece badly damaged the chance for constructive and edifying dialogue. . . . And for this I am mostly to blame."[83]

If Francis Schaeffer was agitated by Noll's and Marsden's interpretation of the founding fathers, it is no surprise that the petulant Franky would be even more so. He jumped into the debate with a letter to Noll the week after Noll had first written to apologize to Francis. Twelve days before his father said the same thing, Franky wrote to Noll saying he was naïve for making a negative statement to Woodward and *Newsweek*. "[W]hat I do find unfortunate is what I must regard as an example par excellence of the political naivete which accompanies so much real or imagined 'Christian' scholarship," Franky wrote. *Newsweek,* he said, had tried to get a negative remark out of him in a recent interview about another person, but had failed and thus did not quote him. "Had I wanted to see my name in print (for some unknown reason), or had I been a 'Christian scholar' attempting to 'give all points of view,' they would have found something substantial and, I dare say, nasty to lend weight to their argument." Peeved that Noll had said his father was not a scholar, Franky wrote in a postscript, "I must add that I find your reasoning in regard to why you do not consider my father 'a scholar' provincial nit-picking in the extreme." Quoting from Noll's first letter to Francis, Franky responded, "I read you when you say, 'Your work does not take advantage of the crucial technical studies (often by Christians) which illuminate the past. I have, for instance, spent much of the last ten years . . .' as really saying, that in order for Dad to be a scholar in your eyes he should have quoted you and your associates more frequently! The 'Christian' academic community has a well deserved reputation for clannish irrelevance which can surely only be enhanced (if that's the word) by those who would make such pettily arrogant distinctions about what is or is not scholarship."[84]

In his response to Franky, Noll included an addendum on scholarship in which he defined the term again, listed several Christian scholars of American history, and said that none of them had ever concluded that the United States government had been founded on a biblical base. Noll closed, "Those in our day who draw such conclusions — and then urge Christians to take public action on the basis of those conclusions — have themselves a burden to show how they can (apparently) disregard all of this excellent work." As he had with Francis, Noll also cited for Franky America's sorry record in dealing with African Americans, Native Americans, and other underrepresented minorities, and he argued that if the U.S. government stepped into the abortion issue to defend the unborn, "it would represent a great and glorious break with precedent, and it would contradict an entire history of benign neglect or active persecution of the unrepresented."[85]

Noll's response apparently had a profound, if momentary, impact on Franky, who responded with an apology for his earlier letter, which he now considered "full of peek and ill humor." Franky said it was one of those letters that was written but should never have been sent.[86] He followed with a reasoned plea that Noll carefully reconsider how the facts and interpretations of history could either serve or stand in the way of the Christian effort to battle the cultural forces of hostility to the faith. Franky, like his father, believed that historical interpretation should serve the interest of the evangelical cultural agenda. This is why the Schaeffers, who disagreed privately with Jerry Falwell's mixing of Christianity and patriotism, were nevertheless unwilling to criticize him publicly. In his correspondence with Noll, Franky cited his differences with Falwell's "God and Country fundamentalism," yet praised Falwell's efforts for good.[87] Noll, by contrast, believed that the Schaeffers and by implication the entire Christian Right, including Falwell, were unlikely to find proper remedies for the present if their views of the past were skewed.

Franky's careful, reasoned engagement would not last long. The next year he published *Bad News for Modern Man,* lambasting Christian colleges, evangelical publishers, and Christian scholars, Marsden and Ronald Wells by name, attacking their motives as well as their interpretations. Franky lumped Wells and Marsden into a "revisionist throng" that was downplaying America's Judeo-Christian heritage and called Marsden's testimony in the Arkansas Creation Science case perhaps "the most blatant example of the evangelical sellout" to liberal culture.[88] Franky did not mention Noll by name, but he referenced evangelical historians who quibble about whether the Enlightenment or the Reformation had more influence in America's founding — which was ironic given that Francis had brought up the issue in the first place in *Manifesto.* Marsden tried to intervene with Crossway editor Lane Dennis in early 1984 before Franky's book was even published, requesting that Dennis require Franky to soften or remove offensive references like the ones that had appeared in an earlier article. In reply, Dennis told Marsden he had tried unsuccessfully to persuade Franky to moderate his criticism. Though Dennis didn't necessarily endorse Creation Science, he lamented Marsden's participation in the Arkansas case, believing a testimony against Creation Science unproductive for the evangelical cause. He then defended Franky on abortion, calling him "the Stokely Carmichael" of the pro-life movement, a reference to the Black Power radical of the 1960s.[89] Marsden wrote back to Dennis, parodying Dennis's logic: "[S]ince Franky is doing such good consciousness raising on the abortion issue," Marsden wrote sarcastically, "it is alright that he attempts to damage the reputation of fellow Christians on other issues."[90] Dennis attended the same church as Noll and several other Wheaton College professors, and the rift created by Crossway's publication of Franky's book, with its repeated criticism of Wheaton, became a point of tension within the congregation.[91] Roger Lundin, who also attended the church, remembers a woman a thousand miles away from Wheaton saying disparaging things about Noll and Wheaton that she obviously got from *Bad News.*[92]

The Schaeffers' objection to Noll's and Marsden's interpretation of American history paled in comparison to their reaction to Ronald Wells's interpretation of the Reformation. Wells was a fellow historian and Marsden's colleague at Calvin College when he published in the *Reformed Journal* a review of *A Christian Manifesto* entitled "Francis Schaeffer's Jeremiad," and a year later an article called "Whatever Happened to Francis Schaeffer?," a clear play on Schaeffer's *Whatever Happened to the Human Race?* Wells had spent time at L'Abri in the 1960s, and he was put off by Schaeffer's embrace of the Christian Right. Like most Christian scholars, Wells had deep reservations about the details of Schaeffer's interpretation of western intellectual history, and he called parts of *Manifesto* "sophomoric bombast and careless simplicity."[93] Wells critiqued Schaeffer's pitting the Renaissance and Reformation against each other and Schaeffer's argument that humanism was a product of the Renaissance but had no part in the Reformation. Wells argued that humanism was a methodology developed during the Renaissance and used to challenge authority. Given that the Protestant Reformation was just such a challenge to the authority of the medieval church, Wells went so far as to say that Protestantism was "the religious form of Renaissance humanism."[94] Schaeffer, Wells continued, missed the tragic and ironic in the story of the Reformation: the very methodology that made the Reformation possible "loosed a methodology on the world which results in modernity."[95]

In a rambling and at times incoherent letter to Noll in early March 1983, Schaeffer said he had recently read Wells's article "Francis Schaeffer's Jeremiad." Responding to Wells's view that Protestantism was "the religious form of Renaissance humanism," Schaeffer wrote, "I would suggest that if those in your school of thought are trying to be responsible and really mean to be taken seriously that this type of thing should not be allowed to come out of this school of thinking."[96] This reference to interpretations that "should not be allowed" was a harbinger of things to come from Schaeffer. Over the next several weeks he asked Noll and Marsden first to repudiate Wells, then possibly to have him silenced.[97] Believing erroneously that Marsden had taken a public stand against an individual in the Christian Reformed Church who was allegedly soft on inerrancy, Schaeffer wrote, "I do not think you will mind my asking if you have taken the same energetic effort concerning this defaming of the Reformation [by Wells] as you have about Sheppard [*sic*]?"[98] Schaeffer again mixed a form of the earlier battle for the Bible with the American culture war: he clearly implied that Marsden should attempt to have the Christian Reformed

Church, Calvin College's sponsoring body, deal with Wells. The same day he asked Marsden to take a public stand against Wells, Schaeffer told Noll that what Wells had written about the Reformation was "about the most destructive as anything [sic] anyone could write in a journal entitled 'Reformed.'"[99] In response, both Noll and Marsden distanced themselves from Wells's interpretation. Noll told Schaeffer that while Wells was a good friend, "I certainly do not agree with his sentiments which you quoted," while Marsden said of Wells's words, "I think they were a bit of hyperbole."[100]

The correspondence debate went on throughout the spring and into the summer of 1983, with Schaeffer intransigent and Marsden increasingly forceful in his critique of Schaeffer's and Whitehead's political project. Referencing his brief stay at L'Abri, Marsden wrote, "To be frank, I think that L'Abri was better off in the 1960s when the most politics that were around were a few tapes about Rushdoony (even though I do not share your estimate of Rushdoony as a political guide)."[101] Marsden told Schaeffer, moreover, that political causes tend to "obscure the Gospel and divide the church if they are put into the forefront of a ministry."[102]

In May, Marsden threw caution to the wind. He told Schaeffer that Whitehead's *The Second American Revolution* was an "embarrassment." Whitehead's work, wrote Marsden, was a "compilation of half-truths slanted to support current causes," so much so that "it automatically loses its influence among almost everyone who knows much about contemporary scholarship on the subject (i.e. history)." Similarly, Marsden classed Creation Science as "a mixture of half-truths and nonsense," and said he was "very embarrassed that my well-intentioned brothers in the faith are promoting such views."[103] Marsden tried to convince Schaeffer that if Christians were going to make any headway in the political world they were going to need moderate allies, and "Creation-science and other half-baked attempts at Christian scholarship do not help at all on this front. . . . The problem is that when the Tim LaHaye's or (I'm afraid) the John Whitehead's get hold of these issues the crucial people you want to reach stop listening as soon as they run into the outrageous statements. Then you are left just preaching to the converted."[104]

Schaeffer saw Marsden's critique of Whitehead and Creation Science as an attempt to divorce Christian scholarship from the issues of the day. Once again mixing the culture war with the battle for the Bible, Schaeffer cited what he believed was a lack of even-handedness when Marsden, and by implication Noll, displayed much greater sensitivity to perceived misinterpretations of American history than to weakened views of scripture. This dynamic reminded Schaeffer of Westminster Seminary after J. Gresham Machen died in 1937, when the faculty became more exercised about fighting against the dispensationalism of other fundamentalists than against liberal theology.[105] As was often the case, Schaeffer wrote to Noll the same day he wrote to Marsden. He chided Noll for not going after Wells with the same vigor Noll displayed against those who overemphasized the Christian origins of America's past.[106] He was effectively accusing both Noll and Marsden of attacking other Christians instead of attacking their true enemies. The overriding concern for Schaeffer was always that the downplaying of the Christian base that he believed existed in America before the twentieth century would weaken the culture war Christians should wage.

Noll, Marsden, and fellow evangelical historian Nathan Hatch believed the interpretation of America's Christian past sufficiently important to warrant co-authoring *The Search for Christian America,* which was a book-length response to Schaeffer's, Whitehead's, and the Christian Right's views. In *Manifesto,* as elsewhere in his late writings, Schaeffer bemoaned the fact that Christians had been "utterly foolish in our concentration on bits and pieces, and in our complete failure to face the total world view that is rooted in a false view of reality."[107] It is only an advantage to see things whole, however, if they really are whole. If the prevailing worldview of American culture is really a hodgepodge of bits and pieces, then attempting to see it whole is a distortion. If the founding of America was a hodgepodge of influences, part Christian and part secular, then attempting to see the founding as largely Christian leads to distortion. In *The Search for Christian America,* Noll, Marsden, and Hatch argued that Schaeffer, Whitehead, and others were engaging in just such a distortion. Like Schaeffer, they acknowledged the importance of Christian influences in the American Revolution. (Indeed, Hatch had previously written an entire book on that subject, as had Noll.)[108] Unlike Schaeffer, however, they saw many other influences at work. They attempted to show that among the American founders even an orthodox Christian such as John Witherspoon failed to develop a distinctly Christian political theory, but rather bought into the very nature/grace dichotomy that Schaeffer critiqued. Using direct quotes from Witherspoon's own lectures, the authors showed that even this devout Presbyterian minister believed that political theory could be done without reference to revelation but by observation of nature alone. In short, the authors argued, there was no genuinely Christian American past to which evangelicals could look for guidance.[109]

The last word from the Schaeffer side came from Franky. In *Bad News for Modern Man* he repeatedly accused moderate and left-leaning evangelicals of wanting to be culturally accepted so badly that they were afraid to speak out. After attacking evangelical colleges such as Wheaton and publishing houses such as Eerdmans, Franky went after left-leaning evangelicals, including Ronald Sider and Jim Wallis and many others, as being driven by ill motives. Franky called for resistance. He wanted Marsden and Wells, and by extension all Christian scholars, to form cells of resistance in academic life rather than trying to synthesize the best secular scholarship with Christian thought. Whitehead was his model, because Whitehead was outside the academy and did not engage scholars. Ironically, when it came to the arts and media, Franky's primary areas of interest, he called for "invasion," by which he meant that Christians should participate in these secular arenas in an attempt to produce Christian art, journalism, and the like. Franky even spent time in Hollywood trying to break in as a screenwriter, but he did not see his own attempt to infiltrate the film industry with Christian thinking as similar to Noll's and Marsden's call for good Christian scholarship within the larger secular academy.

The overriding issue in Franky's call to activism was abortion. In *Bad News* he repeatedly called for "proabortion professors," by which he seemed to mean anyone who supported *Roe v. Wade,* to be fired from Christian colleges. Typical of his critique was the argument that evangelicals were too preoccupied with examining America's Christian origins or debunking "secular bogeymen" or learning from other traditions such as Gandhi's Hinduism to get involved in the real issues of the day — abortion most of all. "But in the end," Franky wrote, "it all comes down to embarrassed, embittered, postfundamentalist evangelicals who had thrown out the baby with the bath water."[110] In other words, in their desire to distance themselves from the worst aspects of fundamentalism and cozy up to liberal culture, evangelicals had lost their evangelicalism. It was an argument reminiscent of Francis's critique of Karl Barth or the National Association of Evangelicals in the fifties and Fuller Seminary in the seventies, but Franky's views were so extreme and his vilification of evangelical individuals and institutions so uncharitable that few sought to engage him as they had his father. Thus he got the last word.

Ironically, Franky himself would soon become an embarrassed, embittered postfundamentalist, leaving evangelicalism for Eastern Orthodoxy in 1990. In May 2005, he acknowledged that people who predicted a secular culture were wrong, as "Muslim Brotherhoods geared up for jihad, a conservative pope took on communism, and the religious right absorbed the Republican Party."[111] His views now changed and chastened, Franky now proffered his own "explanation as to why fundamentalists dominate our world": when fundamentalist holy warriors of whatever stripe confront tolerant liberals afraid to say anyone's religion is wrong, the latter have no chance. "Certainties are what unite all fundamentalists: the fear of disorder and the unknown — in other words, the fear of freedom." "The final irony of fundamentalism, and the scholastic Catholicism represented by the new pope," Franky, now known as Frank, argued, "is that fundamentalists turn out to be rationalists unwilling to abandon any part of their intellectual systems to embrace the mystery of spirituality."[112]

By 2007, Frank viewed the first half of his life as a time when he had been "Crazy for God," as he titled his autobiography. While many evangelicals revere Francis for laying the intellectual foundations of the Christian Right, Frank is convinced that he pushed his father into something that has proven detrimental to the nation. His subtitle, "How I Grew Up as One of the Elect, Helped Found the Religious Right, and Lived to Take All (or Almost All) of It Back," is only slightly less blunt than the one found on the advance copy: "How I Helped Found the Religious Right and Ruin America."

One wonders what fundamentalists Franky had in mind when he wrote about the "unwillingness to embrace the mystery of spirituality." He could very well have been referring to his father, or at least the type of rationalist fundamentalism that produced him. At the end of his life, prodded as he was by Franky, Francis Schaeffer was no more willing to embrace nuance, complexity, and tension than he had been in the 1930s and 1940s, when he was a full-fledged member of McIntire's wing of American fundamentalism. If one disagreed with him, even on what could very well be considered a secondary issue, such as the Christian or secular origins of America's founding, one ran the risk of incurring his judgment that anything less than his own monolithic interpretation was not truly evangelical. This type of thinking was conducive to culture war but not to reasoned reflection about the state of the world, which was what he tried to cultivate at L'Abri.

But even at L'Abri, Schaeffer's agenda was not to explicate carefully the nuances of history. Rather, he was calling Christians to the important task of worldview formation, which is perhaps his signal achievement and most lasting influence. To do this he engaged in a lot of cultural analysis, and here his influence has been at times damaging. The argument that American culture is nearly monolithic in its secular humanistic base leaves too much unexplained to be helpful; interpreting America's founding as Christian-based does likewise. But even his detractors among evangelicals recognize the good he has done. For all Noll's criticism of Schaeffer's Christian Right activism and the interpretation of American history that facilitated it, Noll to this day believes that, on balance, Schaeffer's influence has been mostly positive within evangelicalism, because he called Christians to think in Christian ways about all of life and culture.[113]

Conclusion:
Francis Schaeffer's Legacy

Francis Schaeffer succumbed to cancer on May 15, 1984. A warrior to the end, early that year he completed a ten-city tour, speaking mostly on college campuses. At some venues assistants carried him from his bed to the speaking platform with a tube in his chest delivering medication as he spoke. When he died, six weeks after the tour ended, his last words to Edith came from Psalm 84, "from strength to strength."[1] In the last years of his life he also engaged in street protests at an abortion facility in Rochester, Minnesota, where he and Edith lived while he was being treated.

Schaeffer and American Culture

Schaeffer's life illustrates the interesting and complex ways that American evangelicals harmonize their theological commitments with their cultural and national loyalties. Powerfully seductive forces tempt American evangelicals to interpret their faith through an American lens. This evangelical tendency seems much stronger in America than in Great Britain, the European continent, Australia, or Canada. Schaeffer's life illustrates this temptation most clearly because he lived the middle period of his career in Europe, giving us something with which to contrast his earlier and later periods.

Before he went to Europe to live in 1948, Schaeffer was a typical fundamentalist, deeply concerned with evangelism and nearly obsessed with the militant defense of the faith against the threat of theological liberalism, but with almost no distinctly political or even cultural message. Still, much of the urgency of this fundamentalist fight was borne along by the belief that American culture was at stake in the battle against theological liberalism. One of his closest associates and mentors, Carl McIntire, is remembered as one of America's most colorful, but also most controversial, fundamentalists. At the time Schaeffer broke with McIntire, McIntire and other fundamentalists were launching a veritable crusade against Communism that often merged the theological fight against liberalism with Cold War considerations. They often identified America with the forces of righteousness, as the atheistic Soviet regime was so obviously an enemy of faith. Schaeffer's move to Europe and the break with McIntire that followed helped him steer clear of this virulent anti-Communism and the mixture of evangelical faith and American patriotism that accompanied the Cold War fight.

When Schaeffer returned from Europe, especially in the 1970s, he returned also to the militant defense of the evangelical expression of Christianity that paralleled his activities in the 1940s. He began once again to stress the need for theological purity as he searched for that elusive line in the sand separating true evangelicals from those who were drifting dangerously close to liberalism. That line, of course, was the standard of biblical inerrancy. While taking up the fundamentalist cause once again, usually against evangelical brothers, Schaeffer also began to align his theological commitments with particular political programs — an alignment that has been endemic to evangelicalism since the early twentieth century. Evangelical concerns have often led to particular political programs, whether in the Scopes Trial of 1925 and then the ongoing American debate over science and religion in public schools, the prayer-in-schools controversies that began in the 1960s, the abortion controversy, or, more recently, the debate over gay marriage. American evangelicals struggle to keep the political from becoming ultimate when they bring a religious agenda to cultural issues. This is not to say that Schaeffer should have stayed out of politics; indeed, it would have been hard to avoid, given his passion for and focus on the politics of abortion, to the neglect if not the exclusion of other issues. Schaeffer's late career raised the very question that continually challenges evangelicals: How should we then live? How can Christians be involved in biblical issues that have political implications without aligning the evangelical expression of Christianity with a particular political party and thereby compromising prophetic independence? As we have seen, Schaeffer hitched the evangelical wagon to the Republican Party's ascendancy in the early 1980s, leading some of his warmest supporters to worry that he was being co-opted by the Reagan revolution. In the final years of his life he wove together the defense of evangelical theology with his resolute defense of America's so-called "Christian base," something he had never done before. In that way, American politics had pulled him in a new direction.

By contrast, he escaped both of these tendencies when he lived in Europe, where he could wear his political predilections and his national commitments loosely. When he returned to America Schaeffer began to engage culture through political activity that would have made little sense in a European context — that is, Christian Right politics geared toward saving and refurbishing what remained of the once-Christian culture. To Schaeffer, Europe was lost in this regard; we do not find Schaeffer, for example, attempting to restore Switzerland's Christian base. Moreover, Europe was not his land. It effectively decontextualized him and freed him to focus on those who arrived at his doorstep at L'Abri, and the world they inhabited. America, on the other hand, had a large base of evangelicals and a recent memory of active evangelical political engagement. There Schaeffer was able to engage enthusiastically in Christian Right politics as a natural extension of his fundamentalist desire to defend the truth and his evangelical effort to win the culture for Christ. The result was that while he had been nearly apolitical for most of his career, with a message that spoke to people across the political spectrum and engaged culture without aligning the faith with it, the final years of his life saw him become a partisan of the Republican Party, which offered a strength in numbers that made large-scale cultural change seem possible.

Schaeffer as Fundamentalist and Evangelical

Another way in which Schaeffer's life is instructive has to do with the definitions of fundamentalism and evangelicalism — and where the line between the two exists. Schaeffer's career blurred that line. Over the past thirty years, scholars following the lead of George Marsden have come to see fundamentalism as the militant and separatist form of Protestant evangelicalism. Viewed this way, all fundamentalists are evangelicals, but not all evangelicals are fundamentalists. There is no doubt where Schaeffer stood in the early phase of his career before moving to Europe. He identified fully with fundamentalism, calling for a militant defense of the faith and separation from liberals and even other evangelicals who would not separate from liberals. While in Europe, Schaeffer's emphasis shifted from separatism and the militant defense of the faith to what could be called apologetic evangelism.

For twentieth-century fundamentalists, or at least for Schaeffer, evangelism was a different matter in Europe than in America. In America, fundamentalist evangelism consisted largely of turning people away from sinful lifestyles and toward the saving work of Christ. Generally speaking, fundamentalists preach that all the troubles in life can be traced to sinful behavior. The chief problems are moral and manifested behaviorally, instead of intellectual and manifested in angst. It is indeed hard to imagine a significant number of people in Schaeffer's America coming to a fundamentalist pastor and saying, "I've been reading Nietzsche and I'm struggling with the question of whether there is a transcendent reality." If Schaeffer ever met such a person in the first phase of his career, he made no mention of it. Instead, his evangelism in America was among rural and small-town people in Grove City, Pennsylvania, dock workers and other working-class types in Chester, Pennsylvania, and urban white children and middle-class workers in St. Louis.

In Europe, however, he encountered young people who were struggling intellectually with the kinds of questions Kierkegaard, Nietzsche, or Freud presented, and to his credit Schaeffer recognized that to be effective, he would have to engage them through discussion at the level of ideas and not merely tell them to straighten up and get right with Jesus. His training within the Reformed branch of American fundamentalism by scholars such as J. Gresham Machen and Cornelius Van Til served him well in this regard. As he began to engage European young people intellectually, he continued for a few years to denounce Barth and others he considered liberals, but it became apparent by the time he and Edith founded L'Abri in 1955 that attacking liberals in a largely secular European culture was relatively unproductive. His break with McIntire at this time resulted from Schaeffer's view that American fundamentalists expended too much time and energy attacking any semblance of liberalism and not enough constructing a positive response to modern ideas that competed with Christianity for people's hearts and minds. Few Europeans cared whether theological liberalism was in error, and as for the defense of the evangelical expression of Protestantism, there was not much evangelicalism in Europe to defend. Instead Schaeffer witnessed a conflict between Christianity and secularization of culture bordering often on existential atheism. So Schaeffer turned more and more toward engaging young existentialists, agnostics, and atheists who had concluded that life had no meaning. In this context, Schaeffer turned from the fundamentalist zeal for internecine warfare to the fundamentalist zeal for evangelism aimed at persuading unbelievers, but with a twist: whereas in America Schaeffer's intellectual endeavors consisted of the militant refutation of liberalism, Europe gave him a rare opportunity to put the intellectual side of fundamentalism into the service of evangelizing the lost through persuasive argument. The result was Schaeffer's apologetic evangelism.

That apologetic was bound up with the Schaeffers' sense of Christian love and hospitality, which Francis and Edith demonstrated so effectively at L'Abri. The Schaeffers had no church facility to which they could invite people, so they brought them to their home. In one respect this was merely fundamentalist evangelism — make no mistake, the Schaeffers wanted first and foremost to see their European friends and neighbors converted. But it was more than evangelism. The activities in the Schaeffer home had all the features of the ancient practice of Christian hospitality. They believed hospitality was a calling and command in and of itself. Still, the community served to create what William Edgar, using a term developed by sociologist Peter Berger, called "a structure of plausibility" for the intellectual articulation of the Christian faith. As we saw in chapter four, the structure of the community and the type of Christian hospitality and love practiced there were at least as important as Schaeffer's ideas for the success of L'Abri's apologetic evangelism. Schaeffer disciples have developed other L'Abris around the world, and it will be left to future studies to discern the degree to which they have been able to duplicate the Schaefferian version of community and hospitality.

When Schaeffer first returned to America on the strength of the growing reputation of his work at L'Abri, his apologetic primarily energized evangelicals on Christian college campuses, and his message inspired a generation of Christian scholars and activists. Schaeffer's American audience was made up largely of people who were already converted, and his message to American evangelical college students was that to be effective witnesses they would have to move beyond fundamentalist separation from secular ideas and beyond mere denunciation of liberals. Instead, evangelicals needed to take ideas seriously and to understand and engage their culture. He preached the strategy and carried on the message that had worked so well at L'Abri. Once Schaeffer was back in America, however, it did not take long for the militant defense of the faith to reassert itself in his writing and speaking, and with Franky's reinforcement this militant defense of the faith led Francis deep into politics, where the theological militancy of his early career became political militancy in the Christian Right.

Beginning in the 1940s, neo-evangelicals tried to be theologically orthodox, like fundamentalists, but culturally engaged, like nineteenth-century American evangelicals. After the beginning of the neo-evangelical movement, militant and separatist evangelicals came to be called fundamentalists, while culturally engaged and nonmilitant evangelicals were supposed to be called evangelicals. This neat categorization broke down with Schaeffer, as he became in the 1970s both militant and culturally engaged. He became a culturally engaged fundamentalist. Or was he a militant evangelical? Before 1980, either term was generally considered to be something of an oxymoron. In Schaeffer's wake, and partly as a result of his influence, there have been a host of Christian Right figures who are both militant and culturally engaged.

The advent in the 1980s of militant evangelical figures raises the question as to whether they should be considered evangelicals, fundamentalists, or something else. Their militancy makes them appear to be fundamentalist, and that is what the media pundits call them, but their cultural engagement lends itself to evangelicalism. Recently, Marsden has suggested that the term "fundamentalistic evangelical" might be useful in describing such people. It certainly describes Schaeffer at the end of his career.

But because of Europe, Schaeffer was different than those who followed him in fundamentalistic evangelicalism. There he could avoid questions that too often preoccupy American evangelicals in internecine battles. Being outside America freed Schaeffer to do his broadest work, for it was in Europe after the formation of L'Abri that he worried neither about where the Christian faith stood in relationship to American politics and patriotism nor about who was in and who was out of evangelicalism. Rather, he was liberated for the task of constructing a coherent Christian worldview.

Schaeffer and the Modern World

If Schaeffer complicates the relationship between evangelicalism and fundamentalism, he also complicates the relationship between evangelicalism and the modern world. American evangelicals have been shaped by the modern world that grew out of the Enlightenment at the same time they have often seemingly been at war with modernity. They have been aptly characterized as having "a love affair with the Enlightenment science."[2] But when the scientific world moved toward more theoretical forms of science, including Darwinian evolution, evangelicals, and especially fundamentalists, were often caught flat-footed. There had been an underlying assumption among nineteenth-century evangelicals that the best of orthodox theology and the best of modern science would always be in harmony. Bewildered and distraught to find that their once-esteemed scientific and philosophical systems had fallen wholly out of fashion, twentieth-century fundamentalists either refused to budge or turned to alternative forms of science, such as Creation Science, and relied heavily on dispensational premillennialism as the key to understanding scripture. This has often resulted in significant intellectual disconnect between fundamentalists and the world around them; Mark Noll has labeled this phenomenon "the intellectual disaster of fundamentalism" in his book *The Scandal of the Evangelical Mind.*[3]

In one respect Schaeffer stands as a significant exception to the scandal of the evangelical mind. He was one of those responsible for helping evangelicals reject fundamentalist anti-intellectualism in favor of a renewed emphasis on things of the mind and a reengagement

234

with mainstream intellectual culture. Moreover, Schaeffer was intuitively gifted in understanding young people who had pushed the Enlightenment project to its logical conclusion, with its emphasis on reason alone as the way to the truth. Schaeffer knew there was no way to begin a rational argument without an assumption that something was true. In Schaeffer's apologetic evangelism he put a personal God at the beginning of the reasoning process, then attempted to show that everything else made sense once that presupposition was adopted. By contrast, he argued, when the process starts merely with space, time, and chance, nothing makes sense. The truly modern person must either smuggle meaning into his or her worldview or admit that life has no meaning. Schaeffer argued effectively that individuals could not live consistently with meaninglessness.

This argument seemed to work, although it seems that at times Schaeffer underestimated the degree to which the non-rational aspects of the Christian community of L'Abri were essential for the effectiveness of the message. For all of its strengths, the weakness of Schaeffer's apologetic was that he consistently over-emphasized the power of human reason to lead to correct conclusions about ultimate matters. He had some success with this method in a time period that could be called the last gasp of modernity — that is, the tail end of the era dominated by the Enlightenment — but there is little to commend it in most quarters today. Philosopher and Schaeffer critic Arthur Holmes and lawyer/activist and Schaeffer disciple John Whitehead both agree that Schaeffer's project does not work very well in a postmodern context. Holmes explains this philosophically, saying that today's young people understand their positions and ideas as being products of many sources, not just reason. In light of the postmodern critique of the Enlightenment, Schaeffer's way of reasoning through the plausibility of the Christian faith is less useful than it was in the 1960s. Whitehead has seen firsthand that Schaeffer does not resonate with today's college students. He has tried to get them to discuss Schaeffer's books and films in the Rutherford Institute's summer programs, but with little success. For Whitehead the lack of connection between his students and Schaeffer is partly because the students are amused or put off by Schaeffer's knickers and teaching style in the film *How Should We Then Live?* Whitehead also believes the disconnect results from there being less passion for finding the truth today than in the sixties and early seventies and less interest in the ideas Schaeffer discussed. Talk about presuppositions, Whitehead says, and people don't know what you mean.[4]

Another view, however, has been put forward by Bryan Follis in his book *Truth with Love: The Apologetic of Francis Schaeffer.* Follis believes that Schaeffer's reasoned argument was never divorced from his emphasis on love and community. Understood this way, Schaeffer's apologetic is even more valid today in a postmodern culture that has little use for intellectual notions of truth. As Follis puts the case, "[T]he lack of trust today in the concept of truth makes [Schaeffer's] approach, with his strong emphasis on individual relationships, love, and truth, even more important."[5] Follis arrives at this conclusion by reading the trilogy through *True Spirituality,* which he believes holds the key to our ability to understand and evaluate Schaeffer's apologetic.[6] The debate over whether Schaeffer was overly rational or struck just the right balance between spirituality and logical argument exists because Schaeffer was not a systematic thinker. Readers must decide for themselves whether he struck the right balance between spirituality and rationality. For his part, Os Guinness says of Schaeffer: "He reasoned as if reason alone mattered; he loved as if love alone mattered."[7]

Either way, Schaeffer's appropriation of Enlightenment reason was not a serious handicap in his own time, but it did make him something of a period piece at the level of ideas. Obviously, Schaeffer was by no means the first figure whose ideas were useful almost exclusively in his own lifetime. Few thinkers retain lasting influence like that of Augustine, Aquinas, or, dare we say, Kierkegaard, so it is hardly a criticism to say that Schaeffer's currency is not what it was when he was alive. Some of his books still sell reasonably well, but not nearly as well as his contemporary C. S. Lewis, whose influence seems to be as strong as ever more than forty years after his death in 1963.[8] Perhaps this is because Lewis had a greater appreciation for the nonrational and aesthetic aspects of the Christian faith; perhaps he was simply a more accomplished writer. There does seem to be a sense in which Lewis transcended his time and moved beyond the Enlightenment, and this may be because he was a product of European intellectual life, where the crisis of rationalism and the devastating critique of the Enlightenment hit about a half-century before coming to America.

Schaeffer was certainly picking up on this when he intuitively pushed the Enlightenment to its logical conclusions and ended up discussing something like postmodernism. The irony, however, was that he then fought against postmodernism with the modern weapons of Enlightenment reason.

Schaeffer's life in this regard becomes instructive for twentieth-century evangelicals, many of whom could never decide whether to separate from mainstream intellectual life or to appropriate Enlightenment reason so fully they seemed to project a belief that if their arguments were refuted by modern science and philosophy, all would be lost. Schaeffer sometimes sounded as if he had fallen victim to the latter tendency, and he often wrote and spoke as if the western rational articulation of Christianity were Christianity itself. As Christianity becomes a globalized, non-western phenomenon, often thriving today in a southern hemisphere where western rationalism does not dominate, it appears that the intellectual aspects of Schaeffer's apologetic were both time-bound and culturally relative. While he viewed the de-Christianization of the West as a catastrophe, he could not have foreseen the de-westernization of Christianity and the possibilities that phenomenon has created. He was an ironic figure in this regard: he was a critic of the implications of western Enlightenment rationalism while being at times a captive of Enlightenment presuppositions about how truth is discovered.

At the same time, however, as his books *True Spirituality, The Church before the Watching World,* and *The Mark of the Christian* show, Schaeffer was indeed concerned with the totality of the Christian life. In these works he taught that the final apologetic for the faith was Christian love demonstrated in community. This part of Schaeffer's message is less time-bound than the rational argument that drove the trilogy, and those who knew him at L'Abri remember how well he integrated *The Escape from Reason* with *True Spirituality.* That said, Schaeffer's intellectual work was more widely read and far more significant to a larger number of people than his spirituality-centered books. There were many spiritual aids available within evangelicalism when Schaeffer arrived on the scene; he was one among many who wrote in this genre. Hardly anyone was articulating ideas in the way Schaeffer did, however, so naturally this became the aspect of his work that set him apart. For those who encountered Schaeffer through his books, films, and lectures, the rational argument and the engagement with culture are what tend to endure, while the relatively few who knew Schaeffer personally at L'Abri recall both the arguments and the community of Christian love in which those arguments were made. Those who knew Schaeffer are more likely to see these two aspects of Schaeffer's ministry as a unified whole. Those who only read him or heard him lecture are far more likely to remember the rational arguments. Such arguments, significant in their own time, today seem quaint remnants of a bygone era.

In summary, Schaeffer exhibited both evangelicalism's strengths — a seriousness about culture and ideas and a deep spirituality and emphasis on Christian community — and its weaknesses — over-reliance on Enlightenment categories and a tendency to conflate issues of faith with issues of politics and American patriotism. Across the three periods of his career, he exhibited different tendencies at different times, and his geographic location seemed to determine his agenda. He was not so much transformed from a fundamentalist to an intellectually progressive evangelical and then back into a fundamentalist culture warrior. Rather, he was smart enough and flexible enough to utilize whichever feature of fundamentalism or evangelicalism his cultural context demanded.

The secret to Schaeffer's influence was this sort of ambiguity. One can view Schaeffer in a variety of ways. For fundamentalists, or at least conservative evangelical inerrantists, he was a militant defender of the faith, battling for the Bible. Intellectually oriented evangelicals found in Schaeffer an inspiration for Christian scholarship. Activists looked to him as the mentor of the Christian Right, leading the way in the fight against abortion and the culture of death.

These are three rather distinct constituencies of influence — defenders of the faith, evangelical scholars, and Christian Right culture warriors. Together the three groups comprise something of a Schaeffer trilogy, and all three had key spokespersons at the L'Abri Jubilee celebration in 2005. Representing the conservative evangelical inerrantists was theologian Harold O. J. Brown, who argued that Schaeffer's apologetic defense of the faith against theological liberalism was second to none. For Brown, Schaeffer was rebuilding the foundation of the evangelical faith, whereas Barth and other neo-orthodox theologians had attempted to rebuild the second story of a house whose foundation and first floor had crumbled. Representing Christian scholars at the L'Abri Jubilee was Os Guinness. His address was as wide-ranging as anything Schaeffer ever produced, but informed by deep reading and conversation with the best scholarship of the past forty years in a way that Schaeffer's work was not. Moreover, while retaining Schaeffer's belief that ideas matter, Guinness has come to grips with the postmodern condition, for the most part avoiding Schaeffer's heavy reliance on Enlightenment rationality. Representing the Christian Right activists at L'Abri Jubilee was Charles Colson, who advocated culture war but in a more nuanced form than seen in fundamentalists such as Jerry Falwell, who also counted Schaeffer as an influence.

That Schaeffer heavily influenced these three groups within evangelicalism makes him easily one of the most important evangelicals of the twentieth century, but what his followers seem to have learned most from him were neither the details of his intellectual arguments nor the techniques of his politics. In intellectual matters, those influenced by Schaeffer have gone well beyond their teacher. Instead evangelicals today look to Schaeffer as an example of one who lived deeply within his own time and immersed himself in his own culture while somehow keeping his eye on what was ultimate. Seen this way, the time-bound and culturally relative nature of his message were strengths as well as weaknesses. Whether in Europe or America, he adapted and adjusted the fundamentalist and evangelical message in order to live in the world without being wholly of it. The enduring lesson for evangelicals who count Schaeffer as an influence is not to duplicate his message in its details, but to follow his example as a model for how to bear witness to Christ within a particular time and place. As he said that first day at L'Abri, the central task of the Christian life was to "put your feet in Jordan, and let God take care of you."

Notes

Notes to the Introduction

1. Ranald Macaulay, "L'Abri: The Ministry," L'Abri Jubilee, 11 March 2005, St. Louis, Missouri.

2. Mark Noll, *The Scandal of the Evangelical Mind* (Grand Rapids: Eerdmans, 1994).

3. Michael Hamilton, "The Dissatisfaction of Francis Schaeffer," *Christianity Today*, 3 March 1997, 30.

4. Thomas V. Morris, *Francis Schaeffer's Apologetics: A Critique*, foreword by Arthur Holmes (Grand Rapids: Baker, 1987), 7.

Notes to Chapter One

1. Betty Randall, "Germantown, Pennsylvania," Indiana University Purdue University at Indianapolis, Max Kade German-American Center, www.ulib.iupui.edu/kade/germantown.html.

2. This family history comes from Edith Schaeffer, *The Tapestry: The Life and Times of Francis and Edith Schaeffer* (Waco, Texas: Word Books, 1981), 37.

3. "Day of Discovery: The Story of Francis and Edith Schaeffer," Part 1 (video, RBC Ministries, n.d.). Copy in author's possession.

4. Francis Schaeffer, "Why and How I Write My Books," *Eternity*, March 1973, 64. See also Schaeffer, *Escape from Reason*, 264. Unless otherwise noted, all references to Schaeffer's books are from Francis Schaeffer, *The Complete Works of Francis A. Schaeffer*, 5 vols. (Wheaton, Ill.: Crossway Books, 1982).

5. Edith Schaeffer, *Tapestry*, 51.

6. Schaeffer, "Why and How I Write My Books," 64.

7. Edith Schaeffer, *Tapestry*, 52.

8. Edith Schaeffer, *Tapestry*, 62.

9. Edith Schaeffer, *Tapestry,* 62-63.

10. "Day of Discovery," Part 1.

11. Edith Schaeffer, *Tapestry,* 64-116.

12. Edith tells this story on camera in "Day of Discovery," Part 1.

13. Edith Schaeffer, *Tapestry,* 141. James Sire visited Hampden-Sydney in the 1970s and saw the plaque with Schaeffer's name still on display. James Sire, interview by author, 23 November 2004.

14. Quoted in Edith Schaeffer, *Tapestry,* 119.

15. *The Record of Hampden-Sydney College,* Summer-Fall 1980, 7-8. Also quoted in *Tapestry,* 119.

16. James Sire, interview by author.

17. See William R. Hutchison, *The Modernist Impulse in American Protestantism* (Durham: Duke University Press, 1992).

18. The best history of the development of fundamentalism remains George Marsden's *Fundamentalism and American Culture: The Shaping of Twentieth-Century Evangelicalism* (New York: Oxford University Press, 1980).

19. On Machen, see D. G. Hart, *Defending the Faith: J. Gresham Machen and the Crisis of Conservative Protestantism in Modern America* (Baltimore: Johns Hopkins University Press, 1994).

20. Edith to Francis, 11 February 1935, copy in *Tapestry,* 160-61. The letter from Francis has not actually survived. I have gleaned the gist of his complaints from Edith's response. Edith wrote, "But Franz don't judge a Seminary by comparing the conversation of fresh graduates with that of older Christians who have been softened and have grown through years of Christian work. Probably those fellows aren't all fight either, but they're young and they naturally feel like measuring up everyone because they know of the modernism, and they are interested in the outcome in their own church."

21. For an interpretation of the 1937 split, see George Marsden, "Perspective on the Division of 1937," in *Pressing toward the Mark: Essays Commemorating Fifty Years of the Orthodox Presbyterian Church* (Philadelphia: The Committee for the Historian of the Orthodox Presbyterian Church, 1986), 295-328.

22. Schaeffer to MacRae, 28 February 1939, MacRae Papers, PCA Historical Center, Covenant Theological Seminary, St. Louis, Missouri; Schaeffer to William S. Barker, 29 April 1978, Covenant Theological Seminary Records, PCA Historical Center, Covenant Theological Seminary, St. Louis, Missouri.

23. Schaeffer to Pat Withrow, 17 August 1937, MacRae Papers.

24. See Timothy Weber, *Living in the Shadow of the Second Coming: American Premillennialism, 1875-1982* (Chicago: University of Chicago Press, 1987).

25. Hart, *Defending the Faith,* 151-64. See also D. G. Hart and John Meuther, *Fighting the Good Fight: A Brief History of the Orthodox Presbyterian Church* (Philadelphia: The Committee on Christian Education and the Committee for the Historian of the Orthodox Presbyterian Church, 1995), 41-50.

26. Schaeffer to Bobby (no last name on the salutation), 31 August 1937, MacRae Papers.

27. Schaeffer to Bruce Garnsey, 28 April 1938, MacRae Papers.
28. Schaeffer to MacRae, 11 June 1938, MacRae Papers.
29. Schaeffer to MacRae, 27 June 1938, MacRae Papers.
30. Schaeffer to MacRae, 1 August 1938, MacRae Papers.
31. Schaeffer to MacRae, 28 February 1939, MacRae Papers.
32. MacRae to Schaeffer, 27 June 1940, MacRae Papers.
33. Schaeffer to MacRae, 27 June 1938, MacRae Papers.
34. MacRae to Edith Schaeffer, 6 February 1940, MacRae Papers.
35. Edith Schaeffer, *Tapestry*, 201-22; William S. Barker, interview by author, 12 March 2005. Audio tape in author's possession.
36. Edith Schaeffer, *Tapestry*, 230-31.
37. Edith Schaeffer, *Tapestry*, 231.
38. Barker, interview by author.
39. Edith Schaeffer, *Tapestry*, 233-38; Barker, interview by author.
40. Edith Schaeffer, *Tapestry*, 241.
41. Schaeffer to McIntire, 26 April 1944, MacRae Papers.
42. Schaeffer to McIntire, 26 April 1944, MacRae Papers.
43. Schaeffer to Rev. R. (Scottie) Hastings, 12 April 1944, Schaeffer Papers, PCA Historical Center, Covenant Theological Seminary, St. Louis, Missouri.
44. Hastings to Schaeffer, 18 April 1944, Schaeffer Papers.
45. Schaeffer to Paul Abbott Jr., 7 December 1945; Abbott to Schaeffer, 11 December 1945, Schaeffer Papers.
46. Minutes, Organization Meeting of the Bible Presbyterian Church of Gainesville, Texas, 22 January 1946, Schaeffer Papers.
47. Minutes, Organization Meeting of the Bible Presbyterian Church of Gainesville, Texas, 22 January 1946, Schaeffer Papers.
48. Schaeffer to Peter Stam Jr., 27 April 1946; and Schaeffer to Stam, 11 June 1946, Schaeffer Papers.
49. Schaeffer to Carl McIntire, 20 November 1949, MacRae Papers.
50. Schaeffer to Rev. Jack Murray, Collingswood, New Jersey, n.d., MacRae Papers.
51. See Mark Taylor Dalhouse, *Island in a Lake of Fire: Bob Jones University, Fundamentalism, and the Separatist Movement* (Athens: University of Georgia Press, 1996).
52. McIntire, *A Ministry of Disobedience: Christian Leaders Analyze the Billy Graham Crusade* (Collingswood, N.J.: Christian Beacon Press, n.d.).
53. Schaeffer to MacRae, 21 December 1947, MacRae Papers.
54. MacRae to Schaeffer, 27 December 1947, MacRae Papers.
55. Schaeffer to Rev. Frederick J. Lenk, Kenmore, New York, 9 August 1946, Schaeffer Papers.

Notes to Chapter Two

1. Quoted in Edith Schaeffer, *Tapestry*, 246. In this chapter, general information that is not footnoted comes from *Tapestry*. I have footnoted specific information and all quotations.

2. There is a Children for Christ folder in the Schaeffer papers at the PCA Historical Center that contains an undated article from *The Clarion* and the minutes from the founding meeting on 20 October 1945.

3. Edith Schaeffer, *Tapestry*, 246-47.

4. Quoted in Edith Schaeffer, *Tapestry*, 257.

5. Quoted in Edith Schaeffer, *Tapestry*, 258.

6. Quoted in Edith Schaeffer, *Tapestry*, 258-59.

7. Edith Schaeffer, *Tapestry*, 263.

8. Edith Schaeffer, *Tapestry*, 271; Francis's brief account of this event can be found in Francis Schaeffer, "The Universe and Two Chairs," *Christianity Today* 13:15 (April 25, 1969): 8-11.

9. Quoted in Edith Schaeffer, *Tapestry*, 271.

10. Edith Schaeffer, *Tapestry*, 272.

11. Edith Schaeffer, *Tapestry*, 273.

12. Quoted in Edith Schaeffer, *Tapestry*, 275.

13. See Frank Schaeffer, *Saving Grandma* (New York: Berkley Books, 1997); and Edith Schaeffer, *Tapestry*, 279.

14. See C. Everett Koop, *Koop: The Memoirs of America's Family Doctor* (New York: Random House, 1991).

15. Laurel Gasque, *Art and the Christian Mind: The Life and Work of H. R. Rookmaaker* (Wheaton, Ill.: Crossway Books, 2005).

16. Edith Schaeffer, *Tapestry*, 310.

17. Edith Schaeffer, *L'Abri* (Wheaton, Ill.: Tyndale House Publishers, 1969), 41.

18. Schaeffer to MacRae, 9 November 1948, MacRae Papers.

19. MacRae to Schaeffer, 17 December 1947, Schaeffer Papers.

20. See MacRae to Schaeffer, 17 December 1947; Schaeffer to MacRae, 21 December 1947; and MacRae to Schaeffer, 27 December 1947, 3. MacRae Papers.

21. Schaeffer to Doctor Holdcroft, 2 December 1950, Schaeffer Papers.

22. Schaeffer to MacRae, 8 November 1951, Schaeffer Papers.

23. See Cornelius Van Til, *The New Modernism: An Appraisal of the Theology of Barth and Brunner* (London: Clarke & Co., 1946). It is not clear that Schaeffer read Van Til's book; he may have picked up the term "new modernism" in conversation.

24. Schaeffer, *The New Modernism*, address to the International Council of Christian Churches, Second Plenary Congress, Geneva, Switzerland, 16-23 August 1950 (Philadelphia: The Independent Board for Presbyterian Foreign Missions, 1950), 3.

25. Schaeffer, *The New Modernism*, 7.

26. Schaeffer, *The New Modernism,* 4.

27. Schaeffer, *The New Modernism,* 11.

28. Karl Barth to Schaeffer, 3 September 1950, J. Oliver Buswell Papers, PCA Historical Center, Covenant Theological Seminary, St. Louis, Missouri.

29. Schaeffer to Barth, 17 October 1950, Buswell Papers.

30. J. Oliver Buswell to Barth, 13 September 1950, Buswell Papers.

31. Schaeffer, *The New Modernism,* 11.

32. Schaeffer, *The New Modernism,* 4.

33. Schaeffer, *The New Modernism,* 5.

34. Schaeffer, *The New Modernism,* 11.

35. Schaeffer, *The New Modernism,* 5-6.

36. Schaeffer, *The New Modernism,* 6.

37. Edith Schaeffer, *L'Abri,* 227.

38. Edith Schaeffer, *L'Abri,* 227.

39. Schaeffer, *The New Modernism,* 8.

40. Schaeffer to Bruce Garnsey, 28 April 1938, MacRae Papers.

41. Schaeffer to MacRae, 14 April 1951, MacRae Papers.

42. Schaeffer to Holdcroft, 11 October 1951, MacRae Papers.

43. Edith Schaeffer, *Tapestry,* 354-56.

44. Francis Schaeffer, *True Spirituality,* in Francis Schaeffer, *The Complete Works of Francis A. Schaeffer,* vol. 3 (Wheaton, Ill.: Crossway Books, 1982), 195.

45. Schaeffer to MacRae, 8 November 1951, MacRae Papers.

46. Schaeffer to MacRae, 8 November 1951, MacRae Papers.

47. Schaeffer to MacRae, 8 November 1951, MacRae Papers.

48. Schaeffer to MacRae, 8 November 1951, MacRae Papers.

49. Schaeffer to MacRae, 8 November 1951, MacRae Papers.

50. Revelation 2:4, New American Standard Version.

51. Schaeffer to MacRae, 8 November 1951, MacRae Papers.

52. Schaeffer to MacRae, 8 November 1951, MacRae Papers.

53. Schaeffer to MacRae, 8 November 1951, MacRae Papers.

54. Schaeffer to MacRae, 8 November 1951, MacRae Papers.

55. Schaeffer to MacRae, 1 August 1938, MacRae Papers.

56. Schaeffer to Holdcroft, 9 February 1951, MacRae Papers.

57. Schaeffer to MacRae, 14 April 1951, MacRae Papers.

58. Schaeffer to McIntire, 6 May 1954, George P. Hutchinson Papers, PCA Historical Center, Covenant Theological Seminary, St. Louis, Missouri.

59. Schaeffer to McIntire, 6 May 1954, Hutchinson Papers.

60. McIntire to Schaeffer, 8 May 1954, Hutchinson Papers.

61. Randall Balmer, "McIntire, Carl," *Dictionary of Christianity in America,* ed. Daniel G. Reid, Robert D. Linder, Bruce L. Shelley, and Harry S. Stout (Downers Grove, Ill.: InterVarsity Press, 1990), 690-91. Balmer does not mention the offshore broadcasting incident. See also "Carl McIntire: Creeds, Councils, and Controversies," at www.ptsem.edu/grow/Library/collections/McIntire.htm.

62. Schaeffer to MacRae, 14 September 1965, MacRae Papers.

Notes to Chapter Three

1. Deirdre Ducker (formerly Deirdre Haim), e-mail to author, 1 April 2005. Copy in author's possession.

2. Ducker, e-mail to author.

3. Edith Schaeffer, *Tapestry*, 388.

4. David B. Calhoun, "By His Grace, For His Glory: The Story of Covenant Theological Seminary," in *All for Jesus: A Celebration of the Fiftieth Anniversary of Covenant Theological Seminary,* ed. Robert A. Peterson and Sean Michael Lucas (Ross-Shire, United Kingdom: Christian Focus, 2006), 12-13, manuscript edition. When I wrote this, the Peterson-Lucas book was not yet published. I was working from a manuscript copy of Calhoun's essay, so the page numbers are different than in the book.

5. Edith Schaeffer, *Tapestry*, 399.

6. See *L'Abri*, 65-71.

7. Quoted in *Tapestry*, 404.

8. Unless otherwise noted, the following material on the Schaeffers' struggle to stay in Switzerland and their move to Huemoz comes from *L'Abri*, 73-121. Edith also tells this story in a chapter entitled "L'Abri" in *Tapestry*, 409-36.

9. Edith Schaeffer, *Tapestry*, 408.

10. Quoted in *L'Abri*, 98.

11. Priscilla tells this story on camera in "Day of Discovery: The Story of Francis and Edith Schaeffer," Part II (RBC Ministries, n.d.).

12. *L'Abri*, 154.

13. This sketch of life at L'Abri comes from Os Guinness, interview by author, 31 August 2004, and from *L'Abri*, 11-16. Guinness first visited L'Abri as a guest, returned as a worker, and eventually became a member.

14. Ducker, e-mail to author.

15. Edith Schaeffer, *Tapestry*, 516-17.

16. Ducker, e-mail to author.

17. *L'Abri*, 220-23.

18. *L'Abri*, 128-131.

19. Maria Walford-Dellu, "You Can Have a Family with Us," in Lane T. Dennis, ed., *Francis A. Schaeffer: Portraits of the Man and His Work* (Westchester, Ill.: Crossway Books, 1986), 136.

20. Os Guinness, interview by author, 31 August 2004. Audio tape in author's possession.

21. Guinness, interview by author.

22. Walford-Dellu, "You Can Have a Family with Us," 136.

23. Larry Norman, "Fly, Fly, Fly," *So Long Ago the Garden* (Solid Rock Records, 1973).

24. Guinness, interview by author.

25. Guinness, interview by author.

26. Guinness, interview by author.

27. Nancy Pearcey, *Total Truth: Liberating Christianity from Its Cultural Captivity* (Wheaton, Ill.: Crossway Books, 2004), 53-54.

28. Pearcey, *Total Truth,* 55.

29. "Give Me Shelter: Memories of L'Abri," Marc Mailloux, "The Animal Eaters," *World,* 26 March 2005, 34-35.

30. Harold O. J. Brown, "Francis Schaeffer and L'Abri: The Message," L'Abri Jubilee Conference, 11 March 2005, St. Louis, Missouri.

31. Harold O. J. Brown, conversation with author, 12 March 2005, St. Louis, Missouri.

32. William and Barbara Edgar, interview by author, 15 February 2005. Audio tape in author's possession.

33. William and Barbara Edgar, interview by author.

34. Maria Walford-Dellu, interview by author, 11 March 2005. Audio tape in author's possession.

35. Walford-Dellu, "You Can Have a Family with Us," 131.

36. Walford-Dellu, interview by author.

37. Walford-Dellu, interview by author.

38. John Walford, interview by author, 11 March 2005. Audio tape in author's possession.

39. Walford, interview by author.

40. Walford-Dellu, "You Can Have a Family with Us," 137.

41. Jerram Barrs, "Francis Schaeffer: The Man," L'Abri Jubilee, 11 March 2005, St. Louis, Missouri.

42. Francis Schaeffer, *The Mark of the Christian,* in *The Complete Works of Francis A. Schaeffer,* vol. 4, book 3 (Wheaton, Ill.: Crossway Books, 1982), 187-89 (quote on 187).

43. Schaeffer, *The Mark of the Christian,* 204.

Notes to Chapter Four

1. *Tapestry,* 530-31.

2. "Mission to Intellectuals," *Time,* 11 January 1960.

3. *L'Abri,* 138-40.

4. *Tapestry,* 519-21.

5. *Tapestry,* 537.

6. Maria Walford-Dellu, interview by author, 11 March 2005. Audio tape in author's possession.

7. Ronald Wells, interview by author, 15 October 2004.

8. Chuck Weber, interview by author, 23 November 2004. Audio tape in author's possession.

9. Francis Schaeffer, "Speaking the Historic Christian Position into the 20th Century," transcribed lecture, 1965, Wheaton College Archives and Special Collections, 42.

10. Roger Lundin, interview by author, 19 May 2004. Audio tape in author's possession.

11. George Marsden, "Twentieth Century Fox," *The Spectacle* 1:5 (1 November 1968), 1

12. Marsden, "Twentieth Century Fox," 1.

13. Marsden, "Twentieth Century Fox," 6.

14. Marsden, "Twentieth Century Fox," 6.

15. Schaeffer to Hans Rookmaaker, 1 March 1965, Hans Rookmaaker Papers, Box IIA1, 1945-1965, Wheaton College Archives and Special Collections.

16. *Tapestry* 441-42.

17. James Sire, interview by author, 23 November 2004. Audio tape in author's possession. Others who lived at L'Abri confirm that Schaeffer's books were the product of his taped lectures and conversations.

18. Francis Schaeffer, *The God Who Is There,* in *The Complete Works of Francis A. Schaeffer,* vol. 1, book 1 (Wheaton, Ill.: Crossway Books, 1982), 144. References and citations to Schaeffer's published works will be from the five-volume collected works edition unless otherwise noted.

19. *The God Who Is There,* 155.

20. *The God Who Is There,* 157.

21. *The God Who Is There,* 139.

22. *The God Who Is There,* 8.

23. Francis Schaeffer, *Escape from Reason,* in *The Complete Works of Francis A. Schaeffer,* vol. 1, book 2 (Wheaton, Ill.: Crossway Books, 1982), 229.

24. *The God Who Is There,* 54.

25. *Escape from Reason,* 209.

26. *Escape from Reason,* 209.

27. *Escape from Reason,* 211.

28. Ronald H. Nash, "The Life of the Mind and the Way of Life," in Lane T. Dennis, ed., *Francis A. Schaeffer: Portraits of the Man and His Work* (Westchester, Ill.: Crossway Books, 1986), 59-60.

29. *Escape from Reason,* 211.

30. *Escape from Reason,* 211.

31. *Escape from Reason,* 214.

32. *Escape from Reason,* 218.

33. *Escape from Reason,* 226.

34. *Escape from Reason,* 226.

35. *Escape from Reason,* 227.

36. *Escape from Reason,* 227.

37. *Escape from Reason,* 232.

38. *Escape from Reason,* 232-33.

39. *Escape from Reason,* 233.

40. *The God Who Is There,* 14.

41. *The God Who Is There,* 15.

42. *The God Who Is There,* 16.

43. *Escape from Reason,* 237.
44. *The God Who Is There,* 54.
45. *Escape from Reason,* 240.
46. *Escape from Reason,* 240.
47. *Escape from Reason,* 242.
48. *Escape from Reason,* 243.
49. *Escape from Reason,* 253-54.
50. *Escape from Reason,* 258.
51. *Escape from Reason,* 260.
52. *The God Who Is There,* 197.
53. *The God Who Is There,* 78.
54. *The God Who Is There,* 133.
55. William Edgar, "Two Christian Warriors: Cornelius Van Til and Francis A. Schaeffer Compared," *Westminster Theological Journal* 57 (Spring 1995); Edgar, interview by author.
56. Quoted in Bryan A. Follis, *Truth with Love: The Apologetics of Francis Schaeffer* (Wheaton, Ill.: Crossway Books, 2006), 67.
57. Francis Schaeffer, *He Is There and Is Not Silent,* in *The Complete Works of Francis A. Schaeffer,* vol. 1, book 3 (Wheaton, Ill.: Crossway Books, 1982), 278-85.
58. *He Is There and Is Not Silent,* 287.
59. *He Is There and Is Not Silent,* 288.
60. *He Is There and Is Not Silent,* 302.
61. *He Is There and Is Not Silent,* 302-3.
62. *He Is There and Is Not Silent,* 323.
63. *He Is There and Is Not Silent,* 327.
64. *He Is There and Is Not Silent,* 328, 331.
65. *He Is There and Is Not Silent,* 343-44.
66. Francis Schaeffer, *True Spirituality,* in *The Complete Works of Francis Schaeffer,* vol. 3, book 2 (Wheaton, Ill.: Crossway Books, 1982), 288.
67. Chuck Weber, interview by author, 23 November 2004.
68. For a fairly standard interpretation see Crane Brinton, *Ideas and Men: The Story of Western Thought* (Englewood Cliffs, N.J.: Prentice-Hall, 1963), especially chapters 7 and 8.
69. On Aquinas, for example, see Donald J. Wilcox, *In Search of God and Self: Renaissance and Reformation Thought* (Boston: Houghton Mifflin, 1975; Prospect Heights, Ill.: Waveland Press, 1975), 265. For a sympathetic critique of Schaffer in particular, see Nash, "The Life of the Mind and the Way of Life," 59-60.
70. *Escape from Reason,* 227.
71. Brinton, *Ideas and Men,* 211-20.
72. Brinton, *Ideas and Men,* 233-36.
73. Sire, interview by author.
74. *Escape from Reason,* 217.
75. *The God Who Is There,* 16.

76. Francis Schaeffer, *The God Who Is There* (Downers Grove, Ill.: InterVarsity Press, 1968), 22.

77. *The God Who Is There*, 22.

78. Nash, "The Life of the Mind and the Way of Life," 62.

79. Richard Neuhaus, "Correspondence," *First Things*, January 2005, 4. Among other works on Kierkegaard, see Stephen Evans, *Kierkegaard's Ethic of Love* (New York: Oxford University Press, 2004).

80. William White to Hans Rookmaaker, 12 March 1967, Hans Rookmaaker Papers, Box IIA2, 1966-1970.

81. Harry H. Schat to Schaeffer, 27 January 1967, Hans Rookmaaker Papers, Box IIA2, 1966-1970.

82. See for example, Schaeffer to R. Nicholas, 24 March 1967, Hans Rookmaaker Papers, Box IIA2, 1966-1970; Rookmaaker to Richard Russell, 21 May 1971, Hans Rookmaaker Papers, Box IIA2, 1966-1970; and Rookmaaker to Cornelius Van Til, 10 May 1967, Hans Rookmaaker Papers, Box IIA2, 1966-1970.

83. Francis A. Schaeffer, *No Little People*, in *The Complete Works of Francis A. Schaeffer*, vol. 3, book 1 (Wheaton, Ill.: Crossway Books, 1982), 146.

84. The importance of this decline-and-fall mentality is pointed out nicely in William Edgar's essay "Two Christian Warriors," 57-80.

85. In discussing fundamentalist habits of the mind, I am indebted to Mark Noll's provocative book *The Scandal of the Evangelical Mind* (Grand Rapids: Eerdmans, 1994).

86. *Escape from Reason*, 228.

87. Thomas V. Morris, *Francis Schaeffer's Apologetics: A Critique*, foreword by Arthur Holmes (Grand Rapids: Baker, 1987), 34-35. This book was first published by Moody Press before Schaeffer's death. For a similar argument see Ron Reugsegger, "Francis Schaeffer on Philosophy," *Christian Scholars Review* 10:3 (1981): 238-54.

88. Schaeffer to *Eternity* magazine, 26 May, 1976, James Sire, personal correspondence. Copy in author's possession.

89. Steve Board to James Sire, n.d., James Sire, personal correspondence. Copy in author's possession.

90. Schaeffer to James Sire, 6 June 1976, James Sire, personal correspondence. Copy in author's possession.

91. Morris, *Francis Schaeffer's Apologetics*, 53.

92. *He Is There and Is Not Silent*, 290.

93. Schaeffer, untitled and unpublished response to Thomas Morris, James Sire, personal correspondence. Copy in author's possession.

94. James Sire to Schaeffer, 18 June 1976. Copy in author's possession.

95. Schaeffer, unpublished response to Thomas Morris.

96. *True Spirituality*, 275-81.

97. *He Is There and Is Not Silent*, 340.

98. *The God Who Is There*, 143-44.

99. *The God Who Is There*, 20.

100. *The God Who Is There,* 68.
101. Edgar, "Two Christian Warriors."
102. Edgar, interview by author.
103. Jerram Barrs, "Francis Schaeffer: The Man," L'Abri Jubilee, 11 March 2005.
104. Barbara Edgar, interview by author.

Notes to Chapter Five

1. James Sire, interview by author, 23 November 2004. Audio tape in author's possession.
2. Sire, interview by author.
3. Roger Lundin, interview by author, 19 May 2004. Audio tape in author's possession.
4. Lundin, interview by author.
5. Lundin, interview by author.
6. Lundin, interview by author.
7. Lundin, interview by author.
8. Francis A. Schaeffer, *Death in the City,* in *The Complete Works of Francis A. Schaeffer,* vol. 4, book 4 (Wheaton, Ill.: Crossway Books, 1982), 209.
9. *Death in the City,* 210.
10. *Death in the City,* 211.
11. *Death in the City,* 211.
12. *Death in the City,* 212.
13. *Death in the City,* 217. In the book, the words "death in the city" appear for the first time at the end of chapter one, and they appear only once in that chapter. This appears to be where Schaeffer said the words three times in succession in his Wheaton lectures. Sire, interview by author.
14. Quoted in *Death in the City,* 219. Italics in the original.
15. *Death in the City,* 220-23.
16. *Death in the City,* 227.
17. *Death in the City,* 228.
18. *Death in the City,* 229.
19. *Death in the City,* 235.
20. *Death in the City,* 239.
21. Quoted in *Death in the City,* 239. Schaeffer was quoting Jeremiah 23:1.
22. *Death in the City,* 239.
23. *Death in the City,* 252.
24. Quoted in *Death in the City,* 258.
25. *Death in the City,* 259.
26. *Death in the City,* 264.
27. *Death in the City,* 272.
28. Quoted in *Death in the City,* 272.

29. *Death in the City,* 282.

30. *Death in the City,* 284.

31. *Death in the City,* 285.

32. Francis Schaeffer, "The Universe and the Two Chairs," *Christianity Today,* 25 April 1969, 8-11.

33. *Death in the City,* 289.

34. *Death in the City,* 289.

35. *Death in the City,* 298.

36. Francis Schaeffer, *Pollution and the Death of Man,* in *The Complete Works of Francis A. Schaeffer,* vol. 5 (Wheaton, Ill.: Crossway Books, 1982), 4.

37. *Pollution and the Death of Man,* 6-7.

38. *Pollution and the Death of Man,* 11.

39. *Pollution and the Death of Man,* 17.

40. *Pollution and the Death of Man,* 19.

41. *Pollution and the Death of Man,* 29.

42. *Pollution and the Death of Man,* 32.

43. *Pollution and the Death of Man,* 33.

44. *Pollution and the Death of Man,* 35.

45. *Pollution and the Death of Man,* 41.

46. *Pollution and the Death of Man,* 43.

47. *Pollution and the Death of Man,* 43-44.

48. *Pollution and the Death of Man,* 55.

49. Laurel Gasque, Hans Rookmaaker Seminar, L'Abri Jubilee Conference, 12 March 2005, St. Louis, Missouri; Laurel Gasque, *Art and the Christian Mind: The Life and Work of H. R. Rookmaaker* (Wheaton, Ill.: Crossway Books, 2005), 50-57. Gasque's biography of Rookmaaker can also be found in H. R. Rookmaaker, *The Complete Works of Hans R. Rookmaaker,* ed. Marleen Hengelaar Rookmaaker (Carlisle, England: Piquant, 2002).

50. Rookmaaker to Schaeffer, 4 July 1959, Hans Rookmaaker Papers, Wheaton College Archives and Special Collections; Schaeffer to Rookmaaker, 10 July 1959, Rookmaaker Papers; Gasque, Hans Rookmaaker Seminar, L'Abri Jubilee Conference. Schaeffer sent Rookmaaker a congratulatory letter for becoming professor at the Free University. See Schaeffer to Rookmaaker, 4 July 1964, Rookmaaker Papers. See also Gasque, *Art and the Christian Mind,* 81-86.

51. Gasque, Hans Rookmaaker Seminar, L'Abri Jubilee Conference.

52. Deirdre Ducker to author, e-mail correspondence, 1 April 2005. Copy in author's possession.

53. Francis A. Schaeffer, "The New Modernism," address by Schaeffer to the International Council of Christian Churches, Second Plenary Congress, Geneva, Switzerland, 16-23 August 1950 (Philadelphia: The Independent Board for Presbyterian Foreign Missions, 1950), 5-6.

54. Francis A. Schaeffer, *Art and the Bible,* in *The Complete Works of Francis A. Schaeffer,* vol. 2, book 5 (Wheaton, Ill.: Crossway Books, 1982).

55. *Art and the Bible,* 375.

56. *Art and the Bible*, 376.
57. *Art and the Bible*, 376-91.
58. *Art and the Bible*, 395.
59. William Edgar, interview by author, 15 February 2005. Audio tape in author's possession.
60. *Art and the Bible*, 395.
61. *Art and the Bible*, 400-401.
62. Francis Schaeffer, *How Should We Then Live?* in *The Complete Works of Francis A. Schaeffer*, vol. 4 (Wheaton, Ill.: Crossway Books, 1982), 132.
63. *How Should We Then Live?* 196.
64. *How Should We Then Live?* 197.
65. *How Should We Then Live?* 199.
66. *How Should We Then Live?* 204.
67. *How Should We Then Live?* 208.
68. Francis Schaeffer, *Whatever Happened to the Human Race?* in *The Complete Works of Francis A. Schaeffer*, vol. 5 (Wheaton, Ill.: Crossway Books, 1982), 355.
69. Quoted in *Whatever Happened*, 354-55.
70. *How Should We Then Live?* 186.
71. Francis Schaeffer, "Form and Freedom in the Church," address at the International Congress on World Evangelization, Lausanne, Switzerland, 1974, 365-66 (quote on 366). All Lausanne addresses and position papers can be accessed at http://lausanne.gospelcom.net/statements/covenant.
72. Schaeffer, "Form and Freedom in the Church," 366.
73. Francis Schaeffer, "Race and Economics," *Christianity Today*, 4 January 1974, 394-95.
74. *How Should We Then Live?* 141.
75. *How Should We Then Live?* 142.
76. Francis A. Schaeffer, "Revolutionary Christianity," *Biblical Missions*, February 1948 (Philadelphia: Independent Board of Presbyterian Foreign Missions, 1948), 31.
77. Schaeffer, "Race and Economics," 394-95.
78. Francis Schaeffer, *No Little People*, in *The Complete Works of Francis A. Schaeffer*, vol. 3, book 1 (Wheaton, Ill.: Crossway Books, 1982), 182.
79. *How Should We Then Live?* 211.
80. *How Should We Then Live?* 215.
81. *No Little People*, 182-84.
82. *No Little People*, 186.
83. *No Little People*, 189-90.
84. *No Little People*, 190.
85. *No Little People*, 190.
86. *How Should We Then Live?* 170.

Notes to Chapter Six

1. Schaeffer to Colin Duriez, 17 June 1972, Hans Rookmaaker Papers, Wheaton College Archives and Special Collections.

2. Francis A. Schaeffer, "The Oneness of Unbelief (II)," *Biblical Missions* (Philadelphia: Independent Board for Presbyterian Foreign Missions, n.d.), 23. The copy I found of this article in the Schaeffer Papers at Covenant Seminary in St. Louis was not dated. From the material in the article and its proximity to other articles he wrote in *Biblical Missions*, it seems to have been written in the late 1940s, probably 1948 or 1949. Schaeffer may have used the term "space and time" earlier than this, but this is the first I have been able to find in print.

3. Francis A. Schaeffer, *Genesis in Space and Time*, in *The Complete Works of Francis A. Schaeffer*, vol. 2, book 1 (Wheaton, Ill.: Crossway Books, 1982), 3-4.

4. Francis A. Schaeffer, "The New Modernism," International Council of Christian Churches, Second Plenary Congress, Geneva, Switzerland, 16-23 August 1950 (Philadelphia: Independent Board for Presbyterian Foreign Missions, 1950), 7.

5. *Genesis in Space and Time*, 19.

6. *Genesis in Space and Time*, 27.

7. *Genesis in Space and Time*, 102. See Erich Auerbach, *Mimesis: The Representation of Reality in Western Literature*, trans. Willard R. Trask (Princeton: Princeton University Press, 1952).

8. *Genesis in Space and Time*, 30.

9. *Genesis in Space and Time*, 31.

10. *Genesis in Space and Time*, 71.

11. *Genesis in Space and Time*, 27-28.

12. Francis A. Schaeffer, *No Final Conflict*, in *The Complete Works of Francis A. Schaeffer*, vol. 2, book 3 (Wheaton, Ill.: Crossway Books, 1982), 140.

13. *No Final Conflict*, 140.

14. Quoted in *Genesis in Space and Time*, 111.

15. Quoted in Mark Noll, *The Scandal of the Evangelical Mind* (Grand Rapids: Eerdmans, 1994), 207. See *The Works of Benjamin B. Warfield*, vol. 5, *Calvin and Calvinism* (New York: Oxford University Press, 1931), 304-5.

16. *Genesis in Space and Time*, 86.

17. *Genesis in Space and Time*, 23.

18. Francis A. Schaeffer, *Joshua and the Flow of Biblical History*, in *The Complete Works of Francis A. Schaeffer*, vol. 2, book 3 (Wheaton, Ill.: Crossway Books, 1982), 305-6.

19. *Genesis in Space and Time*, 17.

20. *Genesis in Space and Time*, 52.

21. Quoted in Noll, *The Scandal of the Evangelical Mind*, 183-84.

22. See Charles Hodge, *What is Darwinism?* (New York: Scribner, Armstrong, and Company, 1874).

23. Schaeffer to T. A. Bryant, 16 April 1976, James Sire, personal correspon-

dence. Photocopy in author's possession. Bryant worked for Zondervan, and in the letter, Schaeffer was giving Zondervan the right to quote him on inerrancy. See Harold Lindsell, *The Battle for the Bible* (Grand Rapids: Zondervan, 1976).

24. *Joshua and the Flow,* 169.

25. *Joshua and the Flow,* 169.

26. *No Final Conflict,* 119.

27. *No Final Conflict,* 119.

28. Schaeffer to Rookmaaker, 23 November 1976, Rookmaaker Papers.

29. Schaeffer to Rookmaaker, 23 November 1976, Rookmaaker Papers.

30. "How Should We Then Live?," interview with Francis Schaeffer, *Christianity Today,* 8 October 1976, 25.

31. "Francis A. Schaeffer, "Form and Freedom in the Church," address given at the International Congress on World Evangelization, Lausanne, Switzerland, July 1974, 365, available at http://lausanne.gospelcom.net/statements/covenant. The position paper he submitted before the conference was published as *Two Contents, Two Realities,* in *The Complete Works of Francis Schaeffer* (Wheaton, Ill.: Crossway Books, 1982), vol. 3, 403.

32. Schaeffer, "Form and Freedom in the Church," 364. See also, Schaeffer, "Others Say . . . ," *Christianity Today,* 29 August 1975, 29.

33. Schaeffer to Kenneth Kantzer, 1 November 1976, p. 2, Covenant Theological Seminary Records, PCA Historical Center, Covenant Theological Seminary, St. Louis, Missouri. The Lausanne Covenant can be found online at http://lausanne.gospelcom.net/statements/covenant.

34. Schaeffer to Robert Rayburn, 19 December 1975, Covenant Theological Seminary Records.

35. Schaeffer to Rayburn, 19 December 1975.

36. The Chicago Statement can be accessed online at www.spurgeon.org/~phil/creeds/chicago.htm.

37. I have been unable to find correspondence or other evidence of Schaeffer's involvement in the development of the Chicago Statement. There are those who believe he was influential. Correspondence in Switzerland, inaccessible to scholars at this time, may someday shed more light on his role.

38. Frank Schaeffer, *Crazy for God: How I Grew Up as One of the Elect, Helped Found the Religious Right and Lived to Take All (or Almost All) of It Back* (New York: Carroll and Graf, 2007), 310.

39. Schaeffer, "Form and Freedom in the Church," 361-62.

40. Schaeffer to Kantzer, 1 November 1976, 6.

41. Schaeffer to Kantzer, 1 November 1976, 7.

42. Schaeffer to Hans Rookmaaker, 23 November 1976, 2.

43. Schaeffer, "Form and Freedom in the Church," 365.

44. *No Final Conflict,* 137-38, quote on 138.

45. *No Final Conflict,* 136-37.

46. *No Final Conflict,* 140.

47. *No Final Conflict,* 132.

48. *No Final Conflict,* 134.
49. See *Edwards v. Aguillard* 482 U.S. 578 (1987) and *McLean v. Arkansas Board of Education,* 529 F. Supp. 1255 (1982). For the best history of Creation Science, see Ronald Numbers, *The Creationists: The Evolution of Scientific Creationism* (New York: A. A. Knopf, 1992).
50. *No Final Conflict,* 134.
51. Schaeffer to Kenneth Kantzer, 1 November 1976, p. 3.
52. *No Final Conflict,* 143.
53. *No Final Conflict,* 144.
54. *No Final Conflict,* 144-46.
55. Francis A. Schaeffer, *The New Super-Spirituality,* in *The Complete Works of Francis A. Schaeffer,* vol. 3, book 3 (Wheaton, Ill.: Crossway Books, 1982).
56. *New Super-Spirituality,* 390.
57. *New Super-Spirituality,* 399-400.
58. See Francis A. Schaeffer, *The Mark of the Christian,* in *The Complete Works of Francis A. Schaeffer,* vol. 4, book 3 (Wheaton, Ill.: Crossway Books, 1982), 185; and Francis A. Schaeffer, *The Church before the Watching World,* in *The Complete Works of Francis A. Schaeffer,* vol. 4, book 2 (Wheaton, Ill.: Crossway Books, 1982), 172-73.
59. Francis A. Schaeffer, *The Great Evangelical Disaster,* in *The Complete Works of Francis A. Schaeffer,* vol. 4, book 5 (Wheaton, Ill: Crossway Books, 1982), 329.
60. *Great Evangelical Disaster,* 332 and 338-39 (quote on 338-39).
61. *Great Evangelical Disaster,* 335.
62. *Great Evangelical Disaster,* 336.
63. *Great Evangelical Disaster,* 338.
64. *Great Evangelical Disaster,* 343.
65. Douglas A. Sweeney, "Fundamentalism and the Neo-Evangelicals," *Fides et Historia* 24:1 (Winter/Spring 1992): 81-96.
66. See Mark A. Noll, *Between Faith and Criticism: Evangelicals, Scholarship, and the Bible in America* (San Francisco: Harper and Row, 1987).

Notes to Chapter Seven

1. Edith Schaeffer, *Tapestry: The Life and Times of Francis and Edith Schaeffer* (Waco, Tex.: Word Books, 1981), 574.
2. Evidence for this interpretation comes from interviews with L'Abri residents who spoke off the record on this subject and from Frank (as he is now known) Schaeffer's 2007 autobiography, *Crazy for God: How I Grew Up as One of the Elect, Helped Found the Religious Right, and Lived to Take All (or Almost All) of It Back* (New York: Carroll and Graf, 2007), 253-82.
3. My sources for this decision would not go on record. For his part, Frank refused to be interviewed for this book.
4. Frank Schaeffer, *Crazy for God,* 10-11.

5. This composite was put together from interviews. Some of the sources were willing to go on the record, some not. For the sake of consistency I have decided to keep all of them anonymous.

6. Frank Schaeffer, *Portofino* (New York: Macmillan Publishing Company, 1992).

7. Frank Schaeffer, *Saving Grandma* (New York: Berkley Books, 1997).

8. Frank Schaeffer, *Zermatt* (New York: Carroll and Graf Publishers, 2003).

9. Frank Schaeffer, *Addicted to Mediocrity: Twentieth-Century Christians and the Arts* (Westchester, Ill.: Cornerstone, 1981); Frank Schaeffer, *Sham Pearls for Real Swine* (Brentwood, Tenn.: Wolgemuth & Hyatt, 1990).

10. Robin Galiano Russell, "Evangelical Heavyweight Schaeffer Turned to Orthodox Christianity," *Dallas Morning News,* 27 April 2005. For an attack on evangelicalism see Franky Schaeffer, *Bad News for Modern Man: An Agenda for Christian Activism* (Westchester, Ill.: Crossway Books, 1984).

11. "How Should We Then Live?" interview with Francis Schaeffer, *Christianity Today,* 8 October 1976, 23-24.

12. "How Should We Then Live?" interview with Francis Schaeffer, 23-24. See also Frank Schaeffer, *Crazy for God,* 253-59, and Edith Schaeffer, *Tapestry,* 577-89, for Edith's account of how the films came together.

13. Franky Schaeffer to Hans Rookmaaker, 6 August 1974, Hans Rookmaaker Papers, Wheaton College Archives and Special Collections. See Francis Schaeffer to Rookmaaker, 2 September 1974, in which Francis thanks Rookmaaker for signing on for the film.

14. William and Barbara Edgar, interview by author, 15 February 2005.

15. John Walford, interview by author, 11 March 2005; *How Should We Then Live?,* Episode III: The Renaissance (Muskegon, Mich.: Gospel Films, 1976).

16. *How Should We Then Live?* Episode I: The Roman Age.

17. *How Should We Then Live?* Episode II: The Middle Ages, and Episode V: The Revolutionary Age.

18. Schaeffer to Rookmaaker, 24 May 1976, Hans Rookmaaker Papers, Box IIA3.

19. James Sire to author, 4 September 2005, e-mail correspondence in author's possession.

20. As quoted in Francis Schaeffer, *How Should We Then Live?* in *The Complete Works of Francis A. Schaeffer,* vol. 5 (Wheaton, Ill.: Crossway Books, 1982), 255.

21. *How Should We Then Live?* 81.

22. *How Should We Then Live?* 89.

23. *How Should We Then Live?* 93.

24. *How Should We Then Live?* 123.

25. *How Should We Then Live?* 150.

26. *How Should We Then Live?* 156.

27. *How Should We Then Live?* Episode VI: The Scientific Age.

28. *How Should We Then Live?* 167.

29. *How Should We Then Live?* Episode VI: The Scientific Age.

30. Philip Yancey, "Francis Schaeffer: A Prophet for Our Time?" *Christianity Today,* 23 March 1979, 18.

31. *How Should We Then Live?* 181.

32. *How Should We Then Live?* 182.

33. *How Should We Then Live?* Episode VII: The Age of Non Reason.

34. Frank Schaeffer, *Crazy for God,* 265.

35. *How Should We Then Live?* 218.

36. *How Should We Then Live?* 223.

37. *How Should We Then Live?* 217.

38. *How Should We Then Live?* 226.

39. *How Should We Then Live?* 226-27; see film version, *How Should We Then Live?* Episode X: Final Choices.

40. *How Should We Then Live?* 250.

41. *How Should We Then Live?* Episode X: Final Choices.

42. Bertram M. Gross, *Friendly Fascism: The New Face of Power in America* (New York: M. Evans, 1980).

43. *How Should We Then Live?* 240.

44. *How Should We Then Live?* 254.

45. *How Should We Then Live?* Episode X: Final Choices.

46. Quoted in C. Everett Koop, *Koop: The Memoirs of America's Family Doctor* (New York: Random House, 1991), 267.

47. Edith Schaeffer, *Tapestry,* 601.

48. Koop, *Koop,* 267.

49. *Whatever Happened to the Human Race?* video 1 (Franky Schaeffer V Productions, Gospel Films, Inc., 1980).

50. Barry Hankins, *Uneasy in Babylon: Southern Baptist Conservatives and American Culture* (Tuscaloosa: University of Alabama Press, 2002), 185-86.

51. James Draper Jr., interview by author, 2 June 1997. Tape and transcript available at the Texas Collection, Baylor University.

52. Francis Schaeffer and C. Everett Koop, *Whatever Happened to the Human Race?* in *The Complete Works of Francis Schaeffer,* vol. 5 (Wheaton, Ill.: Crossway Books, 1982), 281.

53. *Whatever Happened,* 281-86.

54. *Whatever Happened,* 329.

55. *Whatever Happened,* 339.

56. See Janet Farrell Brodie, *Contraception and Abortion in Nineteenth-Century America* (Ithaca, N.Y.: Cornell University Press, 1994), 153-58; Linda Gordon, *The Moral Property of Women: A History of Birth Control Politics in America* (Urbana: University of Illinois Press, 2002), 26; and Leslie J. Reagan, *When Abortion Was a Crime: Women, Medicine, and Law in the United States, 1867-1973* (Berkeley: University of California Press, 1997), 8.

57. *Whatever Happened to the Human Race?* video 1.

58. Quoted in *Whatever Happened,* 324; *Newsweek,* 12 November 1973.

59. Quoted in *Whatever Happened,* 324.

60. *Whatever Happened,* 324-25.

61. For an easily accessible abstract of the Quinlan case, see the website www.ascensionhealth.org/ethics/public/cases/case21.asp.

62. *Whatever Happened,* 334.

63. *Whatever Happened,* 327-38.

64. *Whatever Happened,* 345.

65. *Whatever Happened,* 347.

66. *Whatever Happened to the Human Race?* video 1.

67. *Whatever Happened to the Human Race?* video 1.

68. *Whatever Happened,* 356.

69. *Whatever Happened,* 359.

70. *Whatever Happened,* 359, emphasis mine.

71. Yancey, "Francis Schaeffer: A Prophet for Our Time?" 18.

72. *Whatever Happened,* 366-67.

73. *Whatever Happened,* 371.

74. *Whatever Happened,* 408.

75. *Whatever Happened,* 409.

76. "Beyond Personal Piety," *Christianity Today,* 16 November 1979, 13.

77. "Beyond Personal Piety," 13.

78. Francis Schaeffer, *A Christian Manifesto,* in *The Complete Works of Francis A. Schaeffer,* vol. 5 (Wheaton, Ill.: Crossway Books, 1982), 454; and Edith Schaeffer, *Tapestry,* 634.

79. Edith Schaeffer, *Tapestry,* 634.

80. Koop, *Koop,* 268.

81. See, for example, Marvin Olasky, "Francis Schaeffer's Political Legacy," *World,* online edition, 3 March 2005. Olasky, the editor of *World,* argues that Schaeffer is the central figure in the mobilization of conservative Christians over the past twenty-five years, saying that as such Schaeffer was responsible for George W. Bush's reelection in 2004.

Notes to Chapter Eight

1. Philip Yancey, "Francis Schaeffer: A Prophet for Our Time?" *Christianity Today,* 23 March 1979, 14-18. This is a two-part interview with Schaeffer; part one appears in this issue and part two in the 6 April issue. See also Edith Schaeffer, *Tapestry* (Waco, Tex.: Word Books, 1981), 608-10.

2. Frank Schaeffer, *Crazy for God: How I Grew Up as One of the Elect, Helped Found the Religious Right, and Live to Take All (or Almost All) of It Back* (New York: Caroll and Graf, 2007), 139.

3. The background on Whitehead comes from John W. Whitehead, *Slaying Dragons: The Truth behind the Man Who Defended Paula Jones* (Nashville: Thomas Nelson Publishers, 1999). Whitehead wrote this autobiography after nearly two years in the public spotlight that resulted from the Rutherford Institute's repre-

sentation of Paula Jones in her sexual harassment suit against President Bill Clinton.

4. See Rousas John Rushdoony, *The Institutes of Biblical Law* (Nutley, N.J.: Craig Press, 1973); and Gary North and Gary DeMar, *Christian Reconstruction: What It Is, What It Isn't* (Tyler, Tex.: Institute for Christian Economics, 1991).

5. William and Barbara Edgar, interview by author, 15 February 2005. Audio tape in author's possession.

6. Francis Schaeffer to John Whitehead, 10 March 1981, John Whitehead, personal correspondence. Photocopy in author's possession.

7. See Francis Schaeffer, "Looking Back 44 Years for Lessons for Today and Tomorrow," undated, unpublished address, Schaeffer Papers, Box 4, File 55. This address was given in the summer of 1980 to about one hundred Presbyterian ministers in Pittsburgh. Schaeffer was looking back forty-four years to when fundamentalists left the Presbyterian Church in the United States of America, the Northern Presbyterian Church. In the address he referred to the San Francisco case.

8. John W. Whitehead, interview by author, 18 May 2005. Audio tape in author's possession.

9. Quoted in Whitehead, *Slaying Dragons*, 178.

10. Quoted in Whitehead, *Slaying Dragons*, 178.

11. John Whitehead, interview by author.

12. Schaeffer to Whitehead, 10 August 1981, John Whitehead, personal correspondence. Photocopy in author's possession.

13. Schaeffer to Whitehead, 22 May 1982, John Whitehead, personal correspondence. Photocopy in author's possession. Whitehead, *Slaying Dragons*, 188.

14. Francis Schaeffer, *A Christian Manifesto*, in *The Complete Works of Francis A. Schaeffer*, vol. 4 (Wheaton, Ill.: Crossway Books, 1982), 417.

15. *Christian Manifesto*, 424.

16. *Christian Manifesto*, 426.

17. *Christian Manifesto*, 431.

18. *Christian Manifesto*, 432.

19. *Christian Manifesto*, 434.

20. Frank Schaeffer, *Crazy for God*, 265.

21. CM, 436.

22. Whitehead, interview by author.

23. *Christian Manifesto*, 440.

24. Kenneth Woodward, "Guru of Fundamentalism," *Newsweek*, 1 November 1982, 88.

25. *Christian Manifesto*, 440.

26. *Christian Manifesto*, 446.

27. Edith Schaeffer, *Tapestry*, 544-48.

28. Woodward, "Guru of Fundamentalism," 88.

29. *Christian Manifesto*, 460, italics in the original.

30. *Christian Manifesto*, 447.

31. *Christian Manifesto,* 450.

32. Schaeffer to Whitehead, 10 March 1981, John Whitehead, personal correspondence. Photocopy in author's possession.

33. Schaeffer to Whitehead, 10 March 1981.

34. *Christian Manifesto,* 485-86.

35. Edgar, interview by author.

36. James Davison Hunter, *Culture Wars: The Struggle to Define America* (New York: Basic Books, 1991).

37. *Christian Manifesto,* 458.

38. *Christian Manifesto,* 461.

39. *Christian Manifesto,* 462.

40. Francis Schaeffer to John Whitehead, 10 August 1981.

41. For a biography of John Knox see Jasper Ridley, *John Knox* (New York: Oxford University Press, 1968).

42. *Christian Manifesto,* 472-73; quote on 472.

43. *Christian Manifesto,* 474.

44. *Christian Manifesto,* 479-80; quote on 479.

45. See *Edwards v. Aguillard* 482 U.S. 578 (1987).

46. *Christian Manifesto,* 480.

47. *Christian Manifesto,* 482.

48. *Christian Manifesto,* 484-85.

49. *Christian Manifesto,* 491, emphasis in original.

50. *Christian Manifesto,* 493-94; quote on 493.

51. Franky Schaeffer to Cliff Cornelius, 17 June 1983, Mark Noll, personal correspondence. Photocopy in author's possession. See Franky Schaeffer, *Bad News for Modern Man: An Agenda for Christian Activism* (Westchester, Ill.: Crossway Books, 1984). The case citation is *McLean v. Arkansas Board of Education,* 529 F. Supp. 1255 (1982). Marsden's testimony can be accessed at the website http://www.antievolution.org/projects/mclean/new_site/pf_trans/mva_tt_marsden.html#pg62.

52. George Marsden to Francis Schaeffer, 15 February 1982, Mark Noll, personal correspondence. Photocopy in author's possession.

53. Francis Schaeffer to George Marsden, 21 April 1982. Copy in author's possession.

54. Schaeffer to Marsden, 21 April 1982.

55. Marsden to Schaeffer, 15 February 1982.

56. Marsden to Schaeffer, 15 February 1982.

57. Schaeffer to Marsden, 21 April 1982.

58. Quoted in Woodward, "Guru of Fundamentalism," 88.

59. Arthur Holmes, interview by author, 18 May 2004.

60. Quoted in Woodward, "Guru of Fundamentalism," 88.

61. Mark Noll, interview by author, 18 May 2004.

62. Mark Noll to Francis Schaeffer, 3 November 1982, Mark Noll, personal correspondence. Photocopy in author's possession.

63. Noll to Schaeffer, 3 November 1982.

64. Noll to Kenneth Woodward, 3 November 1982, Mark Noll, personal correspondence. Photocopy in author's possession.

65. Francis Schaeffer to Mark Noll, 20 November 1982, 9, Mark Noll, personal correspondence. Photocopy in author's possession.

66. Mark Noll to Francis Schaeffer, 8 December 1982, Mark Noll, personal correspondence. Photocopy in author's possession.

67. Noll to Schaeffer, 8 December 1982.

68. Noll to Schaeffer, 8 December 1982.

69. Noll to Schaeffer, 8 December 1982.

70. Noll to Schaeffer, 8 December 1982.

71. Noll to Schaeffer, 8 December 1982.

72. Noll to Schaeffer, 8 December 1982.

73. Edgar, interview by author.

74. Francis Schaeffer to John Whitehead, 25 November 1982, John Whitehead, personal correspondence. Photocopy in author's possession.

75. Francis Schaeffer to John Whitehead, 14 January 1983, John Whitehead, personal correspondence. Photocopy in author's possession.

76. Francis Schaeffer to Mark Noll, 25 April 1983, 3, Mark Noll, personal correspondence. Photocopy in author's possession.

77. Francis Schaeffer to Mark Noll, 20 December 1982, Mark Noll, personal correspondence. Photocopy in author's possession.

78. Mark Noll to Francis Schaeffer, 13 January 1983, Mark Noll, personal correspondence. Photocopy in author's possession.

79. George Marsden to Francis Schaeffer, 12 January 1983, Mark Noll, personal correspondence. Photocopy in author's possession.

80. Marsden to Schaeffer, 13 January 1982.

81. Lane Dennis to Francis Schaeffer, Mark Noll, and Franky Schaeffer, 16 February 1983, Mark Noll, personal correspondence. Photocopy in author's possession. Apparently Will Barker, president of Covenant Theological Seminary, also attempted to mediate the dispute. Francis Schaeffer to William S. Barker, 27 August 1983, Mark Noll, personal correspondence. Photocopy in author's possession. Also, William S. Barker, interview by author, 12 March 2005. Audiotape in author's possession.

82. Dennis to Schaeffer, Noll, and Schaeffer, 16 February, addendum B.

83. Mark Noll to Lane Dennis, 18 February 1983, Mark Noll, personal correspondence. Photocopy in author's possession.

84. Franky Schaeffer to Mark Noll, 8 November 1982, 1-3, Mark Noll, personal correspondence. Photocopy in author's possession.

85. Mark Noll to Franky Schaeffer, 7 December 1982, 1-2, Mark Noll, personal correspondence. Photocopy in author's possession.

86. Franky Schaeffer to Mark Noll, 15 December 1982, 1, Mark Noll, personal correspondence. Photocopy in author's possession.

87. Franky Schaeffer to Noll, 15 December 1982.

88. Franky Schaeffer, *Bad News for Modern Man,* 69, 83; quote on 83.

89. Lane Dennis to George Marsden, 1 March 1984, Mark Noll, personal correspondence. Photocopy in author's possession.

90. George Marsden to Lane Dennis, 6 March 1984, Mark Noll, personal correspondence. Photocopy in author's possession.

91. Roger Lundin, interview by author, 19 May 2004. Audiotape in author's possession.

92. Lundin, interview by author.

93. Ronald Wells, "Francis Schaeffer's Jeremiad," *Reformed Journal,* May 1982, 17.

94. Wells, "Francis Schaeffer's Jeremiad," 18. See also Ronald Wells, "Whatever Happened to Francis Schaeffer?" *Reformed Journal,* May 1983, 11.

95. Wells, "Francis Schaeffer's Jeremiad," 18.

96. Francis Schaeffer to Mark Noll, 11 March 1983, 2, Mark Noll, personal correspondence. Photocopy in author's possession.

97. Francis Schaeffer to George Marsden, 14 March 1983, Mark Noll, personal correspondence. Photocopy in author's possession.

98. Francis Schaeffer to George Marsden, 25 April 1983, 3, Mark Noll, personal correspondence. Photocopy in author's possession.

99. Francis Schaeffer to Mark Noll, 25 April 1983, 2, Mark Noll, personal correspondence. Photocopy in author's possession.

100. Mark Noll to Francis Schaeffer, 5 April 1983, 1; and George Marsden to Francis Schaeffer, 31 March 1983, Mark Noll, personal correspondence. Photocopies in author's possession.

101. George Marsden to Francis Schaeffer, 31 March 1983, Mark Noll, personal correspondence. Photocopy in author's possession.

102. Marsden to Schaeffer, 31 March 1983.

103. George Marsden to Francis Schaeffer, 7 May 1983, 2, Mark Noll, personal correspondence. Photocopy in author's possession.

104. Marsden to Schaeffer, 7 May 1983.

105. Francis Schaeffer to George Marsden, 22 July 1983, 1, Mark Noll, personal correspondence. Photocopy in author's possession.

106. Francis Schaeffer to Mark Noll, 22 July 1983, Mark Noll, personal correspondence. Photocopy in author's possession.

107. CM, 493.

108. Nathan Hatch, *The Sacred Cause of Liberty: Republican Thought and the Millennium in Revolutionary New England* (New Haven: Yale University Press, 1977); and Mark Noll, *Christians in the American Revolution* (Grand Rapids: Christian University Press, 1977).

109. Mark Noll, Nathan Hatch, and George Marsden, *The Search for Christian America* (Westchester, Ill.: Crossway Books, 1983; expanded edition Boulder, Colo.: Helmers & Howard, 1989).

110. Franky Schaeffer, *Bad News for Modern Man,* 84.

111. Franky Schaeffer, "With God on Their Side," Open Forum, *San Francisco Chronicle,* 22 May 2005, web version, 1-2.

112. Franky Schaeffer, "With God on Their Side," 2.

113. Mark Noll, interview by author.

Notes to the Conclusion

1. *Day of Discovery,* video (RBC Ministries, n.d.).

2. See George Marsden, *Understanding Evangelicalism and Fundamentalism* (Grand Rapids: Eerdmans, 1991), especially his chapter "The Evangelical Love Affair with Enlightenment Science"; and Mark Noll, *The Scandal of the Evangelical Mind* (Grand Rapids: Eerdmans, 1994), especially his chapter "The Evangelical Enlightenment."

3. Noll, *Scandal of the Evangelical Mind.* Creation Science holds that all scientific data must conform to a literalistic interpretation of the Genesis creation accounts. What this means in brief outline is that the world could not have evolved over a long period of time but rather is a mere ten thousand or so years old. The geological strata that seem to indicate an earth that is billions of years old are the result, Creation Scientists say, of formations caused by Noah's flood. Dispensationalism is the form of premillennialism that divides history into several periods, called dispensations. Dispensationalists believe that God relates to human beings differently in each dispensation. Some passages of scripture are believed to be applicable to one dispensation but not to another. For example, the Sermon on the Mount, say many dispensationalists, is not applicable to the present age but instead describes the kingdom age that will come after Christ's return. Noll argues that each of these is unhelpful for the development of the evangelical mind. Creation Science uses an interpretation of the Bible as a grid through which to study the natural world instead of actually studying the natural world itself. Similarly, dispensationalism becomes a grid through which fundamentalists study scripture — often with more attention paid to the grid than to scripture itself.

4. Arthur Holmes, interview by author, 18 May 2004; John Whitehead, interview by author, 18 May 2005, audiotape in author's possession.

5. Bryan A. Follis, *Truth with Love: The Apologetic of Francis Schaeffer* (Wheaton, Ill.: Crossway Books, 2006), 15.

6. Follis, *Truth with Love,* 91.

7. Guinness, interview by author.

8. A check of Amazon.com sales rankings, which according to Amazon "are calculated much like *The New York Times* Bestseller List," showed that in August 2004 *How Should We Then Live?* was ranked 7090, and the trilogy at 10,744. By comparison, C. S. Lewis's *Mere Christianity* was 343 and *Screwtape Letters* 554. The lower the number, the higher the rank. In November 2005 *True Spirituality* had the highest rank among Schaeffer's books at 15,901, followed by the trilogy at

17,988, and *How Should We Then Live?* at 21,970. At that time Lewis's *Mere Christianity* was 269, *Screwtape Letters* 585, and *Miracles* 6389.

Crossway Books reports raw number sales for *How Should We Then Live?* at 9824 for the period January 1 through November 21, 2005; *A Christian Manifesto* at 4431; and the trilogy at 3042. Crossway was the original and only publisher of *A Christian Manifesto* and in November 2005 had sold a total of 404,742 copies. Crossway has sold 304,457 copies of *How Should We Then Live?,* but that book was published for a number of years by Fleming H. Revell before Crossway took over publication. Crossway began publishing the trilogy (*The God Who Is There, Escape from Reason,* and *He Is There and Is Not Silent*) in a single volume in 1990, and by November 2005 had sold a total of 40,634 copies.

Index

Index